# The Men's and Women's Programs

ENDING RAPE THROUGH PEER EDUCATION

# The Men's and Women's Programs

## JOHN D. FOUBERT

Routledge
Taylor & Francis Group
New York   London

Routledge
Taylor & Francis Group
711 Third Avenue
New York, NY 10017

Routledge
Taylor & Francis Group
27 Church Road
Hove, East Sussex BN3 2FA

International Standard Book Number: 978-0-415-88105-0 (Paperback)

### Library of Congress Cataloging-in-Publication Data

Foubert, John.
   The men's and women's programs : ending rape through peer education / John D. Foubert.
     p. cm.
   Includes bibliographical references and index.
   ISBN 978-0-415-88105-0 (pbk. : alk. paper)
   1. Rape--Prevention--Study and teaching. 2. Male college students--Counseling of. 3. Women college students--Counseling of. 4. Peer counseling of students. I. Title.

HV6558.F677 2011
378.1'9786--dc22
                                                                              2010009246

**Visit the Taylor & Francis Web site at**
**http://www.taylorandfrancis.com**

**and the Routledge Web site at**
**http://www.routledgementalhealth.com**

# Contents

# Preface

During the summer of 1993, I wrote what is now known as the first script for *The Men's Program,* an all-male, sexual assault, peer education program. Since that time the program has been implemented in colleges and universities, rape crisis centers, and military units worldwide. Much has happened since then, including three revisions to a book on the Men's Program and now this new volume and set of companion pieces for the Men's and Women's Programs.

This book, and its accompanying volumes for peer educators, is designed to be the complete manual for you to start up all-male and all-female peer education groups on your college campus, in your military unit, in your community, or in your other organization. The format of the book is intended to make program implementation as smooth for you as possible.

When I first wrote the initial script for the Men's Program, I was in my first job after earning my master's degree. At the time I served in the Dean of Students Office at the University of Richmond. A group of students from a sexual assault peer education group came to me and said they were having trouble reaching the men on campus. They asked if I would help them create a program for men on the subject. I eagerly accepted, and went about trying to find successful programs. To my surprise, there were none out there. All of the programs I could get my hands on treated men as potential rapists in a condescending fashion. I saw that a new approach was needed. So, I found a videotape created for police training that graphically described a rape experience. I used this video to create a program to teach men what rape feels like. I couched the message in the context of a program on how to help a friend recover from rape. This appealed to men as potential helpers instead of potential rapists. The program got a strong positive response from men at Richmond. I then began presenting it at conferences, made it the cornerstone of my doctoral dissertation, and wrote a book about it, and it spread nationwide. *One in Four* was the name selected by the first peer education group I built from scratch. The name has since been adopted by scores of peer education groups nationwide who present the Men's Program. Affiliation with this organization is not required to make presentations, though it is recommended. More information can be found at www.oneinfourusa.org.

This manual begins with a complete description of what the Men's Program and the Women's Program are and why they are effective. Chapter 2 provides you with scripts for both programs, additional scripts tailored toward military audiences for both programs, material for a PowerPoint™ presentation for the Men's Program, and a handout for the Women's Program.

Chapter 3 includes detailed training materials that you can use to equip your peer educators with the basic information they will need to teach their peers about sexual assault. More than just information about the program they will present, this chapter provides you with workshops to put your educators through about issues such as gender, rape trauma syndrome, answering difficult questions, and other critical areas of content that they will need to master before giving a presentation.

Chapter 4 provides you with advanced training exercises that you can use to supplement the training of your peer educators as needed. This material can also be used as follow-up training for your peer educators, or even follow-up programs for your intended audience. You will find that many of the training exercises in this chapter are themselves stand-alone programs. If your institution has a more serious commitment to sexual assault prevention than most, you might find that using several of these in addition to the Men's and Women's Programs useful.

Chapter 5 outlines how to recruit and select men and women to be in sexual assault, peer education groups. Ideas for recruiting members, letters to send out, interview questions to select from, rating scales, and ideas on how to choose candidates are included in this comprehensive chapter.

Chapter 6 provides advice from former peer educators for prospective and current peer educators. It includes the perspectives of the president of a One in Four chapter at Western New England College and from a Captain in the U.S. Army who was the president of the One in Four chapter earlier at the University of Virginia.

Chapter 7 provides a great deal of advice and resources for your role as the advisor of a sexual assault peer education group. It begins with material to help you decide whether you should advise such a group. In addition, the chapter includes advice on laying the groundwork for a chapter, how to get your group off to a good start, a sample constitution, advice on getting high attendance at programs, an agenda for a group retreat, motivational speeches to deliver to your group at different times of the year, and several other helpful resources.

To help substantiate your efforts, Chapter 8 describes several evaluation studies of the Men's Program and a study recently completed on the Women's Program. Having all this information will help you and your presenters to know they truly are making a difference. In addition, you can use this research with funding and decision-making authorities on your campus or in your organization to justify the use of these programs.

Thank you for being part of the movement to end men's violence against women! Go forth and make a difference.

**John D. Foubert, PhD**
*Stillwater, Oklahoma*

# Acknowledgments

I don't take credit for a single idea or word printed in this book. Anything I have contributed is a provision from God, for which I can claim no credit.

Since 1993 when I wrote the first script for what is now the Men's Program, I have benefited from the advice, criticism, and wisdom of individuals far too many to count or certainly to fit on these pages. Thanks to all who offered so much assistance.

I have learned most of what I know about how to prevent sexual assault from my interactions with students, most of all from the tremendously rewarding relationships I have been blessed to have with members of many chapters of and staff in the national office of One in Four. Countless ideas and passages in this book were originally drafted by or are in some way attributable to their passion, insight, and hard work. I appreciate their contributions deeply. Thank you.

Thank you to Edsel Erickson for publishing the first edition of *The Men's Program* and for always rooting for me. Thank you, Mary Koss, for conducting the first study to find the one in four statistic and for standing by it regardless of who attacked it or you. Your steadfast passion inspires me. Thank you, Dick Ramon, for creating a scenario that is the catalyst of behavior change. You have changed and continue to change the lives of many. Thank you to David Lisak for helping the field understand perpetrators, and for teaching us about their weaknesses. Your ideas made the Women's Program possible. Thank you, Gail Stern, for showing me how to be a better teacher, Christopher Kilmartin for teaching me about gender and sexual harassment, and to both Gail and Chris for being the best collaborators with whom I have ever worked.

Thank you to so many professional mentors who have invested themselves in me throughout my academic, administrative, and faculty career: Larry Beckhouse, Scott Allison, Barbara Sholley, Dick Mateer, Len Goldberg, Ken Blick, Susan Komives, Marylu McEwen, Bud Thomas, Larry Benedict, David Leslie, Chuck Eberly, and Dale Fuqua.

Dana Bliss from Routledge has provided years of ideas, encouragement, and conceptualization of how to package this work. Thank you, Dana, for believing in this project. Sean Bannon provided critical editorial assistance from a valued perspective as an advisor in training; I am sure he will make a wonderful chapter advisor. Thank you!

My research collaborators have provided highly valued service and support, most notably J. T. Newberry and Jerry Tatum. Thank you both for the unique ways you display courage and character.

Thank you Susan, my wife, for her unconditional love; Meg, my daughter, for her contagious joy; Will, my son, for all he will become; and to Jesus my savior for what he accomplished.

This book is dedicated to the glory of God.

# About the Author

**John D. Foubert, PhD,** received a BA in both psychology and sociology from the College of William and Mary, an MA in psychology from the University of Richmond, and a PhD in college student personnel administration from the University of Maryland at College Park. Dr. Foubert has served as a student affairs administrator at the University of Richmond, the University of Maryland, and the University of Virginia. He also served as an assistant professor, then associate professor of higher education administration at the College of William and Mary.

Since 2009, Dr. Foubert has served as associate professor and Anderson, Farris, & Halligan Professor in the College Student Development Master's Degree Program at Oklahoma State University. Dr. Foubert teaches courses in college student development theory, advanced student development theory, group and cultural interventions, introduction to student affairs, master's theses, and supervision of internship experiences. In addition to the present volume, Dr. Foubert is the author of *The Men's Program: A Peer Education Guide to Rape Prevention* (3rd edition, 2005) and *Lessons Learned: How to Avoid the Biggest Mistakes Made by College Resident Assistants* (2007). He is also widely published in scholarly journals such as the *Journal of American College Health*, the *Journal of Interpersonal Violence*, the *Journal of College Student Development*, the *Journal of Personality and Social Psychology*, *Sex Roles*, and *Violence Against Women*.

In 1998, Dr. Foubert founded what is now the national nonprofit organization One in Four. While serving as its president for 10 years, he led its growth to dozens of campus-based chapters and began a nationwide "RV Tour" with four recent college graduates who present the most effective rape prevention program ever evaluated in the research literature.

Since 1993, his sexual assault prevention work has been used by countless universities, state health departments, the U.S. Naval Academy, the U.S. Army, rape crisis centers, police departments, and correctional facilities to educate men about rape. From 2005 to 2007 he served as the principal investigator for a $275,000 U.S. Department of Education grant which successfully completed the most comprehensive evaluation study of a rape prevention program ever attempted. This grant project helped produce the only program in history ever shown to lead to a decline in sexual assault among high-risk men who saw a program relative to a control group.

Dr. Foubert has also conducted numerous studies on the development of college students in the psychosocial, moral, and spiritual realms. His current research is identifying the areas of spiritual struggle for college students and elements that lead to religious conversion. He is also studying the effects of men's use of pornography on bystander behavior in sexual assault situations.

An award-winning practitioner, scholar, and programmer, Dr. Foubert was identified by the American College Personnel Association in 2001 as an "Emerging Scholar" and was the runner-up for the National Dissertation of the Year Award from the National Association of Student Personnel Administrators for his work in rape prevention in 2000. In 2007, he won the William and Mary President's Award for Service to the Community. His work has appeared in the *Washington Post*, the *Chronicle of Higher Education*, *Inside Higher Education*, and numerous television news programs, and he has been a featured guest on the National Public Radio program *Talk of the Nation*. Dr. Foubert is a regular keynote speaker and consultant to universities, state health departments, and the military; has testified before Congress; and has presented before state sexual assault coalitions on how to end sexual assault on college campuses and in the military.

# Chapter 1

# Introduction to the Men's and Women's Programs

Do you have responsibility for educating college students about sexual assault? Do you work in the military and seek an effective program to prevent military sexual trauma? Do you work in a rape crisis center or other community organization and seek effective training material for men or women about sexual violence? Do you advise an antiviolence group and want ideas about how to freshen up your training? Do you wonder how you can get more people—men or women—involved in your educational efforts? Do you want to use the only program in the scholarly literature shown to reduce sexual assault among men and one of the only programs shown to increase bystander behavior among women? If so, this book is designed for you.

Whether you are a student affairs or health education professional working on a college campus, a sexual assault response coordinator or program director in the military, a prevention educator in a rape crisis center, or some other educator who is looking for a research-based approach to ending rape, this book was written to take you from just wanting to do rape awareness programming through every step to the outcome of a successful program.

What you will find in these pages is a complete guide for how to start up your own sexual assault peer education group, or groups. Some readers will be familiar with the precursor to this book, *The Men's Program*. The several editions of that book focused on how to create all-male peer education groups. This volume overhauls that program and includes materials for all-female groups along with a new focus on areas such as bystander intervention, alcohol, and the military.

Throughout this book you will be provided with resources and recommendations; it will be up to you to make choices about how to use them. You will find that there will be recommendations made to follow the guidance from research; in the end, the book is designed for you to make choices on what to use, whether to use it, and if so, how.

There are two main "programs" included in this book. Scripts for each of them are provided in Chapter 2. One is written for men, the other for women—thus they are referred to as "The Men's Program" and "The Women's Program." Both take about an hour for peer educators, or others, to present to an audience. Both are based on theories of attitude and behavior change. Both have outcomes research to demonstrate their effectiveness.

Both the Men's Program and the Women's Program are designed to be first-time sexual assault presentations for young adults. Both introduce the topic of sexual assault and set the course for future educational experiences you might offer them. I recommend that you use other research-based programs with the target population of your educational efforts after you have used the Men's and Women's Programs as part of a comprehensive sexual assault prevention effort. Some of the training materials in this manual could serve as follow-up programs. In addition, programs that have research support, for example, the Green Dot program, are worth trying in addition to the programs described herein.

## The Men's Program

In the Men's Program, participants learn what a rape feels like, how to help a woman recover from a rape experience, and how to intervene as a bystander if they observe a situation that could turn into a rape. As you will read, not only do they become more effective bystanders who intervene in situations that could turn into a sexual assault; they also become less likely to commit sexual assault in the first place (Foubert, Newberry, & Tatum, 2007; Langhinrichsen-Rohling, Foubert, Brasfield, Hill, & Shelley-Tremblay, in press).

The Men's Program is designed as an all-male, peer education workshop because research shows that for sexual assault programs, single-sex, peer education formats are much more likely to result in attitude and behavior change (Brecklin & Forde, 2001; Stein, 2007). However, the program can be presented by anyone.

The Men's Program focuses on increasing men's empathy toward women who survive rape and encouraging men to intervene when they see that a rape situation might occur. It convinces men that being raped is a traumatic experience and shows men how they can help women recover from the experience, if a woman comes to them asking for help. Presenters often use preprinted posters or PowerPoint™ with pertinent information to reinforce key points. Toward the end of the program, peer educators open the floor for questions.

### *The Program Begins*

The Men's Program opens by establishing the nonconfrontational nature of the program. Peer educators give an overview of what will be covered in the subsequent hour, and make sure that everyone knows that he can leave at any time.

Participants view a 15-minute video, prefaced by an introduction that it describes "a rape situation" that will help them to better understand how to help a sexual assault survivor. Participants are not told that the video describes two men raping a *male* police officer. They know only that the video describes a rape situation.

## The Video

The video shows a speech by a male police officer who describes another male police officer who is moving a trash can in an alley. Two attackers surprise him and take control of the situation. The police officer is told not to move; he quickly assesses the situation. He ends up submitting to a rape out of fear that greater harm might be done to him. Later, he endures a difficult hospital examination, becomes concerned about sexually transmitted infections, and is subjected to insensitive comments from his colleagues that perhaps he had met his attackers before and that maybe he really wanted the incident to happen. These segments of the video are processed as they relate to experiences commonly endured by women who survive rape.

At the conclusion of the video, peer educators break the stunned silence by explaining that a video in which an officer describes a male-on-male rape was used because it is the closest parallel available for helping men understand what it might feel like to be assaulted. The peer educators use the video to draw parallels from the police officer's experience to experiences commonly endured by female survivors.

A pair of peer educators then takes turns reminding the audience of several segments of the video and relating these to common experiences of women who survive rape. These common survivor experiences include having a rape happen in an everyday situation that turns bad, being frozen with fear, eventually submitting to the act to avoid further violence, worrying about long-term physical consequences, enduring a hospital examination, and suffering the questions about why she didn't resist the attack. As men are led through these parallels, research shows that they develop a deeper empathy for rape survivors (Foubert & Newberry, 2006). The message they receive is that rape is a violent crime that is not the fault of the survivor.

## Helping a Survivor

At this point in the program, the peer educators note that one in four college women have survived rape or attempted rape. This statistic is used to show the men that learning to help a survivor is relevant to them, as it is likely that someone they know has survived rape. Peer educators review the importance of encouraging proper medical attention, listening, believing, referring the survivor to counseling, and resisting the temptation to suggest further violence.

### Other Ways Men Can Prevent Rape

The next section of the program focuses on what men can do to help prevent rape. Men are encouraged to communicate openly during their own sexual encounters, to recognize that cooperation does not equal consent, and to pay attention to verbal and nonverbal cues during intimate encounters. Peer educators then discuss the effects of joking about rape and encourage participants to confront other men when they say things that put women down.

### Bystander Intervention

At this point in the program, there is lively audience participation. To introduce the topic of bystander intervention, men are led through a guided imagery exercise where a woman special to them experiences rape and a man who is in a position to do something about it does nothing. Attention is focused on the man who does nothing and his responsibility for intervening, motivating everyone to see the need to intervene in such situations.

Participants are then asked to consider two scenarios involving alcohol-related sexual assault. Men are asked what they could do to stop such incidents from becoming sexual assault. Peer educators lead the audience through a lively dialogue where effective bystander behavior is brainstormed and discussed.

### Closing

A question-and-answer period then allows participants to request additional information or to ask for clarification of key points. After answering questions and identifying resources on campus, the program ends on a serious yet solemn tone, noting that if the hour in which the program took place was an average hour in the United States, approximately 114 women would have survived rape (Kilpatrick, Resnick, Ruggiero, Conoscenti, & McCauley, 2007).

## The Women's Program

Because few women perceive themselves as potential victims of rape, the Women's Program focuses on how women can be effective bystanders to assist their friends in situations that pose a high risk for rape, particularly those involving alcohol. The Women's Program also focuses on identifying characteristics of dangerous men and how to help a friend recover from sexual assault without blaming the survivor.

### Research Basis

The Women's Program was written based on research, both quantitative and qualitative. Research has shown that active resistance is more likely to result in averting a rape than passive resistance (Lonsway, 2009). Lack of ability to perceive danger is related to victim status, with forceful physical resistance, forceful verbal resistance, and fleeing the most effective resistance strategies (Söchting, Fairbrother, & Koch, 2004). In addition, women who take a longer time to notice danger signs in intimate situations with men they know are more likely than other women to experience rape more than once. Such previously victimized women are more likely to try to leave a dangerous situation only when it gets to the point when they are isolated, which is often too late. This delayed response to cues alerting them to danger increases the likelihood that they will be revictimized (Messman-Moore & Brown, 2006). These studies all point to the need to teach women about effective resistance strategies, characteristics of perpetrators, and danger signals in situations that could lead to rape.

The characteristics women can benefit from knowing about perpetrators are lengthy. Men who rape are particularly more likely to drink higher amounts of alcohol when a sexual encounter is or might be taking place (Abbey, Clinton-Sherrod, McAuslan, Zawacki, & Buck, 2003; Abbey, McAuslan, Zawacki, Clinton, & Buck, 2001; Carr & VanDeusen, 2004). Sexually coercive men also believe that women are dishonest about not wanting to have sex on a particular occasion. This is especially evident when both parties involved in the incident have consumed alcohol (Norris, George, Davis, Martel, & Leonesio, 1999). In addition, men who admit to being sexually coercive with women are more likely than other men to be more physically aggressive toward women, adhere to adversarial beliefs between men and women, and display lower levels of empathy (Abbey et al., 2001). Men who have been sexually coercive with women are also more likely to support traditional gender-role stereotypes, to initiate sexual encounters, and to justify aggressive behaviors by supporting rape myths (e.g., "women enjoy forced sex") (Abbey et al., 2001). Thus, there are important characteristics that can be singled out that women can be taught about dangerous men and dangerous situations. Of course, this must be done with careful regard not to blame survivors for rape and to place the blame squarely on perpetrators.

The intent of the Women's Program is to engage women as potential bystanders, rather than as potential victims, by teaching them how to intervene to help protect their friends from sexual aggression, and by teaching them how to respond better to a friend who discloses victimization. Traditional programs for women have focused too much on women's behavior and not enough on educating women about recognizing the behavior of potential perpetrators (Rozee & Koss, 2001). The more women can recognize threatening cues in a situation that could turn into a sexual assault situation, the more likely they could be to resist or escape (Turchik, Probst, Chau, Nigoff, & Gidycz, 2007). Thus, preparing women to respond assertively to threatening situations has the potential for helping women to resist assaults (Turchik et al., 2007). Teaching women bystander intervention strategies empowers women to help others to begin to be free from the burden of rape (Banyard, Moynihan, & Plante, 2007).

## Goals

The Women's Program has three goals. First, the Women's Program was written to enable women to recognize characteristics of high-risk perpetrators. Second, it is intended to enable and empower women to intervene in potentially high-risk situations. The third goal is to enable women to help rape survivors by giving them pertinent information about rape, a victim's recovery from rape, and resources where more information can be found.

## Program Overview

The Women's Program begins by defining rape, mental incapacity and physical helplessness. Next, participants watch a short video, *The Undetected Rapist*. This video illustrates important characteristics of potential rapists by reenacting an interview between a male college student and a researcher. Program presenters then discuss the interview with the audience, identifying characteristics of high-risk men to prepare audience members for situations in the future where they could help their friends avoid high-risk men and get out of dangerous situations.

Peer educators then discuss ways participants can help sexual assault survivors and explain that helping sexual assault survivors involves understanding the needs of the survivor as well as personal limitations. A strong emphasis in this section is encouragement to avoid blaming the victim. This is obviously good advice; in addition, research has shown that when women blame themselves for experiencing rape, it increases their risk for experiencing rape an additional time (Miller, Markman, & Handley, 2007). Thus, blaming the victim can be a risk factor for revictimization, making education on this issue highly important.

Then they ask audience members to talk about how they could intervene as active bystanders if a potential rape situation were about to occur in their presence. Finally, presenters end by asking audience members what they personally are willing to do after the program to intervene as bystanders in rape situations.

Peer educators then engage the participants in discussion and talk about how they can help their friends avoid risky situations. Finally, participants have the opportunity to request additional information or clarify key points from the presentation.

## Proven Results for Both Programs

Most programs have not been shown to decrease rape-supportive attitudes for men. Even successful programs have not shown that effects are long lasting (Söchting et al., 2004). In Chapter 8, you will read how the Men's and Women's Programs are different when you see detailed descriptions of several studies showing their effects on several different populations and on several different variables.

## The Men's Program

The Men's Program combines the characteristics that research literature shows to be the most effective with an approach to changing attitudes and behaviors that fit a well-tested theoretical model. The Men's Program uses an all-male, peer education, victim empathy approach. In addition, by framing the program in the context of a "how to help a sexual-assault survivor" program, the likelihood increases that men will use a type of thinking called "central-route processing." Such processing, characterized by the motivation to hear the message, the ability to understand the message, and the perceived personal relevance of the program material, has been shown to be more strongly associated with long-term attitude and behavior change (Petty & Cacioppo, 1986).

By framing the workshop as a training workshop in which men learn how to help women recover from a rape experience, the Men's Program appeals to a "potential helper" persona, rather than the "potential rapist" persona found in many other rape-prevention approaches. In the Men's Program, men listen as potential helpers and are presented with information that has been shown to be most effective in content and format, making long-term changes in attitude and behavior more likely.

Early research on the Men's Program showed that 75% of men who indicated some likelihood of raping before seeing the program reported lower likelihood of raping immediately after the program, and 7 months later. In essence, this showed that the program reaches three quarters of the men we are most trying to reach (Foubert, 2000).

Men who see the Men's Program have also reported that they have more empathy toward female rape survivors after the program than they did before the program (Foubert & Newberry, 2006). This finding, determined through pre- and post-testing with a measure of victim empathy, is important given that one of the emphases of this program is to build empathy with survivors.

Men who see the Men's Program also report an increased willingness to intervene as a bystander in situations that could turn into rape and an increased sense of efficacy of how to intervene (Langhinrichsen-Rohling et al., in press).

In a study of first-year college men, those who joined fraternities reported committing fewer and less severe cases of sexual assault if they had seen the Men's Program at the beginning of the year than if they had not seen the program (Foubert, Newberry, & Tatum, 2007). This very important study was the first in the research literature ever to show a decline in sexual assault in a college population attributable to a prevention program. Specifically, 10% of untreated fraternity men committed sexual assault while 6% of treated men committed sexual assault. Moreover, the severity of the acts of sexual assault committed by untreated men was eight times higher than by those who had seen the Men's Program. This behavioral difference shown by research can give you a great deal of confidence in the potential for effectiveness in using the Men's Program. Another noteworthy study found that the effects of the Men's Program on men of color are strikingly similar to its effects on white men (Foubert & Cremedy, 2007). More information on these and other studies is provided in Chapter 8 and by visiting http://okstate.academia.edu/JohnFoubert.

### The Women's Program

As a much newer program, the Women's Program has not been subjected to the level of evaluation as has the Men's Program. It was developed with the written input of several expert women and other experts on gender during the initial stages and during its first year of presentation. Input in writing was gathered from 1,000 women and used for script revisions. These women included professional women at sexual assault conferences and women on college campuses. One question we asked was whether they thought the program should continue to be used with no changes, minor changes, or major changes, or never used again. Results showed that 95% of women said it should be used again with either no changes or minor changes.

A formal evaluation was then undertaken using a quasi-experimental design. A sample of 179 mostly first-year women at a large southern university was divided into a treatment group and a control group based on class sections in which they were enrolled. Treatment participants saw the Women's Program. All participants completed measures of rape myth acceptance, bystander efficacy, and bystander willingness to help.

Women who participated in the Women's Program reported a significant increase in their perceived ability to intervene in a potential sexual assault situation (bystander efficacy) and a significant increase in their willingness to intervene in a sexual assault situation. Both of these effects were significantly different from a control group.

In addition, women who saw the Women's Program experienced a significant decline in their rape myth acceptance. Women in the control group did not. Thus, program participants' attitudes moved significantly in the desired direction.

This study is an initial affirmation that the Women's Program is successful in motivating women to intervene as bystanders and is successful in changing their attitudes. Further research is needed to confirm these findings, to establish their longitudinal nature, and to extend them to new populations (Foubert, Langhinrichsen-Rohling, Brasfield, & Hill, in press).

## Contexts

The Men's Program and the Women's Program have been presented to a wide variety of groups and organizations. Given the length of time that it has existed, the Men's Program has been presented to a wider variety of audiences.

## College Campuses

Since 1993, the Men's Program has been presented to tens of thousands of college students on hundreds of college campuses in North America. As of the writing of this book, there are approximately 40 college campuses with peer education groups that actively present the Men's Program as part of their ongoing efforts to educate students about sexual assault.

The Women's Program has been presented on approximately a dozen college campuses and at national conferences. Data on the program has been presented at several conferences.

## The Military

The U.S. Military has used the Men's Program to educate its members in several contexts. Presentations have been made to cadets at West Point; annual presentations are made at the U.S. Naval Academy; presentations have been made to Sheppard Air Force Base, Cape Canaveral Air Force Base, Patrick Air Force Base, and the U.S. Air Force Academy. Presentations have been made at Fort McCoy, Fort Drum, Fort Eustis, Fort Monroe, and Widbey Island Naval Air Station.

In addition, the U.S. Army, Europe, is currently using the Men's Program to educate several hundred soldiers while conducting an evaluation study to determine the effects of the program versus their current training model.

A plan for using the Women's Program in the military is currently in the works and is ready for immediate implementation by contacting the author of this book.

## Additional Venues

The Men's Program has also been presented successfully to boys in high schools, at high school conferences, to nonprofit organizations, at state sexual assault coalition conferences, at national sexual assault conferences, to police officers and other law enforcement personnel, to medical students, and to rape crisis center workers.

Presentations of the Women's Program have thus far been limited to colleges and sexual assault conferences. Presentations to women in the military, nonprofit organizations, male and female law enforcement personnel, medical students, rape crisis center workers, and high school girls are recommended.

The rest of the book provides you with the tools to make these presentations possible. Good luck!

# Chapter 2

# Making Presentations

This chapter contains scripts for each program. For both the Men's Program and the Women's Program you will need to order DVDs to show during these programs. The DVD for the Men's Program is sold by Routledge and can be purchased on Amazon.com or wherever good books are sold. Simply search for the *Police Rape Training* video. To order the DVD for the Women's Program, *The Undetected Rapist*, use the order form in this book located at the end of the script for the Women's Program.

## Dividing Up Parts

Each script is broken down into several parts (A, B, C, etc.). Each part is divided in half, with sections intended to be delivered separately by presenters who are members of "Team 1" and "Team 2." It is recommended that peer educators spend their first few months learning to present the parts assigned to either Team 1 or Team 2. This will allow time to get to know half of the script well. Later, when more experienced, each peer educator can spend time learning the entire script. Presenting the entire program by oneself is extremely difficult.

Each presentation will require at least one peer educator from Team 1 and at least one from Team 2. Typically, at least four peer educators are sent to each presentation. When four people are present, each peer educator presents the lines assigned to the team for alternating parts of the program. For example, one peer educator might present the lines in the Men's Program for Team 1, parts A, C, and E. For larger and/or tougher audiences, you may want to send more than four presenters.

Of course, you may find that a different way of breaking up the script works for you or your group. While it is recommended that peer educators stick to the script as much as possible, it is also encouraged that they adapt the language to fit their own personal style and vernacular. Presenters should focus on making each point rather than on getting every word exactly as written.

## Setting Up

Before presenting, it is important to do several things.

- Arrive early at the presentation site (at least 20 to 30 minutes ahead of time).
- Meet the person who invited you to present. If attendance is voluntary, encourage him or her to round up people to come to the presentation. Offer to have some of your group help with this process.
- Have the others in your presenting group set up the audio/visual equipment. Test the DVD to make sure that the sound can be heard in the back. Cue the video to the start.
- Set up chairs in the room so that every seat is facing the presentation area.
- Put resource fliers of local counseling and support services for rape survivors at the entrance/exit area of the room in which you are presenting.
- To build rapport, informally chat with people as they arrive.

## Script for the Men's Program
## How to Help a Sexual Assault Survivor: What Men Can Do

### *Part A: Establishing Rapport*

*Team 1*

Thank you all for coming out. We are members of the One in Four chapter (state only if you are an officially recognized chapter of One in Four; for recognition go to www.oneinfourusa.org. Note: you do not have to be a recognized chapter to present this program) here at (insert name of your institution). The first thing we have to say to you today is—

*We are not here to blame you for rape.* We are not here to talk down to you about rape. And we are not here because of any particular incident that happened. The reason we're here is because when someone is sexually assaulted, the first person she usually goes to for help is a friend. And often that friend is a guy, one of you. So we want you to be prepared in case a sister, a friend, or someone else close to you asks for your help.

We are not going to stand up here and lecture you about why you shouldn't rape women. We already know you don't want to do that; so let's move on. We will discuss what we as guys can actually do about sexual assault. Let's talk about how to help sexual assault survivors and let's talk about some things we can do to make sure it isn't happening around us in the first place. Right now, we will introduce ourselves. (Introduce selves.)

Our name One in Four comes from the statistic that one in four college women has survived rape or attempted rape. When I first heard this statistic, it shocked me. It was hard for me to believe that *one quarter of the women that I knew* had experienced something as bad as sexual assault.

The truth is, the statistic has been found numerous times for over 20 years. The U.S. Department of Justice published a study in 2006 of over 4,000 college women: 3% of those women had survived rape or attempted rape in a 7-month academic year (Fisher, Cullen, & Turner, 2006). An additional 21% had survived rape or attempted rape at some point in their lives prior to that academic year. When you take those two figures and add them up—the 3 and the 21—you get 24%, or roughly one in four.

*Team 2*

### Disclaimer

Obviously, rape is a disturbing subject. There are parts of this program that are disturbing. If you need to leave the room at any time, that's okay. Obviously, we hope you will stay. We believe it is important to remember that both women and men survive rape, and both women and men commit rape. If you are a rape survivor, or someone close to you has experienced rape, you may be particularly upset by this program, and especially by the DVD we will show you. If you'd like to talk privately, we will be available at the end of the program. In addition, if you go to www.rainn.org, that's "rainn" with two "n"s—you can find the location of a rape crisis center anywhere in the country. Also, we have placed flyers by the door with an overview of resources available.

## Team 1

### Overview

In the next hour, we are going to do several things:

■ We will define rape.
■ Next, we will show and discuss a police training video that describes a rape situation. This DVD will help you learn what rape is like so that you will be better able to help a survivor in case she comes to you.
■ We will then talk about how to help a sexual assault survivor.
■ After that we will talk about some ways guys talk with and about women.
■ Next, we'll talk about how we can intervene as men if we see a sexual assault about to occur.
■ Finally, we will end by answering any questions you have.

## Team 2

### Definitions (You may want to insert your institution's or state's definitions here)

If a friend comes to you and isn't sure if what has happened meets the definition of rape or sexual assault, knowing the definitions will help you figure this out. One of the things that makes this complicated is that laws are different in every state, and often the policies of different institutions differ from state laws. However, in order that you have a basic understanding of how most states define rape and sexual assault, we'll go over a couple definitions. A basic definition of rape is:

*Rape:* Sexual intercourse with another person that is
    A. Against that person's will, by force, threat, or intimidation;
    B. Mentally incapacitated or physically helpless; or
    C. A child under the age of legal consent.

So basically, rape is having intercourse with someone who *does not* or *cannot* agree to it. Part B of that definition covers those situations where a person may be in a position where she *cannot* agree to it, so let's talk about those.

*Mental incapacity:* The person is in a condition where he or she cannot understand the nature or consequences of the sexual act involved and the accused knew or should have known the survivor's condition.

*Physical helplessness:* Unconsciousness or any other condition, such as intoxication, that made the person physically unable to communicate an unwillingness to act and the accused knew or should have known the survivor's condition.

Basically, this includes cases when someone is passed out, unconscious, asleep, or too intoxicated by alcohol or other drugs, or has some sort of temporary or permanent handicap which prevents the person from being able to understand or communicate during a sexual encounter.

When you hear the word *rape*, lots of things can come to mind. Before I saw this presentation, I always thought of what I saw on the news or on TV every week. There's a woman running alone late at night, and some guy she doesn't know jumps out from behind the bushes, pins her down, and rapes her. That of course is stranger rape, and it occurs far too often. What we want you to remember is this:

*Four of five times when a man chooses to rape a woman, it is a man the woman knows. It could be an acquaintance. It could be a friend. It could be someone from class. It could be a boyfriend. But four of five times, it is someone she knows, and the average length of time she has known him is 1 year. So it's usually not someone she just met. But on average, she's known her attacker for an entire year.*

## Team 1

Right now we're going to show you a 15-minute DVD that describes a rape situation. We're showing this to you so that you will understand what rape survivors go through so you'll be better able to help them, if they come to you. The tape itself is of Seattle police detective Dick Ramon who is training new officers about how to handle rape situations as a police officer. We've found that it is also a great way for us to learn about what rape is all about so we can better help women we know who have had this experience.

Again, we want to let you know that the video is graphic and disturbing. After the video is over, we'll talk more about what it might feel like to be raped.

(Show DVD here.)

## *Part B: Understanding Rape*

### *Team 1*

We showed you this DVD to help you understand what it might feel like to experience rape. If a woman comes to you asking for help after experiencing rape, it is important that you understand what it might have felt like. Obviously, both men and women can be raped and there are differences between a man raping a woman and a man raping a man. Discussing a situation in which a man is forcibly and unwillingly penetrated by another man is the closest parallel we could find to help you understand what rape feels like. As with many male-on-male rapes, what you watched described a case in which presumably *heterosexual* perpetrators (one had a wife, the other had a girlfriend) used rape and battery to assert power and control over another man.

Now we are going to draw some parallels between the police officer's experience and common experiences women have before, during, and after being raped. This will help you learn more about what it may feel like for women to be raped, and will make you better prepared in case a woman comes to you asking for help.

| Team 1 | Team 2 |
|---|---|
| *Police Officer's Experience* | *Survivor's Experiences* |
| **A Cop Moves a Trash Can** | **Everyday Situation Turns Bad** |
| Think back to when the police officer decided to move the trash can. He was just doing his job; in fact, he was just being helpful. It was just another normal thing he did as he went about his daily routine. Of course, he had no way to know what was about to happen. | In the same way, when men rape women, many of these incidents arise out of situations the woman can't predict. She may be hanging out with a trusted male friend, she may be on duty, doing her job, she may even be with a guy she wants to hook up with. But these are all things that she has control over, and the thing about rape is that, at some point, control is taken away from her. There is no flashing sign that goes off to say "you are about to be raped." These are just everyday situations that turn bad. |
| **"Don't Make a Move"** | **Frozen With Fear** |
| In the next part of the video, the police officer is told not to make a move. His first reaction, as he is being threatened, is to remain still, play for time, and figure out what is going on. | Keep in mind that four of five times when a man rapes a woman, the woman knows who he is. So, usually, this person who is threatening her is someone she trusts, and that trust is being violated. If someone we trust suddenly threatens us, our first reaction might not be to fight back, run, or scream. In fact, in most cases, what most people do immediately is tense up. In most rape cases, what happens is that the woman freezes and tries to figure out what is going on. This freeze reaction is the same psychological process involved when soldiers on the front lines of battles don't fire, given the stress involved. Both involve traumatic circumstances, and both can immobilize people. |

| **"Get on Your Knees"** | **Desire to Avoid Violence** |
|---|---|
| Later, the police officer is told to get on his knees, and it becomes more obvious what is about to happen. It's hard to tell what anyone would do in this situation, without living through it, but he decided the most important thing was to stay alive. | Most men who rape women weigh a lot more than the woman they are attacking. This physical difference poses a threat, especially in an intimate situation where trust is on the line. Sensing this threat, a survivor may find that if she kicks or screams, he may become even more violent toward her. So it makes sense that some women might suddenly freeze in an intimate situation where a guy is doing something she doesn't want, out of fear that he might become more violent. Even so, the U.S. Department of Justice found that 70% of sexual assault survivors physically resist, but they end up being overpowered physically or psychologically. |
| **Fear of STIs** | **Fear of STIs and Pregnancy** |
| In this situation, the police officer is worried that, given the high-risk contact that is involved, he has to think about catching a whole variety of sexually transmitted infections. | Today, there are a lot of sexually transmitted infections to worry about. Being raped could mean catching a potentially fatal disease. According to the Centers for Disease Control, 1 of every 500 college students is infected with HIV (Gayle, Keeling, Garela-Tunon, Kilbourne, Narkunas, Ingram et al., 1990). In addition, at least one of five adults in the United States has genital herpes.

Although men sometimes experience rape, usually we can protect ourselves from these things—we can choose to have sex or we can have unprotected sex. Rape survivors don't have these options.

Also, for female survivors, they face the possibility that the rape could result in pregnancy. In fact, pregnancy occurs in about 5% of rape cases. These survivors must then consider the ramifications of that pregnancy on their lives. |
| **Humiliating Hospital Visit** | **Another Painful Process** |
| Remember how the officer felt in the waiting room? He wasn't the first one treated because he wasn't a gunshot victim and he wasn't in immediate danger of dying. He was then put on a table and had a doctor probing around his body collecting evidence. Clearly this was an uncomfortable exam. | Even though the rape exam is extremely important for her health, many survivors describe it as another painful process. She has to tell and retell her story to people who come in and out of the exam room. She has a person she's never met thoroughly examining the most intimate parts of her body. Really, how many of us would want to have pubic hairs plucked out of our groin? And this is just one thing that has to happen during a rape exam. Thankfully, medical facilities have done a lot recently to make these exams go as well as possible, but as you can imagine, these rape exams are much more intrusive than other kinds of visits to the doctor, are quite painful, and happen right after she experienced something extremely traumatic. |

*(Continued)*

**(Continued)**

| Team 1 | Team 2 |
|---|---|
| *Police Officer's Experience* | *Survivor's Experiences* |
| **Did You Fight?** | **Did You Resist?** |
| Remember how the officers reacted to the raped officer. "What? You did what? You didn't pull your gun? Didn't you scream, didn't you yell, kick him in the balls?" (with disbelieving look). Then later on, the cop has his friend say, "Yeah, the guys have been talking and we think you knew those guys and maybe this was something consensual that kinda just got out of hand. Is that true?" | [With disbelieving tone of voice]. Where were you? Were you drinking? You were with *that* guy? You hooked up with him before, didn't you? [With passionate disbelief] So you were alone with that guy again? What were you wearing? Well, if you really were raped, why didn't you scream, push him away, and leave? Are you sure it was rape, or did you want this to happen!? [Pause; speak in normal tone of voice] Rape survivors get asked these questions all the time, and none of them matters. The point is, her instinct was to stay alive and no matter what, no one, *no one,* ever asks to be raped. |

## Team 1

This rape experience we just described is similar to what many college women experience. In fact, one out of every four college women has survived rape or attempted rape at some point in her lifetime. One of four college women has gone through an experience similar to the one we just talked about. Knowing that, what can we do?

## *Part C: Helping a Survivor*

### *Team 1*

Now that you've heard more about how it might feel to survive rape, we are going to talk about how to help a sexual assault survivor who comes to you asking for your help.

Every rape survivor is different, so there is no perfect step-by-step plan that will work every time. She will recover in her own way and on her own schedule. With that said, there are a few things you can *do*, and a few things to *avoid*, that will usually make her recovery easier.

### Encourage Medical Attention

It is important that she goes to the hospital for medical attention, particularly within the first 3 days after the assault. There she will get tested for STIs and have any injuries treated. If she gets there in the first 3 days she can also have evidence collected that will allow her to decide later about whether to be a witness in a criminal case against the rapist. Because of the forced physical contact, she is likely to be injured and may have internal injuries that she cannot feel. So one of the best things you can do is encourage her to go to the hospital, even offer to go with her. But remember; recommend that she go, but if she doesn't want to right away, respect her decision.

### *Team 2*

### No More Violence

I don't know about you, but if one of my friends came up to me and told me that some guy raped her, that some guy has caused *her* the kind of pain the cop went through on that video, my first instinct would be to go find that guy and beat the crap out of him. Maybe this would be your instinct too; a lot of guys feel this way at first. That is one of the worst things you can do if you want to help her recover.

You need to decide whose needs are more important—yours or hers. Take a step back and think—she has already tried to calm down one violent man. The last thing she needs as she is trying to tell you what happened is to feel like she has to calm you down and try to control your anger too. She may also worry that if you go beat him up, he may come back and hurt her, or even rape her again. Instead of more violence, let her know calmly that you will do anything you can to help.

### *Team 1*

### Listen

This next suggestion can be one of the toughest: *Talk less and listen more.*

You may be curious to know the details about what happened. If your goal is to help her, it is better if you don't ask for details about what she was wearing or where she was. A lot of guys think they can fix the problem by suggesting why it happened. If you do this, she may think that you are trying to blame her.

Many rape survivors say that one of the worst parts of their experience is having control taken away from them. As a friend, your instinct may be to hug her, but it is important for you to listen to her carefully about whether or not she wants to be held at all. If you think she does, ask her. Of course, she should also always have control over who knows about her story. Remember that if you tell others about what happened to her without her permission, she has lost even more control. So be sure to keep her information confidential.

## Team 2

### Believe Her

According to a study done by the U.S. Department of Justice (Tjaden & Thonnes, 2006), only 5% of rapes are reported to the police, making rape the most under-reported crime by far. Why is that? Why are so many rape survivors not telling the police what happened to them?

It is because survivors don't feel like they're going to be believed, and being believed is the most important thing to a survivor's recovery. In another study funded by the U.S. Department of Justice (Lonsway, Archambault, & Berkowitz, 2007) it was found that only 2 to 4% of rape reports were unfounded. That's a very low percentage by any standard. Even if we take it at its highest point, 4%, what that means is that, at a bare minimum, 96% of the time when people say they've been raped, there is no evidence contradicting their story and every bit of proof to say that what they said is exactly what happened.

Of course, you don't need a bunch of statistics to believe your friend, but it's important to know how harmful skepticism toward rape survivors can be. Also, if you think about it, it doesn't make sense for someone to go through every-thing that happens to women who report rape if it didn't happen—it is so tough on those to whom it did happen that most don't even report it. It just doesn't make sense to go through that if it didn't even happen.

## Team 1

### Advise Her to See a Counselor

It takes a long time to heal emotionally from rape. Several months to several years is quite common (Kilpatrick, Resnick, Ruggiero, Conoscenti, & McCauley, 2007). The best thing to help her feel better as quickly as she can is to see a counselor on a regular basis. So, please, recommend she see someone; even find out some names of good therapists she can go see. Also, it may be a good idea for you to seek a coun-selor yourself. Not only will you have a confidential setting to talk about what hap-pened, but that counselor will give you more suggestions on how to help your friend.

### *Part D: Other Ways Men Can Help End Rape*

*Team 1*

Now that you've heard advice about how to help a sexual assault survivor, let's switch gears and discuss other ways in which we can affect this issue in our day-to-day lives.

## Communicate During Encounters

One important thing we can do is make sure we are careful in our intimate experiences, if we choose to have them. The best way to do that is to keep an open line of communication when hooking up with someone.

None of us goes into an intimate situation intending to hurt the person we're with—that's just not how guys think. But I do know good guys who have gotten themselves into risky situations and it usually boiled down to their lack of establishing consent. So it's important to communicate clearly if you choose to hook up. Be sure to listen to what the other person wants and does not want and, of course, make sure she is in a clear state of mind to be consenting in the first place.

## Cooperation Does Not Equal Consent

Just because a person is going along with something in an intimate situation doesn't mean she has necessarily agreed to it. She might be overwhelmed by how fast things are moving, she could be intimidated by our size difference, or she could just be uncomfortable. The only way to be sure that she is comfortable with what's happening is to *ask*.

Asking *doesn't* have to be awkward. We're certainly not talking about agreeing to terms on a written contract. It can be really simple. It could be a few words such as, "Is this okay?" Ask her what she wants to do. The important thing is to ask her, give her time to respond, and then respond appropriately.

## The Freeze

A way we can know that someone might be *uncomfortable* is what we call "The Freeze." Sometimes in an intimate situation, a person may freeze up. Some guys may think the person just needs to be "loosened up." He may push a little harder, try again, pour a drink, or turn on some music. But think back to the video. When did the police officer freeze up? Of course, it was when he was scared and surprised by someone when he didn't expect it.

We're not saying that if someone freezes up, it means she thinks she's going to be raped. But it's a good sign that we should find out why she's uncomfortable, and the best way to do that is simple: Stop and ask. So if you're initiating something new, think the other person is uncomfortable, or if you are unsure, be sure to stop and clear up what you will do together. We've all grown up hearing that *no* means *no*: of course that is true. We also have to remember that just because a person *hasn't* said "no," *doesn't* mean that the person has said "yes."

## Team 2

### Changing Language

Along with those things that we hope you'll think about in your own personal lives, I want to take a couple of minutes to discuss some things in the broader picture. These suggestions are related to language and behavior, and on the surface, they may seem minor or unrelated to rape. But in a subtle way, they can encourage people to accept or tolerate sexual assault. We think it is important that when we hear these types of things we step up and find a way to let other guys know how their language can hurt women, even if that's not what they intended.

### Joking About Rape

Obviously, from seeing the video and discussing the experiences common to sexual assault survivors, there's nothing funny about the crime of rape. But the word "rape" gets thrown around jokingly all the time. This is something my friends and I used to do, and I'm sure you know what I mean. Maybe you're walking out of a test, and someone says "man, that test raped me." Or maybe watching a football game with some friends and one says "man, the (sports team) got raped." Of course, guys mean no harm by it, but the problem with talking about rape in a joking way, and using the word to mean something that it doesn't, is that it starts to lose its meaning. Think about the fact that one in four of your classmates may have survived rape or attempted rape. That's a lot of survivors coming out of class with you or watching those football games. For survivors to hear us belittle their experience could be very painful. So we'd just suggest that if you hear friends using *rape* in this way, let them know there's another word they could use.

### Phrases That Put Women Down

This next section has to do with attitudes that are hurtful to women. This might be the kind of thing that comes up during a touch football game—one guy drops back and throws a pass, but it falls 10 yards short. So, of course, his buddies are gonna jump on his case—"you throw like a bitch, take off your skirt." They're just joking around, and while there's nothing wrong with joking around, there is a problem with using those kinds of expressions. When we do that, we make being a woman synonymous with weakness and inferiority and that can make it a lot easier for some guys to justify treating women as though they *are* inferior. So we hope you'll encourage your friends to avoid using these kinds of expressions.

## Stories of Abuse

Maybe you've been around sometime with a bunch of guy friends before a meeting or in a locker room or someplace where only the guys are around listening to one guy telling a story. He talks about the party he was at Friday night, and how there was this drunk girl there who could barely stand up straight, but how he got her upstairs, and "sealed the deal." Of course, guys tell hookup stories all the time. But as you're listening to this story, you start to realize that he's not just talking about hooking up or sex. What he's really saying is that he took advantage of that woman and may have caused her a lot of pain. We strongly suggest that if you find yourself in this situation, be the brave one who stands up and lets your friend know that you don't think what he did was right. And I know that that can be a really hard thing to do. But remember, if you think what he did was not right, there's a good chance the rest of the guys feel the same way. If you say something they'll probably respect you for having the guts to speak your mind. At a bare minimum, we hope you don't laugh or prod for information to make him think you approve.

As you might guess, some guys have a hard time with this part of the program. The first time I saw it, I did too, because I think it's tough to see the connections between word choice and an issue as serious as rape. But I hope that having discussed the attitudes that these choices can encourage in some people, you'll make these changes, because while they're small for us, they could make a huge difference for someone we care about.

## *Part E: Bystander Intervention*

### *Team 1*

There are many situations where you or someone else can do something to help prevent a sexual assault from occurring. Of course, it is important to remember that you shouldn't always rush in and try to save the day by yourself; sometimes that is too dangerous. But in most situations, there is some way you can at least get help from others to stop a sexual assault from occurring.

We want you to think about some social situations where rape might occur. We are going to talk about what you can do to step up as leaders and do something. This will give you the chance to think about this now, before it happens, so you can be ready for these kinds of situations when they do occur.

### *Team 2*

### Guided Imagery

Now, we are going to ask you to imagine a situation happening as vividly as you can. We will talk you through it and have you imagine different things happening. The situation we will guide you through is upsetting; we hope you'll participate as fully as possible though.

This really works best if you close your eyes, so right now, please close your eyes and think about this situation as vividly as you can. (Wait until they actually do.) Think for a moment about a woman *your age* about whom you care a lot—a girlfriend, a sister, a best friend (pause). Once you get that person in your mind, picture her at a party (pause) with about 10 people or so (pause) in someone's apartment (pause). Picture what she looks like (pause), her being happy and having a good time (pause), laughing and maybe dancing a little (pause). On this night, she's had a lot to drink (pause), and she is really drunk (pause). So she decides to sit down on the couch (pause), and a guy her age who she's known for a year or so sits down next to her (pause). The party runs out of beer, so most of the people leave to go to another party (pause). Your friend is there on the couch with this guy (pause) alone (pause). He asks if she wants a shot (pause). Before she can respond, he puts it in her hand (pause) and she drinks it (pause). Now I want you to imagine that as she gets more and more intoxicated (pause) and almost passes out (pause), he starts to rape her (pause). She tries to push him away (pause), but he's bigger than she is and she can't really move (pause). Think about this as vividly as you can (pause). Think back to the police video, where the cop was bent over the trash can (pause). Remember how he felt right then (pause)? This is how a woman important to you feels right now (pause).

Now imagine that there's another man who comes back to the apartment to get his car keys (pause). He notices your friend and this guy (pause) and sees what is going on (pause). He was at the party, so he knows how completely drunk she was (pause). He knows that this is wrong (pause). He chooses to do nothing (pause). He just gets his keys (pause) and walks away (pause). Open your eyes (very long pause).

Okay, now we are going to ask you guys to talk a little bit about the scene we just went through. It doesn't have to be much, just give us your first reaction.

1. How did you feel imagining a woman close to you being raped?
2. How do you feel toward the man who saw what was happening and walked away? What words would you use to describe him? (Wait for them to say a word that does not demean another group of people; reinforce the words that don't demean groups of people.)
3. Raise your hand if you feel that the man who watched and then walked away should have done something to stop it instead.

## Team 1

Okay, now that you've thought about a situation in which a (insert words they called him here) who was in a position to prevent or interrupt a rape did nothing; let's talk about a different situation in which some action on your part could help prevent a lot of pain and suffering.

## Scenario 1

What would you do if you had a roommate who came back to your room with a woman who was so drunk that she was stumbling over her own feet and looked like she was about to pass out? He tells you to leave so they can hook up.

What are some of the possible responses you could have that would help keep a rape from happening?

If audience says nothing, or nothing positive, here are possible responses for presenters to suggest:

■ You could talk with your roommate privately in the hallway and suggest she's too drunk to hook up.
■ You could offer to help take care of her because she is so drunk.
■ You could call and order a pizza.
■ You could say you aren't going to leave the room.

Follow-up questions (use as necessary):

■ What could happen if you just leave the room?
■ What are some of the things you could *say* to your roommate to get his attention?
■ What are some of the things you could *do* to get his attention?
■ What are some other resources you might be able to use for help?

- What is the worst thing that could happen if you try to prevent your room-mate from doing what he has planned?
- How does this differ from the worst that could happen if you just leave the room?

## Scenario 2

Okay, in this next scenario, let's say you're in a more social setting with other people around. You see two people there including one of your friends. He is hitting on this woman and she is so drunk she is holding herself up by hanging on to the wall. You overhear your guy friend ask someone for a room so the two of them can go have sex. He then puts his arm under her shoulder and starts to head to a private room. What could you do to make it less likely that a rape could occur?

If audience says nothing, or nothing positive, here are possible responses to suggest:

- Ask him about the STI he got last week and suggest he not give it to her.
- Look for her friends to see if they can help take her home.
- Tell him the police are on the way to break up the party and everyone is leaving.
- "Accidentally" pour a cold or noxious substance on him that will distract him long enough to convince the woman to go home.

Follow-up questions (use as needed):

- What could happen if you do nothing?
- What could happen if you try to prevent your friend from taking the woman to the private room?
- What are some of the things you could *say* to get the guy's attention?
- What are some of the things you could *do* to get his attention?
- What are some of the things you could do at the party to get other people's attention?
- What are some other resources you might be able to use for help?
- What is the worst thing that could happen if you intervene?
- How does this differ from the worst that could happen if you don't intervene?

## *Team 2*

### Some Advice

We hope that no matter what, in these scenarios you would choose to do *something*. Our best advice is to approach your friend as just that, a friend. Appeal to his loyalty to you as a friend, to a group you both belong to, to his hall, team, whatever. No one wants to be talked down to, so if you approach him as a friend, he will be more likely to follow your lead. Of course, like many important things in life, it's not easy to step up and intervene without risking feeling like a jerk or even losing your friendship. However, in the end, we hope you agree with us that it is the right thing to do; and the right thing to do isn't always easy.

Another way to take action is to get involved in a group like this. Please come talk to us after the program if you are interested in being part of One in Four and giving this same presentation to educate other guys about this issue.

So before we close, what questions do you have? (Take questions as time allows.)

We have flyers available with resources that you can give to a friend who has been raped. We will also stay after if you would like to talk to us individually.

## Team 1

In closing, we have one final statistic. A recent study by the National Crime Victims Research and Treatment Center found that every year in the United States, over 1,000,000 women survive rape (Kilpatrick et al., 2007). Over 1,000,000! If you do the math, that works out to 114 women every hour. We've been here for over an hour. If the last hour was an average hour in this country, while you sat here, at least 114 women had an experience similar to the one you saw on the video.

## Team 2

114 women have just been raped. 114 women just had an experience like to the one we showed you on that video. That's 114 best friends, 114 sisters, 114 daughters. 114 women have just been raped.

## Team 1

Please go forth and make a difference.

## Team 2

Thank you for coming.

## Material for the Men's Program to Print on Poster Board or PowerPoint™ Slides

How to Help a Sexual Assault Survivor: What Men Can Do—
A Presentation by One in Four

**Rape:** Sexual intercourse with another person that is
   A.  Against that person's will, by force, threat, or intimidation
   B.  Mentally incapacitated or physically helpless, or
   C.  A child under the age of legal consent

**Mental incapacity:** The person is in a condition in which he or she cannot understand the nature or consequences of the sexual act involved and the accused knew or should have known the survivor's condition.

**Physical helplessness:** Unconsciousness or any other condition, such as intoxication, that made the person physically unable to communicate an unwillingness to act and the accused knew or should have known the survivor's condition.

| Police officer | Survivors |
|---|---|
| Cop Moves a Trash Can | Everyday Situation Turns Bad |
| Don't Make a Move | Frozen With Fear |
| Get on Your Knees | Desire to Avoid Violence |
| Fear of STIs | Fear of STIs, Pregnancy |
| Humiliating Hospital Visit | Another Painful Process |
| Did You Fight? | Did You Resist? |

- Encourage Medical Attention
- No More Violence
- Listen
- Believe
- Advise Her to See a Counselor

- Communicate During Encounters
- Cooperation Does Not Equal Consent
- The "Freeze"

- Changing Language
  - Joking About Rape
  - Phrases That Put Women Down
- Stories of Abuse

- Scenarios
  - What Would You Do?

## Script for the Women's Program Empowering Women: Learning About Dangerous Men and Helping Rape Survivors

### Part A: Establishing Rapport and Definitions

> Do: *Distribute the handout for the Women's Program: "Characteristics of Men Who Rape and Commit Other Types of Sexual Assault" as people enter the room.*

### Team 1

Thank you for coming out.

*Insert if men are presenting instead of women*: Many women are passionate about this issue, and as a result, many sexual assault programs are presented by women. We recognize that there are many more things women often do in their daily lives to reduce their risk for rape than men do; and though many men are rape survivors, a *whole* lot more women are. All of us are here because we realize that rape is wrong, and we firmly believe that men need to take an active role in helping to end sexual assault, because if we are not part of the solution, then we are still part of the problem. So we are here today to add our perspectives as men to what you already know about the issue. We have been trained to offer you a research-based program about sexual assault. Our hope is that what you hear today will be useful to you as you help your friends avoid risky situations and recover from very difficult experiences.

### Team 2

Today we are going to present a program called "Empowering Women: Learning About Dangerous Men and Helping Rape Survivors." We're not here to give you "the answer" about how to avoid being raped, because there is no definite answer. Rape happens when someone chooses to rape, and according to the National Crime Victimization survey, 95% of the time (U.S. Department of Justice, 2010), this choice is made by a man.

So while we can't offer you a solid rule that will guarantee the safety of your friends, or even you, we can give you the most statistically reliable information we can find on high-risk men so you can help your friends identify characteristics of high-risk guys and high-risk situations.

### Overview

We believe that we can share some information with you that will empower you to help your friends reduce their risk for experiencing sexual assault, and help your friends recover from it in case it does happen. We will do five basic things:

1. First, we're going to go over some basic definitions.
2. Next, we are going to show you a video where a researcher interviews a college guy who set a woman up for rape. This will help you identify characteristics of high-risk men so that you can better help your friends get out of dangerous situations.
3. After that, we're going to talk about how to help a friend who survives rape.
4. Then we'll ask you to talk with us about how you think you can intervene as an active bystander to help your friends get out of bad situations if you are actually there when something happens.
5. Finally, we'll wrap up by asking you what you personally are willing to do after today's program.

## *Team 1*

### Disclaimer

Obviously, rape is a disturbing subject. Any part of today's program could disturb you. If you need to leave the room at any time, that's okay. We hope you will stay with us.

If you are a rape survivor, or are a friend or relative of a survivor, you may be particularly affected by our discussion. If you'd like to talk privately, we will be available at the end of the program. Also, just so you know, our college has on- and off-campus resources available for counseling and judicial referral. In addition, if you go to www.rainn.org, that's "rainn" with two "n"s—you can find the location of a rape crisis center anywhere in the country.

## *Team 2*

### Definitions

If a friend comes to you and isn't sure if what has happened to her is rape, knowing the definitions will help you figure this out. One of the things that makes this complicated is that laws are different in every state, and often the policies at different institutions differ from the laws of the state. However, in order that you have a basic understanding of how most states define rape and sexual assault, we'll go over a couple definitions. A basic definition of rape is

*Rape:* Sexual intercourse with another person that is

   A. Against that person's will, by force, threat, or intimidation

   B. Mentally incapacitated or physically helpless, or

   C. Under the age of legal consent

Basically, rape is having intercourse with someone who *does not* or *cannot* agree to it.

Part B of that definition covers those situations where a person may be in a position where the person *cannot* agree to it, so let's talk about those.

> *Mental incapacity:* The person is in a condition in which he or she cannot understand the nature or consequences of the sexual act involved and the accused knew or should have known the survivor's condition.
>
> *Physical helplessness:* Unconsciousness or any other condition, such as intoxication, that made the person physically unable to communicate an unwillingness to act and the accused knew or should have known the survivor's condition.

Basically, this includes cases when someone is passed out, unconscious, asleep, or too intoxicated by alcohol or other drugs, or has some sort of temporary or permanent handicap which prevents the person from being able to understand or communicate during an intimate situation.

When you hear the word "rape," lots of things can come to mind. Before I saw this presentation, I always thought of what I saw on the news or on TV every week. There's a woman running alone late at night, and some guy she doesn't know jumps out from behind the bushes, pins her down, and rapes her. That of course is stranger rape, and it occurs far too often. What we want you to remember this:

*Four out of five times when a man chooses to rape a woman, it is a man the woman knows. It could be an acquaintance. It could be a friend. It could be someone from class. It could be a boyfriend. But four out of five times, it is someone she knows, and the average length of time she has known him is 1 year. So it's usually not someone she just met. But on average, she's known her attacker for an entire year.*

## Part B: Recognizing Dangerous Men

### Team 1

One of the things that research shows is that women can reduce their risk for being sexually assaulted if they are more able to detect danger signals from a man who is setting them up for sexual assault. That is a foundation of our program. Of course, even if every danger sign is detected, nobody is ever at fault for experiencing rape—rape is only the fault of the rapist.

There has actually been a lot of research done on men who rape—both those who rape strangers and those who rape women they get to know. A lot of this research is detailed on the handout we gave you in the beginning of the presentation.

We are going to show you a video where a college guy is interviewed by a college professor who studies men who rape. This college guy is actually an actor, but he is reading—word for word—the transcript of an interview with a real person on a campus who set up a woman for rape.

The woman never reported the rape, so of course he never got in trouble. In this case the rape happened in a fraternity, but it could have happened almost anywhere on campus. The video is a few years old, but we hope you will pay attention and see how it relates to stuff today. Of course it talks about rape, which can be upsetting. Again, you can leave any time. After this brief video we'll talk about some of its key points.

(Show DVD here)

### Team 2

I'm sure we all agree that what Frank did was wrong, was his choice, was his responsibility, and was his fault. It was also the shared responsibility of the others in his organization who supported him. The first-year woman he raped was certainly in no way at fault.

Of course not all rapists are just like Frank. Some are close friends, some are family members, and some are romantic partners. They can be almost anyone. What we're going to do now is pick apart Frank's tactics so we can all better understand how men like Frank operate. These tactics come from the research on men who rape women.

### Team 1

Research shows that men who rape actually plan things out much as Frank did in this DVD. As the researcher says at the end of this interview, we can all learn a lot from Frank's language. He uses words like *prey*, *targets*, and *staked out* to describe what he does. These are all words that dehumanize his victim. Like most men who rape, Frank shows that he views women as sexual objects to be conquered, coerced, and used solely for his own desires.

Frank also shows no empathy for his victim. When she was scared, he got angry. This lack of empathy is consistent with the research about men who rape.

## Team 2

Frank doesn't believe it when women say no to sex. He also makes light of the violence he used, even cutting off her breathing. Like most men who rape, Frank used only as much violence as was needed to terrify and coerce his victim into submission.

Also consistent with men who rape, Frank didn't seem to think he was doing anything wrong, and if he is like most men who rape, he will do it over and over again. In fact, Lisak & Miller (2002) released a study that showed that a guy like Frank commits an average of six rapes. So odds are, he's done this before, and he will do it again.

Also like most men who rape, the weapons he used were psychological—manipulation—backed up by physical force. Men like Frank also tend to use alcohol deliberately so that women will be easier to rape—either because they pass out or are less physically coordinated. Men who rape women almost never use weapons like knives or guns.

## Team 1

This video helps us see a little more clearly the red flags to watch out for in the type of guy who targets women for rape. You can see how open Frank was about what he did to this woman when he was talking with the male researcher. He would never share such secrets with a potential "target"—a woman. That is one of the reasons we are showing this to you. An even more detailed list is on the handout we gave you.

We want you to be better informed about the tactics of men like Frank so you can be better prepared if you run into guys like him. We also want you to help your friends notice if they are getting attention from guys like Frank. Knowing all of this, sadly, anyone can still experience a rape. And certainly there are guys who are nothing like Frank who commit rape. But many guys who rape can be recognized by the characteristics we've just talked about. A little later we'll talk about some ways to intervene if you see some potentially dangerous situations starting to unfold.

## *Part C: Helping a Friend*

### *Team 1*

We are sure you know how to help a friend through an everyday problem. But if a friend comes to you having survived rape, it can be really difficult to know what to do, or even where to start. And worse than wondering how best to help is the knowledge that some things can hurt. Even with the best intentions, some behaviors can come across to survivors as blaming them for what happened. And blaming a survivor is the last thing any of us should ever do if we want her to recover. So right now we're going to go over some things you can do, and some things we recommend that you avoid, that can help a survivor recover.

### Encourage Medical Attention

Getting to the hospital, especially within the first 3 days, is important for STI testing, evidence collection, and treatment of internal and external injuries. Often it can help if you offer to go with her. Staying in control is crucial to the survivor, so if she doesn't want to go, respect her decision.

### *Team 2*

### Listen

Here's a simple rule to remember: *Talk less and listen more.*

Along with listening, it is important that you avoid asking for details about what she was wearing or where she was. You may be curious about this, but if your goal is to help her, it's best to avoid such questions. That is where victim blaming can start to occur. Obviously you wouldn't mean to do this. We aren't talking about what you mean to do, we are talking about how a survivor hears what you say.

Asking a survivor what she was wearing or suggesting why it happened can come across to her as saying she deserved it. Instead, *listen* to what she wants to say, respect what she wants to keep private, and don't say anything that judges her statements. Even if deep down you do think she made some poor decisions, you have to decide what is more important—her recovery or pointing out her faults. If you want to make her recovery most important, listen to her in a nonjudgmental way and help get her the support she needs.

Many rape survivors say that one of the worst parts of their experience is having control taken away from them. Of course, she should always have control over who knows about her story. Remember that if you tell others about what happened to her without her permission, she has lost even more control. So be sure to keep her information confidential.

## *Team 1*

### Believe Her

Nationwide anonymous surveys of women who have survived rape in college show that they report the rape to police only 5% of the time. This makes rape the most underreported crime by far. Why is that? Why are so few rape survivors telling the police what happened to them? It is actually pretty simple: they don't feel like they're going to be believed.

All too often, people think women lie about being raped. This happens despite evidence from the U.S. Department of Justice that only 2 to 4% of rape reports are unfounded (Lonsway et al., 2007).

Of course, no one here needs to read a study to believe a friend. We all need to remember how harmful our skepticism toward rape survivors can be. Not believing her can traumatize her all over again. Guys like Frank, and the friends who support him, want everyone to think that women lie about being raped. It is up to all of us to decide if we want to create a community where survivors are believed, or to live with a culture that allows survivors to be retraumatized by disbelief.

Part of believing a survivor is making sure she knows that *what happened to her was not her fault*. Many survivors may start blaming themselves for being raped, asking themselves questions, such as "Why did I drink so much?" or "Why did I sit down with that guy?" I'm sure you've heard lots of reasons that it's important to tell her it isn't her fault. Well, here's another one: a study released in 2007 showed that women who experience sexual assault *and* blame themselves for what happened are significantly more likely to be sexually assaulted again within the next 4 months.

I'll say that again. A study released in 2007 (Miller, Markman, & Handley, 2007) showed that women who experience sexual assault *and* blame themselves for what happened are significantly more likely to be sexually assaulted again within the next 4 months. So it is extremely important that if a friend of yours is sexually assaulted and blames herself, you instead place *all* of the blame on the person who decided to commit the rape, not on the survivor.

## *Team 2*

### Advise Her to See a Counselor

Rape isn't something people get over in a short period of time; if they ever really get over it. Survivors take several months to several years to recover (Kilpatrick et al., 2007). The best thing a survivor can do to feel better as quickly as possible is to see a counselor on a regular basis. So please, recommend she see someone; even find out some names of good therapists she can go see.

Also, it may be a good idea for you to seek a counselor yourself. Not only will you have a confidential setting to talk about your emotions, but that counselor will give you more suggestions on how to help your friend.

## Part D: Becoming an Active Bystander

### Team 1

Right now we're going to ask you to talk with us about things that you personally can do to help stop rape. Given that 95% of rapes are committed by men (U.S. Department of Justice, 2010), we believe that guys should be taking much more responsibility than they currently are for ending it. Still, we believe that there are ways that women can intervene if they see their friends are in risky situations. By identifying roles for women to intervene to help stop rape from happening, women can be empowered to be part of the solution for ending rape in society—and that is a good thing!

Any time we talk about intervening in a risky situation, the first thing we need to address is personal safety. Everyone, regardless of sex, should consider whether or not it is best to call the police for help, enlist the support of other friends, do something to divert attention, or make a carefully timed comment. Ultimately, it has to be a personal decision; we hope everyone keeps their personal safety a top priority.

With that said, let's talk about a couple of hypothetical situations together. We want to hear about what you would consider doing in response to these situations.

### Team 2

In this first scenario, let's say you and a friend go out to an off-campus party together. You know a few people there, but not many. People are drinking beer and doing shots. After having a beer, your friend Julia talks to this guy Mike for about 5 minutes. Later that night Julia has had a lot to drink and is so intoxicated that she is having trouble standing up on her own. At this point Mike approaches her again, but this time he offers her a shot of vodka. She drinks it, and he grabs her hand and leads her back to his room saying something that you know means that he's going to try to have intercourse with her.

What would you do in this situation? We don't want to hear what you think you *should* do, but what *would* you do?

Follow-up questions:

- What could happen if you do nothing?
- What are some of the things you could *say* to Mike to get his attention?
- What are some of the things you could *do* to get his attention?
- What are some of the things you could do at the party to get other peoples' attention?
- What are some other resources you might be able to use for help?

■ If Julia said she "wanted" to hook up with Mike, what is the worst thing that could happen if you suggest she do otherwise? (She could resent you/get angry.)

■ How does this differ from the worst that could happen if you don't intervene? (Rape)

## Team 1

Okay, let's take a different situation. Think about what you would do if you had a roommate come to your room with a guy and you noticed that your roommate was so drunk that she was stumbling over her own feet. As she stumbled into the room, she mumbled, "Can you get out of here for a while so we can hang out?" You can tell by looking at the guy that he has no intention of just innocently hanging out. What do you think you would actually do in this situation?

If the audience says nothing, or nothing positive, here are possible responses for presenters to suggest:

■ You could talk with your roommate privately in the hallway and suggest that she's too drunk to hook up.

■ Ask the guy to go home and offer to help take care of her because she is so drunk.

■ You could say you aren't going to leave the room.

■ You could ask your roommate if she was able to pick up her medication for the STI she caught last week and hope the guy leaves.

Follow-up questions:

■ What could happen if you do nothing?

■ What are some of the things you could *say* to your roommate, or to the guy, to get their attention?

■ What are some of the things you could *do* to get their attention?

■ What are some other resources you might be able to use for help?

■ If your roommate said she "wanted" to hook up with the guy, what is the worst thing that could happen if you suggest she do otherwise? (She could resent you/get angry.)

■ How does this differ from the worst that could happen if you don't intervene? (Rape)

## *Part E: Closing*

### *Team 1*

Before we take your questions, think back to the discussion we had about the guy on the video, Frank. What are some of the danger signals that stood out to you about Frank and guys like Frank?

**Note:** When people bring up different ones, discuss them in the group as desired.

Optional questions:

■ Why did that danger signal stand out to you?
■ Why do you think that is a danger signal?
■ What do you think women should do if they see a guy do that?

For years, people who spoke to women about sexual assault have focused just on how they can reduce their risk for rape. While that is important, we think women deserve better than that. We think women can be empowered to make a much bigger difference. We think women can do more than just hope they survive rape. We think women can help *prevent* the rape of others by being active bystanders. To do that, to really help *prevent* rape, you need to commit to stepping up and doing something when you see something that just doesn't seem quite right—as the hypothetical situations we just talked about.

We hope that you'll use what we've talked about today to help prevent rape by being active bystanders. Our goal today wasn't to tell you what to do, where to go, who to talk to, anything like that. It was to encourage you if you pick up on those danger signals or something just creeps you out, please don't suppress that feeling to do something. If you speak up or intervene in some way, and there was nothing wrong, well that's awkward. But you can move on. The consequences can be much worse if you have a chance to prevent something horrible from happening to a friend, and you just let it pass.

We hope you'll trust your instincts and do what you can to help keep others safe.

### *Team 2*

We hope that by a show of hands you will commit to doing something to help prevent rape. Having heard our advice, and having great ideas of your own, we want to hear back from you.

Right now, will someone say one thing she is willing to do as a bystander to intervene to help end rape if she is in one of the types of situations we just talked about?

(Wait for someone to say something like "I'm willing to call the police"; "I'm willing to say I won't leave the room"; "I'm willing to get an RA.")

**Note:** When an audience member mentions an action, thank her and say "How many others are willing to (insert action here)?

Okay, how about another thing someone is willing to do?

*Repeat this until there are no more actions mentioned.*

## Team 1

What questions do you have?

If you would like to speak to us on a more individual basis for any reason, we will stick around after the presentation for as long as necessary. Also, remember that the counseling center on campus is a good resource for you if you want to talk with someone about something that has happened to you or someone else. Finally, if you log onto www.rainn.org, (that's "rain" with two "n"s), you can get the information for the nearest rape crisis center anywhere in the United States.

Thank you for coming, and thank you for committing to help end rape.

---

## *Handout for the Women's Program*

## CHARACTERISTICS OF MEN WHO RAPE AND
## COMMIT OTHER TYPES OF SEXUAL ASSAULT

This handout summarizes several recent studies that looked at characteristics of men who choose to rape and how they differ from men who choose not to rape. Section A covers research on men who admit committing a wide variety of behaviors of alcohol-related sexual assault in their past. Section B covers research on men who have committed rape. This section is based on research of men who have *not* been reported to the police for their crimes (84 to 95% of rapists) and has been collected through anonymous surveys of men on college campuses.

### SECTION A: MEN WHO HAVE SEXUALLY ASSAULTED (BUT NOT NECESSARILY RAPED) WOMEN IN THE PAST

*Men who have committed sexual assault (compared to men who have not committed sexual assault):*

1. Drink more alcohol (Abbey, Clinton-Sherrod, McAuslan, Zawacki, & Buck, 2003).
2. Are more likely to commit sexual assault, particularly if they have had four to eight drinks. Sexual assault is even more likely the more intoxicated the victim is (Abbey et al., 2003).
3. Think women lie about not wanting to have sex (Bernat, Calhoun, & Stolp, 1998).
4. Believe that if a woman is drinking it is a sign of sexual interest (Zawacki, Abbey, Buck, McAuslan, & Clinton-Sherrod, 2003).

### SECTION B: MEN WHO ADMIT TO RAPE

[all research from Dr. David Lisak including (Lisak & Miller, 2002)]
   *Men who admit to behaviors that meet the legal definition of rape on anonymous surveys.*

1. Are extremely adept at identifying "likely" victims and testing prospective victims' boundaries.
2. Plan and premeditate their attacks, using sophisticated strategies to groom their victims for attack and to isolate them physically.
3. Use only as much violence as is needed to terrify and coerce their victims into submission.
4. Use psychological weapons—power, control, manipulation, and threats—backed up by physical force, and almost never resort to weapons such as knives or guns.

5. Use alcohol deliberately to render victims more vulnerable to attack, or completely unconscious.
6. Rape multiple times.
7. Commit other forms of violence, such as battery and child abuse.
8. Are more sexually active than other men.
9. Believe that if they are not very sexually active then they are neither "successful" nor adequate as men.
10. View women as sexual objects to be conquered, coerced, and used for self-gratification.
11. Are much more likely to hold stereotyped beliefs about the "proper" roles for women and men in society.
12. Adhere to "rape myths" that both justify their aggressive acts and foster them, tell themselves that "women say no to sex even when they really want it," and disregard their victims' obvious signs of terror and resistance.
13. Harbor chronic, underlying feelings of anger and hostility toward women.
14. Easily feel slighted by women, and carry grudges against them. This underlying hostility is easily evoked and leads them to see women as "teases" who either "secretly" want to be coerced into sex or else "deserve" it.
15. Consistently have strong needs to dominate and to be in control of women; fearful of being controlled by women.
16. View sexual relations as "conquests," and all women as potential "targets" of conquests.
17. Are more emotionally constricted, much less emotionally expressive, less empathetic.
18. Tend to be part of sexually violent all-male subcultures that normalize sexual conquests through violent pornography, and explicit images of rape as being acceptable, noncriminal, and the sign of male virility.
19. Strive always to behave in rigidly and stereotypically masculine ways, are always on the alert for any perceived slight to their masculine identities, and are made very anxious by any situation that might cast doubt on their perceived masculinity. Tend to view aggression and violence as crucial markers of their adequacy as males.
20. When a woman resists his coercive sexual pressure, he is very likely to perceive this as a challenge and affront to his masculinity and to react with anger and aggression, behaviors which restore his sense of adequacy.

# Video Order Form for the Women's Program

## THE "UNDETECTED" RAPIST

Re-enactment of an interview conducted by Dr. David Lisak, excerpted from the National Judicial Education Program's video curriculum, *Understanding Sexual Violence: The Judge's Role in Stranger and Nonstranger Rape and Sexual Assault Cases.*

### *Video Order Form*

**Contact Name:**_____

Organization Name:_____

Address:_____

_____

Phone:_____ Fax:_____

Email:_____

Number of Videos at $15.00 each: _____
*Running time: 6 minutes, 18 seconds.*

Please remit your enclosed payment in the amount of _____ to NOW Legal Defense and Education Fund, earmarked for NJEP. You may pay by check or credit card. If you wish to pay by credit card, please complete the following:

Check one: ___ Visa ___ Mastercard ___ American Express

Card Number:_____ Exp. Date:___/____

Billing Address:_____

Signature:_____

Mail your order form and payment to:

**National Judicial Education Program**
**395 Hudson Street, 5ᵗʰ Floor**
**New York, NY 10014**

*Orders cannot be processed until payment is received. Our federal tax ID number, which you may need for ordering, is 23-7085442. Please allow two to three weeks for delivery. These prices include regular postage within the United States. If you are outside the United States, postage will depend on your location and postal preference, i.e., surface or air.*

For more information, contact the National Judicial Education Program at NOW Legal Defense and Education Fund at (212) 925-6635; Fax: (212) 226-1066, 395 Hudson Street, 5ᵗʰ Floor, New York, NY 10014-3684, njep@nowldef.org.

## Script for the Military Version of the Men's Program How to Help a Sexual Assault Survivor: What Men Can Do

### Part A

#### Team 1

Thank you for coming. Today we are going to present a brief called "How to Help a Sexual Assault Survivor: What Men Can Do." The first thing we have to say to you today is:

*We are not here to blame you for rape.* We are not here to talk down to you about rape. And we are not here because of any incidents that have happened in the military or anywhere else. The reason we're here is because when someone is sexually assaulted, usually the first person she goes to for help is a friend—not a counselor, not an MP, not an officer, *a friend.* And often that friend is a guy, one of you. So we want you to be prepared in case a friend, or someone close to you from back home, asks for your help after going through something like this. At this point we will introduce ourselves.

(Introduce selves, give name, rank, and hometown.)

So, we are not going to lecture you about why you shouldn't rape women. We already know you don't want to do that. Instead, we will talk about what we as guys can do about it. We will talk about how to help rape survivors and we will discuss some things we can do to make sure it isn't happening around us in the first place.

#### Team 2

The program we are presenting is part of the One in Four initiative. One in Four refers to the statistic that one in four women in the U.S. Military has experienced rape *during* her military service (Sadler, Booth, & Doebbeling, 2005). What is even more awful is that the same study found that 96% of the time, the person who raped her came from our own military.

When I first heard this statistic, it shocked me. And maybe like you, I even doubted it a little. But when you look at the numbers, they don't lie. *One quarter of the women with whom we serve* have experienced something as bad as rape, by a guy who wears our uniform.

Now, our goal isn't to shame those guys into changing their ways. That doesn't work. Rather, our goal is to help us all understand what rape feels like so we can better help women recover from rape. And our goal is to teach all the good guys out there—the overwhelming majority—to stand up and step in when we see something that just doesn't look right. It is you, the good guys, who can stop rape from happening before it starts. That is our focus today.

*Team 1*

## Disclaimer

Obviously, rape is a serious subject. There are parts of this program that can be upsetting. If you need to excuse yourself at any time, that's okay. We hope you will stay.

Now, both women and men survive rape, and both women and men commit rape. If you are a rape survivor, or someone close to you has experienced rape, you may be particularly affected by the DVD we will show you. If you'd like to talk privately, we will be available at the end of the brief. Also, we have placed flyers by the door with an overview of resources available.

*Team 2*

## Overview

We are going to do several things in this brief.

- We will show you and discuss a police training video that describes a rape situation.
- This DVD will help you learn what rape is like so that you will be better able to help a survivor in case she comes to you.
- We will then talk about how to help a sexual assault survivor.
- After that, we will talk about some ways guys talk with and about women.
- Next, we'll talk about how we can intervene as men if we see a sexual assault about to occur.
- Finally, we will end by answering any questions you have.

*Team 1*

When you think about rape, what is it that you usually imagine? Before I saw this presentation, I always thought of what I saw spotlighted on the news or on TV. There's a woman running alone late at night and some guy she doesn't know jumps out from behind the bushes, pins her down, and rapes her. That of course is stranger rape, and it occurs far too often. What we want you to remember is this:

*Four out of five times when a woman is raped, it is by someone she knows. It could be an acquaintance. It could be a friend. It could be a boyfriend. But four out of five times, it is someone she knows, and the average length of time she has known him is 1 year. So it's usually not someone she just met. But on average, she's known her attacker for an entire year.*

### Team 2

Right now we're going to show you a 15-minute DVD that describes a rape situation. This will help you understand what rape survivors go through so you'll be better able to help them if they come to you. The video itself is of Seattle police detective Dick Ramon who is training new officers about how to deal with rape situations. It doesn't show a rape happening, but it describes a rape in detail and just to be clear, it can be upsetting, particularly to people who have survived rape. After the video is over we'll talk more about what it might feel like to experience rape.

(Show DVD here.)

## Part B: Understanding Rape

### Team 1

We showed you this DVD to help you understand what it might feel like as a guy to experience rape. If a woman comes to you asking for help after experiencing rape, it is important that you understand what it might have felt like. Obviously, both men and women can be raped, and there are differences between a man raping a woman and a man raping a man. Discussing a situation in which a man is forcibly and unwillingly penetrated by another man is the closest parallel we could find to help you understand what rape feels like. As with many male-on-male rapes, what you watched showed a case where presumably heterosexual perpetrators (one had a wife, the other had a girlfriend) used rape and battery to assert control over another man.

Now we are going to draw some parallels between the police officer's experience and common experiences women have before, during, and after being raped. This will help you learn more about what it may feel like for women to be raped, and will make you better prepared in case a woman comes to you asking for help.

| Team 1 | Team 2 |
|---|---|
| *Police Officer's Experience* | *Survivor's Experiences* |
| **A Cop Moves a Trash Can** | **Everyday Situation Turns Bad** |
| Think back to when the police officer decided to move the trash can. He was just doing his job; in fact, he was just being helpful. It was just another normal thing he did as he went about his daily routine. Of course, he had no way to know what was about to happen. | In the same way, when men rape women, many of these incidents arise out of situations the woman can't predict. She may be hanging out with a trusted male friend, she may be on duty, doing her job, she may even be with a guy she wants to hook up with. But these are all things that she has control over, and the thing about rape is that, at some point, control is taken away from her. There is no flashing sign that goes off to say "you are about to be raped." These are just everyday situations that turn bad. |
| **"Don't Make a Move"** | **Frozen With Fear** |
| In the next part of the video, the police officer is told not to make a move. His first reaction, as he is being threatened is to remain still, play for time, and figure out what is going on. | Keep in mind that four of five times when a man rapes a woman, the woman knows who he is. So, usually, this person who is threatening her is someone she trusts, and that trust is being violated. If someone we trust suddenly threatens us, our first reaction might not be to fight back, run, or scream. In fact, in most cases, what most people do immediately is tense up. In most rape cases, what happens is that the woman freezes and tries to figure out what is going on. This freeze reaction is the same psychological process involved when soldiers on the front lines of battles don't fire, given the stress involved. Both involve traumatic circumstances, and both can immobilize people. |

*(Continued)*

**(Continued)**

| "Get on Your Knees" | Desire to Avoid Violence |
|---|---|
| Later, the police officer is told to get on his knees, and it becomes more obvious what is about to happen. It's hard to tell what anyone would do in this situation, without living through it, but he decided the most important thing was to stay alive. | Most men who rape women weigh a lot more than the woman they are attacking. This physical difference poses a threat, especially in an intimate situation where trust is on the line. Sensing this threat, a survivor may find that if she kicks or screams, he may become even more violent toward her. So it makes sense that some women might suddenly freeze in an intimate situation where a guy is doing something she doesn't want, out of fear that he might become more violent. Even so, the U.S. Department of Justice found that 70% of sexual assault survivors physically resist, but they end up being overpowered physically or psychologically. (Fisher et al., 2006) |
| **Fear of STIs** | **Fear of STIs and Pregnancy** |
| In this situation, the police officer is worried that, given the high-risk contact that was involved, he had to think about catching a whole variety of sexually transmitted infections. | Today, there are a lot of sexually transmitted infections to worry about. Being raped could mean catching a potentially fatal disease. According to the Centers for Disease Control, 1 of every 500 college students is infected with HIV (Gayle et al., 1990). In addition, at least one of five adults in the United States has genital herpes. |
|  | Although men sometimes experience rape, usually we can protect ourselves from these things—we can choose to have sex or we can have unprotected sex. Rape survivors don't have these options. |
|  | Also, for female survivors, they face the possibility that the rape could result in pregnancy. In fact, pregnancy occurs in about 5% of rape cases. These survivors must then consider the ramifications of that pregnancy on their lives. |
| **Humiliating Hospital Visit** | **Another Painful Process** |
| Remember how the officer felt in the waiting room? He wasn't the first one treated because he wasn't a gunshot victim and he wasn't in immediate danger of dying. He was then put on a table and had a doctor probing around his body collecting evidence. Clearly this was an uncomfortable exam. | Even though the rape exam is extremely important for her health, many survivors describe it as another painful process. She has to tell and retell her story to people who come in and out of the exam room. She has a person she's never met before thoroughly examining the most intimate parts of her body. Really, how many of us would want to have pubic hairs plucked out of our groin? And this is just one thing that has to happen during a rape exam. Thankfully, medical facilities have done a lot recently to make these exams go as well as possible, but as you can imagine, these rape exams are much more intrusive than other kinds of visits to the doctor, are quite painful, and happen right after she experiences something extremely traumatic. |

**(Continued)**

| Team 1 | Team 2 |
|---|---|
| *Police Officer's Experience* | *Survivor's Experiences* |
| **Did You Fight?** | **Did You Resist?** |
| Remember how the officers reacted to the raped officer. "What? You did what? You didn't pull your gun? Didn't you scream, didn't you yell, kick him in the balls?" (with disbelieving look). Then later on, the cop has his friend say, "Yeah, the guys have been talking and we think you knew those guys and maybe this was something consensual that kinda just got out of hand. Is that true?" | [With disbelieving tone of voice]. Where were you? Were you drinking? You were with *that* guy? You hooked up with him before, didn't you? [With passionate disbelief] So you were alone with that guy again? What were you wearing? Well, if you really were raped, why didn't you scream, push him away, and leave? So with all of your training, you let this happen? Are you sure it was rape, or did you want this to happen!? [Pause; speak in normal tone of voice] Rape survivors get asked these questions all the time, and none of them matters. The point is, her instinct was to stay alive and no matter what, no one, *no one,* ever asks to be raped. |

## Team 1

This rape experience we just described is similar to what many women experience. In fact, one of every four women in the military has survived rape during her military service. One of four military women has gone through an experience similar to the one we just talked about while she was serving our country. Knowing that, what can we do?

## *Part C: Helping a Survivor*

### *Team 1*

Now that you've heard more about how it might feel to survive rape, we are going talk about how to help a sexual assault survivor who comes to you asking for your help. If the situation happened within the military, you of course need to remember to follow all military protocols, the UCMJ, and the expectations set within your chain of command. The advice we are giving here is generic advice about how to be helpful to people you know who experience rape.

Every rape survivor is different, so there is no perfect step-by-step plan that will work every time. She will recover in her own way and on her own schedule. With that said, there are a few things you can *do*, and a few things to *avoid*, that will usually make her recovery easier.

### Encourage Medical Attention

It is important that she gets medical treatment, particularly within the first 3 days after the assault. She will need testing for STIs and have any injuries treated. If she gets treated in the first 3 days after the assault, she can also have evidence collected that will allow her to decide later about whether to be a witness in a case against the rapist. Because of the forced physical contact, she is likely to be injured and may have internal injuries that she cannot feel. So one of the best things you can do is encourage her to go get medical treatment, even offer to go with her. But remember; don't try to force her to do anything after a rape. Recommend that she go, but if she doesn't want to right away, respect her decision.

### *Team 2*

### No More Violence

I don't know about you, but if one of my friends came up to me and told me that some guy raped her, that some guy has caused *her* the kind of pain the cop went through on that video, my first instinct would be to go find that guy and beat the crap out of him. Maybe this would be your instinct too; a lot of guys feel this way at first. Actually, that is one of the worst things you can do if you want to help her recover.

You need to decide whose needs are more important—yours or hers. Take a step back and think—she has already tried to calm down one violent man. The last thing she needs as she is trying to tell you what happened to her is to feel like she has to calm you down, and try to control your anger too. She may also worry that if you go beat him up, he may come back and hurt her, rape her again, ruin her military career, or depending on who he is, shoot her with his sidearm. Instead of more violence, let her know calmly that you will do anything you can to help.

## *Team 1*

### Listen

This next suggestion can be one of the toughest: *Talk less and listen more.*

If your goal is to help her, don't ask for details about what she was wearing or where she was and don't suggest why it happened. If you ask these kinds of things she may think that you are trying to blame her for what happened. You may be curious about details, but if you want to help, it is better to avoid such questions. You need to focus on helping her understand that what happened to her was not her fault. Be sure to just listen to what she wants to say and don't judge her statements.

Many rape survivors say that one of the worst parts of their experience is having control taken away from them. As a friend, your instinct may be to hug her, but it is important for you to listen to her carefully about whether or not she wants to be held at all. If you think she does, ask her. Of course, she should also always have control over who knows about her story. Remember that if you tell others about what happened to her without her permission, she has lost even more control. So be sure to keep her information confidential.

## *Team 2*

### Believe Her

According to a study done by the U.S. Department of Justice, only 5% of rapes are reported to the authorities, making rape the single most underreported crime by far. Why is that? Why are so many rape survivors not telling the police what happened to them?

It is because survivors don't feel like they're going to be believed; and being believed is the most important thing to a survivor's recovery. In another study funded by the U.S. Department of Justice, it was found that only 2 to 4% of rape reports were unfounded. That's a pretty low percentage by any standard. Even if we take it at the highest point, 4%, that means at a bare minimum, 96% of the time when someone says she's been raped, there is no evidence contradicting her story, and every bit of proof to say that what she said is exactly what happened.

Of course you don't need a bunch of statistics in order to believe your friend, but it's important to know how harmful skepticism toward rape survivors can be. Also, if you think about it, it doesn't make sense for someone to go through everything that happens to women who report rape if it didn't happen—it is so tough on who it did happen to that most don't even report it. When women in the military report rape, think about it—does their status go up or down? In all likelihood, it goes way down. Very few women even report rape in the first place. So why on earth would a woman report rape when it *didn't* happen? It just doesn't make sense to go through after rape exams, lower status, and so much trauma if it didn't even happen.

*Team 1*

## Advise Her to See a Counselor

It takes several months to several years to heal from the trauma of rape to the point where someone can become mission ready (Kilpatrick et al., 2007). To feel better, seeing a counselor on a regular basis is critical. So please, recommend she see someone; even find out some names of good therapists she can go see when possible. Also, it may be a good idea for you to seek a counselor yourself. Not only will you have a confidential setting to talk about what happened, but that counselor will give you more suggestions on how to help your friend.

## Part D: Other Ways Men Can Help End Rape

### Team 1

Now that you've heard advice about how to help a sexual assault survivor, we're going to discuss other ways in which we can affect this issue in our day-to-day lives.

### Communicate During Encounters

One important thing we can do is make sure we are careful in our intimate experiences, if we choose to have them. The best way to do that is to keep an open line of communication when hooking up with someone.

None of us goes into intimate situations intending to hurt the person we're with—that's just not how guys think. But I do know good guys who have gotten themselves into risky situations, and it usually boiled down to their lack of clearly establishing consent. So it's important to communicate clearly if you choose to hook up. Be sure to listen to what the other person wants and does not want, and of course make sure the person is in a sober state of mind to be consenting in the first place.

### Cooperation Does Not Equal Consent

Just because a person is going along with something in an intimate situation doesn't mean she has necessarily agreed to it. She might be overwhelmed by how fast things are moving, she could be intimidated by your size difference, or she could just be uncomfortable. The only way to be sure that she is comfortable with what's happening is to *ask*.

Asking *doesn't* have to be awkward. We're certainly not talking about agreeing to terms on a written contract; that would be awkward. It can be real simple. It could be a few words, "Is this okay?" Ask her what she wants to do. The important thing is to have a situation where you ask her, give her time to respond, and then respond appropriately.

### "The Freeze"

A way we can know that someone might be *uncomfortable* is what we call "the freeze." Sometimes in an intimate situation, a person may freeze up. Some guys may think the person just needs to be "loosened up." He may try the same thing again, pour her a drink, or turn on some music. But think back to the video. When did the police officer freeze up? Just like the stories you hear sometimes of someone in combat for the first time, people will often freeze initially when they are scared and surprised.

We're not saying that if someone freezes up, it means she thinks she's going to be raped. But it's a good sign that we should find out why she's uncomfortable, and the best way to do that is simple: Stop and ask. So if you're initiating something new and think the other person is uncomfortable, or if you are unsure, be sure to stop and clear up what you two will do together. We've all grown up hearing that *no* means *no*; of course that is true. We also have to remember that just because a person *hasn't* said "no," *doesn't* mean that she's said "yes,"

*Team 2*

## Changing Language

Along with those things that we hope you'll think about in your own personal lives, I want to take a couple of minutes to discuss some things in the broader picture. These suggestions are related to language and behavior, and on the surface, they may seem minor or unrelated to rape. But in a subtle way, they can encourage people to accept or tolerate sexual assault. We think it is important that when we hear these types of things, we step up and find a way to let other guys know how their language can hurt women, even if that's not what they intended. And hurting women means we are less mission ready, and that hurts all of us.

## Joking About Rape

Obviously, from seeing the video and discussing the experiences common to sexual assault survivors, there's nothing funny about the crime of rape. But the word "rape" gets thrown around jokingly all the time. This is something my friends and I used to do years ago, and I'm sure you know what I mean. Maybe you're walking out of a test, and someone says "man, that test raped me." Or maybe watching a football game with some friends and one says "man, the (sports team) got raped." Of course, guys mean no harm by it, but the problem with talking about rape in a joking way, and using the word to mean something that it doesn't, is that it starts to lose its meaning. Think about the fact that one in four women survives rape during her military service. That's a lot of women you serve alongside who could hear you tell a joke that you don't mean to hurt anyone, but does. For survivors to hear us belittle their experience could be very painful. So we'd just suggest that if you hear a friend using the term *rape* in this way, suggest the friend use another word.

## Phrases That Put Women Down

This next section has to do with attitudes that are hurtful to women. This might be the kind of thing that comes up during a touch football game—one guy drops back and throws a pass, but it falls 10 yards short. So of course, his buddies are gonna jump on his case—"you throw like a bitch, take off your skirt." They're just joking around, and while there's nothing wrong with joking around, there is a problem with using those kinds of expressions. When we do that we make being a woman synonymous with weakness and inferiority. And that can make it a lot easier for some guys to justify treating women as though they *are* inferior. So in the same way as with the word *rape*, we hope you'll encourage your friends to avoid using these kinds of expressions.

## Stories of Abuse

This final suggestion has to do with condemning the abuse of women. Maybe you've been around sometime with a bunch of guys on an exercise or someplace where only the guys are around listening to one guy telling a story. He talks about having leave, going out, and how there was this drunk girl or "slut" who could barely stand up straight, but how he got her and "sealed the deal." Of course, guys tell hookup stories all the time. But as you're listening to this story, you start to realize he's not just talking about hooking up or sex. What he's really saying is that he took advantage of that woman, and may have caused her a lot of pain. We strongly suggest that if you find yourself in this situation, be the brave one we are taught to be. Stand up and let your friend know that you don't think what he did was right. I know that can be a really hard thing to do. But remember, if you think what he did was not right, there's a good chance the rest of the guys feel the same way. If you say something, they'll probably respect you for having the guts to speak your mind. At a minimum, we hope you don't laugh or prod for details to make him think you approve.

We know some guys have a hard time with this part of the program. It's tough to see the connections between word choice and rape. But I hope that having discussed the attitudes that these choices can encourage in some people, you'll make these changes, because while they're small for us, they could make a huge difference for someone we care about.

## *Part E: Bystander Intervention*

### *Team 1*

There are many situations where you can do something to help prevent a sexual assault from occurring. In this final section we want you to think about some situations where rape might occur, and talk about what you could do to step up as leaders and do something. This will give you the chance to think about this now, before it happens, so you can be more ready for these kinds of situations if and when they do occur.

### *Team 2*

### Guided Imagery

Now, we are going to ask you to imagine a situation happening as vividly as you can. We will talk you through it and have you imagine different things happening. The situation we will guide you through can be upsetting; we hope you'll participate as fully as possible though.

This really works best if you close your eyes, so right now, please close your eyes and think about this situation as vividly as you can. (Wait until they actually do.) Think for a moment about a woman *your age* about whom you care a lot—a girlfriend, a sister, a best friend (pause). Once you get that person in your mind, picture her at a party (pause) with about 10 people or so (pause) in someone's apartment (pause). Picture what she looks like (pause), her being happy and having a good time (pause), laughing and maybe dancing a little (pause). On this night, she's had a lot drink (pause), and she is really drunk (pause). So she decides to sit down on the couch (pause), and a guy her age whom she's known for a couple years, sits down next to her (pause). The party runs out of beer, so most of the people leave to go to another party (pause). Your friend is there on the couch with this guy (pause) alone (pause). He asks if she wants a shot (pause). Before she can respond, he puts it in her hand (pause) and she drinks it (pause). Now I want you to imagine that as she gets more and more intoxicated (pause) and almost passes out (pause), he then starts to rape her (pause). She tries to push him away (pause) but he's bigger than she is and she can't really move (pause). Think about this as vividly as you can (pause). Think back to the police video, where the cop was bent over the trash can (pause). Remember how he felt right then (pause)? This is how the most important woman to you feels right now (pause).

Now imagine that there's another man who comes back to the apartment to get his car keys (pause). He notices your friend and this guy (pause) and sees what is going on (pause). He was at the party, so he knows how completely drunk she was (pause). He knows that this is wrong (pause). He chooses to do nothing (pause). He just gets his keys (pause) and walks away (pause). Open your eyes (very long pause).

Okay, now we are going to ask you guys to talk a little bit about the scene we just went through. It doesn't have to be much, just give us your first reaction.

1. How did you feel imagining the woman closest to you being raped?
2. What do you think about the man who saw what was happening and walked away? What words would you use to describe him? (Wait for them to say a word that does not demean another group of people.)
3. Raise your hand if you feel that the man who watched and then walked away should have done something to stop it instead.

## Team 1

Okay, now that you've thought about a situation in which a (insert words they called him here) who was in a position to prevent or interrupt a rape did nothing; let's talk about a different situation in which some action on your part could help prevent a lot of pain and suffering.

## Scenario 1

In this first scenario, let's say you are sharing an apartment with one other guy who is a friend of yours. It's a small one bedroom apartment with two twin beds in the bedroom and a couch in the living room. It isn't much, but it's what you call home for now. One night, your roommate comes back to the apartment with a female who is so drunk that she is stumbling over her own feet and looks like she is about to pass out. He tells you to go sleep on the couch so they can hook up.

What are some of the possible responses you could have that would help keep a rape from happening?

If audience says nothing, or nothing positive, here are possible responses for presenters to suggest:

■ You could talk with your roommate privately and suggest she's too drunk to hook up.
■ You could offer to help take care of her because she is so drunk.
■ You could say you aren't going to leave the room.
■ You could invite a bunch of friends over for a party.

Follow-up questions (use as needed):

■ What could happen if you do nothing?
■ What could happen if you try to step in and do something?
■ What are some of the things you could *say* to get your roommate's attention?
■ What are some of the things you could *do* to get your roommate's attention?
■ What are some of the things you could do to get other people's attention?

- What are some other resources you might be able to use for help?
- What is the worst thing that could happen if you intervene?
- How does this differ from the worst that could happen if you don't intervene?

## Scenario 2

Okay, in this next scenario, let's say you're in a more social setting with other people around. You see two people there including one of your friends, Alan. He is hitting on this woman, which is normal for him. He's a bit aggressive with her. She is just sitting there, listening to him, not paying a lot of attention. He keeps at it. You aren't too surprised, it is Alan after all. Alan can be a bit of a bully, and that's Alan's style. You notice that the woman starts to look at her watch, and mostly look away from Alan. Alan moves in closer and closer to her. You start to think that it doesn't look quite right but you are having a good time with your other friends and don't want to be bothered. You remember that earlier that night Alan said he was going to "slay the first bitch he saw" that night. Next, you see Alan grab the woman by the hand and start to walk off. She doesn't look like she wants to go anywhere, seems to be looking around for a friend, and doesn't seem to know what to do.

What could you do to make it less likely that a rape could occur?

- Ask Alan about the STI he got last week and suggest he not give it to her.
- Look for her friends to see if they can help take her home while you distract Alan.
- Tell Alan the MPs are on the way to break up the party and everyone is leaving.
- "Accidentally" pour a cold or noxious substance on Alan that will distract him long enough for you to help the woman go home.

Follow-up questions (use as needed):

- What could happen if you do nothing?
- What could happen if you try to step in and do something?
- What are some of the things you could *say* to get Alan's attention?
- What are some of the things you could *do* to get Alan's attention?
- What are some of the things you could do to get other people's attention?
- What are some other resources you might be able to use for help?
- What is the worst thing that could happen if you intervene?
- How does this differ from the worst that could happen if you don't intervene?

## Team 2

### Some Advice

We hope that no matter what, in these scenarios you would choose to do *something*. If we could offer one piece of advice on approaching your friend, approach him as just that, a friend. Appeal to his loyalty to you as a friend, to your mission, your unit, or whatever works in the situation you find yourself in. No one wants to be talked down to, so if you approach him as a friend, he will be more likely to follow your lead. Of course, like many important things in life, it's not easy to step up and intervene without risking feeling like a jerk or even losing your friendship. However, in the end, we hope you agree with us that it is the right thing to do; and the right thing to do isn't always easy. And if there is anyone in here who got into the military because it is easy, go ahead and say so. Otherwise, it's time for us to lead by doing the right thing—step up and prevent rape.

So before we close, what questions do you have? (Take questions.)

We have flyers available with resources that you can give to a friend who has been raped. We will also stay after if you would like to talk to us individually.

## Team 1

As we close, we leave you with one final statistic. At the beginning of this program, we told you that a national study found that one in four of U.S. women veterans experienced rape during their military service. Almost all those women, 96%, are raped by members of the military. That's over one in four women in the U.S. military who experience rape during their military service.

## Team 2

This high percentage is a major reason we must lead the way. It is time for men in the military to take control of the one in four statistic and obliterate it by intervening when we see a rape about to happen. And if we decide to stand up and intervene when things look like they might get out of hand, we can. We hope you will join us.

Thank you.

## Script for the Military Version of the Women's Program Empowering Women: Learning About Dangerous Men and Helping Rape Survivors

### Part A: Establishing Rapport and Definitions

> Do: *Distribute the handout for the Women's Program: "Characteristics of Men Who Rape and Commit Other Types of Sexual Assault" as people enter the room.*

### Team 1

Good morning/afternoon. Today's brief is called "Empowering Women: Learning About Dangerous Men and Helping Rape Survivors."

*Insert if men are presenting:*

Many women are passionate about this issue, and as a result, many sexual assault programs are presented by women. We recognize that there are many more things women often do in their daily lives to reduce their risk for rape than men do; and though many men are rape survivors, a *whole* lot more women are.

All of us are here because we realize that rape is wrong, and we firmly believe that men need to take an active role in helping to end sexual assault, because if we are not part of the solution, then we are still part of the problem. So we are here today to add our perspectives as men to what you already know about the issue. We have been trained to offer you a research-based brief about sexual assault. Our hope is that what you hear today will be useful to you as you help your friends avoid risky situations and recover from very difficult experiences.

### Team 2

There are several things we are going to cover in this brief. One thing we aren't going to do is give you "the answer" about how to avoid being raped, because there is no definite answer. Rape happens when someone chooses to rape, and according to the National Crime Victimization survey (U.S. Department of Justice, 2010), 95% of the time, this choice is made by a man.

So while we can't offer you a solid rule that will guarantee the safety of your friends, or even you, we can give you the most statistically reliable information we can find on high-risk men so you can help your friends identify characteristics of high-risk guys and high-risk situations.

One thing we do know is that when women experience rape, it is usually by someone they know. That means that it is usually someone in their immediate environment. So when women in the military experience rape, the man who rapes them is usually a man in the military.

Several studies show that over one in four women serving in the military experiences rape during her military service. That is, of course, a very high number. What is just as disturbing is that research also shows that 96% of the perpetrators are men who wear their same uniform; 96% of the time when a woman in the U.S. military experiences rape, the perpetrator is a man in the U.S. military.

The responsibility for this, of course, lies with the perpetrators themselves. We also believe that knowledge is power. So we are here to share information with you today, so you can turn that information into knowledge, and use that knowledge to empower yourself and other women.

## Team 1

### Overview

In the next 45 minutes or so, we will share some information with you that will empower you to help your friends reduce their risk for experiencing sexual assault, and help your friends recover from it in case it does happen. We will do four basic things:

1. First, we are going to show you a video where a researcher interviews a guy who set a woman up to rape her. This will help you identify characteristics of high-risk men so that you can better help your friends get out of dangerous situations.
2. After that, we're going to talk about how to help a friend who survives rape.
3. Then we'll ask you to talk with us about how you think you can intervene as an active bystander to help your friends get out of bad situations if you are actually there when something happens.
4. Finally, we'll wrap up by asking you what you personally are willing to do after today's program.

## Team 2

### Disclaimers

Obviously, rape is a disturbing subject. Any part of today's brief could disturb you. If you need to leave the room at any time, that's okay. Obviously, we hope you will stay.

If you are a rape survivor, or are a friend or relative of a survivor, you may be particularly affected by our discussion. If you'd like to talk privately, we will be available at the end of the program. Also, just so you know, there are resources available to you through your chain of command and through the Department of Defense. In addition, if you go to www.rainn.org, that's "rainn" with two "n"s— you can find the location of a rape crisis center anywhere in the country. They also operate an online hotline 24 hours a day, 7 days a week.

When you hear the word "rape," lots of things can come to mind. Before I saw this presentation, I always thought of what I saw on the news or on TV every week. There's a woman running alone late at night, and some guy she doesn't know jumps out from behind the bushes, pins her down, and rapes her. That of course is stranger rape, and it occurs far too often. What we want you to remember this:

*Four of five times when a man chooses to rape a woman, it is a man the woman knows. It could be an acquaintance. It could be a friend. It could be someone from her unit. It could be a boyfriend. But four of five times, it is someone she knows, and the average length of time she has known him is 1 year. So it's usually not someone she just met. But on average, she's known her attacker for an entire year.*

## Part B: Recognizing Dangerous Men

*Team 1*

One of the things that research shows is that women can reduce their risk for being sexually assaulted if they are more able to detect danger signals from a man who is setting them up for a sexual assault. That is a foundation of our program. Of course, even if every danger sign is detected, nobody is ever at fault for experiencing rape—rape is the fault only of the rapist.

There has actually been a lot of research done on men who rape—both those who rape strangers and those who rape women they get to know. A lot of this research is detailed on the handout we gave you in the beginning of the presentation.

We are going to show you a DVD where a guy is interviewed by a college professor who studies men who rape. This guy is actually an actor, but he is reading—word for word—the transcript of an interview with a real person on a college campus who set up a woman for rape. Although this situation occurred on a college campus and not in a military environment, research shows that the characteristics of rapists are very similar across different situations.

In the situation on the DVD we will show you, the woman never reported the rape, so of course the guy never got in trouble. Of course it talks about rape, which can be upsetting. Again, you can leave anytime. After this brief video we'll talk about some of its key points.

(Show DVD)

*Team 2*

I'm sure we all agree that what the character Frank did was wrong, was his choice, was his responsibility, and was his fault. It was also the shared responsibility of the others in his organization who supported him. The woman he raped was certainly in no way at fault.

Of course, not all rapists are just like Frank. Some are close friends, some are family members, and some are romantic partners. They can be almost anyone. Just as it is important for us to understand the enemy—a terrorist, a foreign power attacking the United States, or whomever, what we're going to do now is pick apart Frank's tactics so we can all better understand how men like Frank operate. These tactics come from years of research on men who rape women.

*Team 1*

Research shows that men who rape actually plan things out much as Frank did in this DVD. As the researcher says at the end of this interview, we can all learn a lot from Frank's language. He uses words like *prey*, *targets*, and *staked out* to describe what he does. These are all words that dehumanize his victim. Like most men who rape, Frank shows that he views women as sexual objects to be conquered, coerced, and used solely for his own desires.

Frank also shows no empathy for his victim. When she was scared, he got angry. This lack of empathy is consistent with the research about men who rape.

## Team 2

Frank doesn't believe it when women say no to sex. He also makes light of the violence he used, even cutting off her breathing. Like most men who rape, Frank used only as much violence as was needed to terrify and coerce his victim into submission.

Also consistent with men who rape, Frank didn't seem to think he was doing anything wrong, and if he is like most men who rape, will do it over and over again. In fact, Lisak & Miller (2002) released a study that showed that a guy like Frank commits an average of six rapes. So odds are, he's done this before, and he will do it again.

Also like most men who rape, the weapons he used were psychological—manipulation—backed up by physical force. Men like Frank also tend to use alcohol deliberately so that women will be easier to rape—because they either pass out or are less physically coordinated. Men who rape women almost never use weapons like knives or guns.

## Team 1

This video helps us see a little more clearly the red flags to watch out for in the type of guy who targets women for rape. You can see how open Frank was about what he did to this woman when he was talking with the male researcher. He would never share such secrets with a potential "target"—a woman. That is one of the reasons we are showing this to you. An even more detailed list of red flags is on the handout we gave you.

We want you to be better informed about the tactics of men like Frank so you can be better prepared if you run into guys like him. We also want you to help your friends notice if they are getting attention from guys like Frank. Knowing all of this, sadly, anyone can still experience a rape. And certainly there are guys who are nothing like Frank who commit rape. But many guys who rape can be recognized by the characteristics we've just talked about. A little later we'll talk about some ways to intervene if you see some potentially dangerous situations starting to unfold.

## *Part C: Helping a Friend*

### *Team 1*

We are sure you know how to help a friend through an everyday problem. But if a friend comes to you having survived rape, it can be really difficult to know what to do, or even where to start. And worse than wondering how best to help is the knowledge that some things can hurt. Even with the best intentions, some behaviors can come across to survivors as blaming them for what happened. And blaming a survivor is the last thing any of us should ever do if we want them to recover. So right now we're going to go over some things you can do, and some things we recommend that you avoid doing, that can help a survivor recover. Of course, you always need to keep in mind the current policies in place in the military and how they relate to any disclosures made to you.

### Encourage Medical Attention

Getting to a clinic or hospital, especially within the first 3 days, is important so that survivors can be tested for STIs, evidence collection, and treatment of internal and external injuries. If you are able, it can help if you offer to go with her. Staying in control is crucial to the survivor, so if she doesn't want to go, respect her decision.

### *Team 2*

### Listen

Here's a simple rule to remember: *Talk less and listen more.*

Along with listening, it is important that you avoid asking for details about what she was wearing or where she was. You may be curious about this, but if your goal is to help her, it's best to avoid such questions. That is where victim blaming can start to occur. Obviously you wouldn't mean to do this. We aren't talking about what you mean to do, we are talking about how a survivor hears what you say.

Asking a survivor what she was wearing or suggesting why it happened can come across to her as saying she deserved it. Instead, *listen* to what she wants to say, respect what she wants to keep private, and don't say anything that judges her statements. Even if deep down you do think she made some poor decisions, you have to decide what is more important—her recovery or pointing out her faults. If you want to make her recovery most important, listen to her in a nonjudgmental way and help get her the support she needs.

Many rape survivors say that one of the worst parts of their experience is having control taken away from them. Of course, she should always have control over who knows about her story. Remember that if you tell others about what happened to her without her permission, she has lost even more control. So be sure to keep her information confidential.

## Team 1

### Believe Her

Nationwide anonymous surveys of women who have survived rape show that they report the rape to police only 5–15% of the time (Fisher et al., 2006; Kilpatrick et al., 2007). This makes rape the most underreported crime by far. Why is that? Why are so few rape survivors telling the police what happened to them? It is actually pretty simple: most don't feel like they're going to be believed.

All too often, people think women lie about being raped. People think this despite evidence from a study done by the U.S. Department of Justice that only 2 to 4% of rape reports are unfounded.

Of course, no one here needs to read a study to believe a friend. We all need to remember how harmful our skepticism toward rape survivors can be. Not believing her can traumatize her all over again. Guys like Frank, and the friends who support him, want everyone to think that women lie about being raped. It is up to all of us to decide if we want to create a community where survivors are believed, or to live with a culture that allows survivors to be retraumatized by disbelief.

Part of believing a survivor is making sure she knows that *what happened to her was not her fault.* Many survivors may start blaming themselves for being raped, asking themselves questions, such as "Why did I drink that night?" or "Why did I sit down with that guy?" I'm sure you've heard lots of reasons that it's important to tell her it isn't her fault. Here's another one: a study released in 2007 showed that women who experience sexual assault *and* blame themselves for what happened are significantly more likely to be sexually assaulted again within the next 4 months.

I'll say that again. A study released in 2007 showed that women who experience sexual assault *and* blame themselves for what happened are significantly more likely to be sexually assaulted again within the next 4 months. So it is extremely important that if a friend of yours is sexually assaulted and blames herself, you instead place *all* of the blame on the person who decided to commit the rape, not on the survivor.

## Team 2

### Advise Her to See a Counselor

Rape isn't something people get over in a short period of time; if they ever really get over it. Survivors take several months to several years to recover (Kilpatrick et al., 2007). The best thing a survivor can do to feel better as quickly as possible is to see a counselor on a regular basis. So please, recommend she talk with a counselor; even find out some names of good counselors she can go see if you have access to this information.

Also, it may be a good idea for you to seek a counselor yourself if one is available to you. Not only will you have a confidential setting to talk about your emotions, but that counselor will give you more suggestions on how to help your friend.

## Part D: Becoming an Active Bystander

### Team 1

As women in the military, we aren't known for sitting around and letting things just happen. We make things happen. Being an active bystander fits right into that. It means acting when we see something isn't right. It also means stepping up when someone needs help. It means making sure nobody gets hurt who wears our uniform.

We're going to ask for you to talk with us about things that you personally can do to help stop rape. Given that 95% of rapes are committed by men, we believe that guys should be taking much more responsibility than they currently are for ending it. Still, we believe that there are ways that women can intervene if they see their friends are in risky situations. By identifying roles for women to intervene to help stop rape from happening, women can be empowered to be part of the solution for ending rape in society—and that is a good thing!

Any time we talk about intervening in a risky situation, the first thing we need to address is personal safety. Everyone, regardless of sex, should consider whether or not it is best to get other people involved for help or go it alone. Ultimately, it has to be a personal decision; we hope everyone keeps their personal safety a top priority.

With that said, let's talk about a couple of hypothetical situations together. We want to hear from you about what you would consider doing in response to these situations.

### Team 2

In this first scenario, let's say you and a friend go out to a party together. You know a few people there, but not many. People are drinking beer and doing shots. After having a beer, your friend Julia talks to this guy Mike for about 5 minutes. Later that night Julia has had a lot to drink and is so intoxicated that she is having trouble standing up on her own. At this point Mike approaches her again, but this time he offers her a shot of vodka. She drinks it, and he grabs her hand and leads her back to his room saying something that you know means that he's going to try to have intercourse with her.

What would you do in this situation?

Follow-up questions:

■ What could happen if you do nothing?
■ What are some of the things you could *say* to Mike to get his attention?
■ What are some of the things you could *do* to get his attention?
■ What are some of the things you could do at the party to get other peoples' attention?
■ What are some other resources you might be able to use for help?

■ If Julia said she "wanted" to hook up with Mike, what is the worst thing that could happen if you suggest she do otherwise? (She could resent you/get angry.)
■ How does this differ from the worst that could happen if you don't intervene? (rape)

## Team 1

Okay, let's take a different situation. Think about what you would do if you had a roommate come to your room with a guy and you noticed that your roommate was so drunk that she was stumbling over her own feet. As she stumbled into the room, she mumbled, "Can you get out of here for a while so we can hang out?" You can tell by looking at the guy that he has no intention of just innocently hanging out. What do you think you would actually do in this situation?

Here are possible responses for presenters to suggest:

■ You could talk with your roommate privately in the hallway and suggest that she's too drunk to hook up.
■ You could ask the guy to go home and offer to help take care of her because she is so drunk.
■ You could say you aren't going to leave the room.
■ You could ask your roommate if she was able to pick up her medication for the STI she caught last week and hope the guy leaves.

Follow-up questions:

■ What could happen if you do nothing?
■ What are some of the things you could *say* to your roommate, or to the guy, to get their attention?
■ What are some of the things you could *do* to get their attention?
■ What are some other resources you might be able to use for help?
■ If your roommate said she "wanted" to hook up with the guy, what is the worst thing that could happen if you suggest she do otherwise? (she could resent you/get angry)
■ How does this differ from the worst that could happen if you don't intervene?

## *Part E: Closing*

### *Team 1*

Before we take your questions, think back to the discussion we had about the guy on the video, Frank. What are some of the danger signals that stood out to you about Frank and guys like Frank?

**Note:** When people bring up different ones, discuss them in the group as desired.

### Optional Questions:

Why did that danger signal stand out to you?
Why do you think that is a danger signal?
What do you think women should do if they see a guy do that?

For years, people who spoke to women about sexual assault have focused just on how they can reduce their risk for rape. While that is important, we think women deserve better than that. We think women can be empowered to make a much bigger difference. We think women can do more than just hope they survive rape. We think women can help *prevent* the rape of others by being active bystanders. To do that, to really help *prevent* rape, you need to commit to stepping up and doing something when you see something that just doesn't seem quite right—as in the hypothetical situations we just talked about.

We hope that you'll use what we've talked about today to help prevent rape by being active bystanders. Our goal today wasn't to tell you what to do, where to go, who to talk to, anything like that. It was to encourage you, if you pick up on those danger signals or something just creeps you out, to not suppress that feeling to do something. If you speak up or intervene in some way, and there was nothing wrong, well that's awkward. But you can move on. The consequences can be much, much worse if you have a chance to prevent something horrible from happening to a friend, and you just let it pass.

We hope you'll trust your instincts and do what you can to help keep others safe.

### *Team 2*

We hope that by a show of hands you will commit to doing something to help prevent rape. Having heard our advice, and having great ideas of your own, we want to hear back from you.

Right now, will someone say one thing she is willing to do as a bystander to intervene to help end rape if she is in one of the types of situations we just talked about?

*(Wait for someone to say something like "I'm willing to say I won't leave the room"; "I'm willing to get an MP"; "I'll beat the guy senseless.")*

**Note:** When an audience member mentions an action, thank her and say "How many others are willing to (insert action here)?

Okay, how about another thing someone is willing to do?

*(Repeat this until there are no more actions mentioned.)*

## Team 1

What questions do you have?

If you would like to speak to us on a more individual basis for any reason, we will stick around after the presentation for as long as necessary. Also, remember that if you log onto www.rainn.org, (that's "rain" with two "n"s) you can get the information for the nearest rape crisis center anywhere in the United States.

Thank you for coming, and thank you for committing to help end rape.

# Chapter 3

# Basic Training for Peer Educators

This chapter provides what I believe to be the most critical training exercises necessary for peer educators to go through prior to serving as peer educators. Chapter 4 consists of "Advanced Training" exercises that you might choose to supplement these "basic" exercises for your peer educators before they present. Exercises in Chapter 4 can also serve as refresher training for current peer educators.

Some training modules in this chapter are intended for male audiences, some for female audiences, and some can be used with either group. Ultimately, it is up to you how many modules you want to use in your training program for peer educators and which modules you wish to use—even which part of each module. As with everything, the choice is yours!

The size of your training group should be around 12 to 16 people. More than 20 people in a training group can make the climate prohibitive for small group discussion.

# Module 1

## *Introductions, Overview, and Ground Rules*

**Time needed: 45 minutes**
**Intended audience: Men or women**

Do: *Greet and mingle with new group members as they arrive. Work to create a "we're all in this together" atmosphere. Start with a lot of energy, especially if it is early in the morning.*

Do: *Introduce yourself and talk about your background and interest in sexual assault issues.*

Ask: Let's go around the room and have everybody introduce themselves so we can start to get to know each other. At this point, give us your name, your hometown, and something unique about you that you want the group to know.

Do: *Pass out a copy of the schedule. Review the schedule so people have a basic idea of what to expect. If you are doing any exercises that could be upsetting, such as showing a movie clip of a rape scene, warn people now so that they can know ahead of time to anticipate this.*

Do: *Tell peer educators that they will be learning to present a program that has been shown by research to be effective. They can have confidence that when they present they will be making a measurable difference. They will learn during training about this difference.*

Do: *Facilitate a conversation to set ground rules for discussion during training. You might start like this:*

State: Many of the training exercises we will go through will require your active participation. There will be times when you will be able to share your personal experiences. There will be times when you will be asked to talk about your opinions.

Ask: As we go through training, what kinds of norms or rules do you all want to set to guide these discussions?

Do: *As each suggestion is made, ask the group:*

Ask: Do people like this idea?

Do: *If you see most of the group nod or say yes,*

Ask: Can everyone agree to this?

Do: *If everyone says yes, write it on newsprint or a dry erase board up front. Continue until there are no more rules to suggest.*

Note: *The following list includes some suggestions, in case your group isn't sure where to start.*

Personal information that is shared in the room stays in the room.

Listen to what everyone has to say and respect everyone's opinions.

When in doubt, share it and get the chance to get feedback on an idea.

If we disagree with someone's idea, it is okay to confront the idea, but don't attack the person.

# Module 2

## *Team Builder: Strengths and Experiences*

**Time needed: 30 minutes**
**Intended audience: Men or women**

State:  I want you to be able to share why you are here because some people come to this training program having had an experience with sexual
assault—with themselves or with someone close to them—that they want to
share upfront and let the group know about. For others, they really want to
help out but haven't been touched personally by the issue, or wish not to
share a personal experience if they've had one.

State:  Whatever your reason for being here, feel free to share on your own
comfort level. Second, in order to be a strong group we need to determine
where our strengths lie. I know it's not comfortable for everyone to say, but
please let us know what you do well and how you can contribute best to
our group and to each other.

Ask:  Why are you here? What strengths do you believe you bring to the group?

# Module 3

## The Men's Program Presentation

**Time needed: 2 hours (presentation and discussion of program)**
**Intended audience: Men**

Do: *Show participants the Men's Program, presented either by you or by trained peer educators. Alternatively, have peer educators read through the script as a group and show them the police rape training video at the appropriate time when it comes up during the program. Presenting the program should take just over an hour.*

Do: *After the presentation, spend time talking about their reactions to the program. You are unlikely to need questions to facilitate a discussion of the Men's Program. Participants are likely to be initially quiet and then have a bunch of questions about it. Some may be just comments "Wow, that was powerful"— some may be specific, "Why shouldn't you beat the guy up?" Some of their questions may be about what it is like to present.*

Do: *See if you can get them to talk about their emotional, visceral experience during the program—how it felt for them so it can solidify in their minds (but try not to use the word* emotional; *some guys don't like that word). We want them to feel the experience as much as possible so that they can remember what they are trying to match for others in the future.*

Ask: What are some of your initial reactions to the Men's Program?

Ask: What did you notice about how the program approached you as a person (as a helper/bystander, not as a rapist)?

Ask: How did you react to the victim in the video being a man?

Ask: Did you suspect beforehand the victim would be male?

Ask: How did you react to being asked to consider what it might feel like to experience rape?

Note: *This gets them to go back and reconsider that feeling so they can think about how to then recreate that for others.*

Ask: What are some challenges you think you'll have in learning to present the program?

# Module 4

## *The Women's Program Presentation*

**Time needed: 90 minutes (presentation and discussion of program)**
**Intended audience: Women**

Do: *Show participants the Women's Program, presented either by you or by trained peer educators. Alternatively, have peer educators read through the script as a group and show them The Undetected Rapist video at the appropriate time when it comes up during the program. Presenting the program should take about 40 minutes.*

Do: *After the presentation, spend time talking about their reactions to the program.*

Ask: What are some of your initial reactions to the Women's Program?

Ask: In what way did the program's approaching you as a potential helper and as someone who could intervene to help prevent the rape of a friend affect you?

Ask: What are some of your other thoughts about the program?

Ask: What are some challenges you think you'll have in learning to present the program?

## Module 5

### *Theory, Research, and Outcomes Assessment on the Men's Program*

**Time needed: 60 minutes**
**Intended audience: Men**

One of the things that will help motivate your peer educators is knowing that what they do makes a difference. Providing them with an overview of the theory, research, and outcomes of the Men's Program will give them the confidence that what they do really works.

The handouts below, also found in *The Men's Program: A Guide for Male Peer Educators*, provides you with the structure for this discussion. If you would like copies of the articles evaluating the Men's Program, they are available at http://okstate.academia.edu/JohnFoubert. Future research on both the Men's Program and the Women's Program will be posted on this Web site as well.

# Handouts

## *Theories of Attitude and Behavior Change*

### *Belief System Theory*

To produce lasting attitude change, interventions must be designed to maintain people's existing self-conceptions (Grube, Mayton, & Ball-Rokeach, 1984). Grube et al. (1994) conclude that it is possible to change many different types of attitudes, values, and behaviors by using a single intervention. Such interventions, if delivered in such a way that existing self-conceptions are maintained or enhanced, can last for years.

### *The Elaboration Likelihood Model*

Behavior change is most likely when people:

■ Are motivated to hear the message
■ Can understand it well
■ Perceive it as personally relevant (Petty & Cacioppo, 1986)

These three conditions—motivation, understanding the message, and personal relevance—make "central route processing" more likely. Central route processing is a type of thinking characterized by the thoughtful evaluation of the material being presented. Central route processing produces greater attitude change, more strongly predicts behavior, and shows greater resistance to later arguments than its opposite, peripheral route processing. Peripheral route processing occurs when participants base their decisions concerning whether to alter their attitudes on the perceived expertness, trustworthiness, and attractiveness of the presenter. If attitude change occurs when processing is peripheral, it is less enduring (Petty & Cacioppo, 1986).

The Elaboration Likelihood Model is visually displayed in the following diagram:

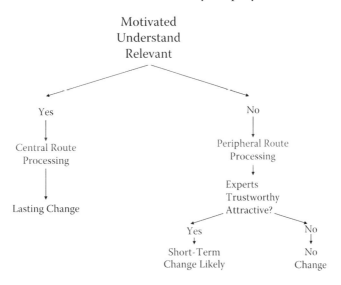

## Research Underlying the Men's Program

- One in four college women has experienced rape or attempted rape (Douglas, Collins, Warren, Kann, Gold, Clayton, Ross et al., 1997; Fisher, Cullen, & Turner, 2006; Koss, Gidycz, & Wisniewski, 1987).

- A substantial amount of research has shown that sexual assault programs presented to single-sex audiences are more effective than those presented to coed audiences (Brecklin & Forde, 2001; Schewe, 2007).

- Research has shown that sexual assault programs presented by peer educators are more effective than those presented by administrators, faculty, and others (Stein, 2007).

- Programs that emphasize getting men to focus on respecting women's "no"; not having sex with women who are intoxicated; not expecting sex (e.g., as a payment for dinner); not interpreting women's flirting, dress, and behaviors as an invitation to sex; challenging gender stereotypes and belief of rape myths, such as blaming the victim and legitimizing rape are rejected by men because they did not see themselves in the same group as rapists and therefore did not interpret the information as applicable to them and do not identify educational efforts of challenging rape myths and rape-supportive attitudes as relevant to them. Teaching men to support survivors and act as allies was viewed by men positively (Scheel, Johnson, Schneider, & Smith, 2001).

- A thorough review of the research found that all eight programs evaluated in the research literature that discuss male-on-male rape report positive outcomes. Both programs that evaluate the impact of discussing male-on-female rape with male audiences report negative outcomes (i.e., a greater likelihood of sexual aggression and increased rape myth acceptance). Thus, research strongly supports the use of describing a male-on-male rape experience in programs for men (Schewe, 2007).

- Bystander intervention training is an effective way to help decrease sexual assault (Banyard, Plante, & Moynihan, 2004).

## Effects of the Men's Program

- Lowers men's rape myth acceptance for 7 months (Foubert, 2000).
- Lowers men's intent to rape for 7 months (Foubert, 2000).
- Helps men understand what rape feels like, and increases their empathy and sensitivity to rape 5 months after seeing the program (Foubert & Perry, 2007).
- Leads to a decline in telling rape jokes (Foubert & Perry, 2007).
- Makes men less likely to believe "she asked for it," "she lied," and "it wasn't rape" (Foubert & Newberry, 2006).
- Increases men's empathy toward female rape survivors (Foubert & Newberry, 2006).

■ Of those who see the Men's Program who reported any degree of likelihood of committing sexual assault before seeing the program, 73% decrease their likelihood after the program, 63% fall to no likelihood at all (Foubert & Newberry, 2006).

■ Men of color react to the Men's Program in profoundly similar ways as white men (Foubert & Cremedy, 2007).

■ Men who see the Men's Program report a significantly greater sense of personal effectiveness about how to intervene if they see a potential sexual assault situation about to occur, and a significantly greater willingness to intervene as a bystander if they see a sexual assault about to occur (Langhinrichsen-Rohling, Foubert, Brasfield, Hill, & Shelley-Tremblay, in press).

■ The Men's Program is *the only program* in the research literature on young adult men ever to report a decline in sexual assault among men who see the program. A study found that 10% of fraternity men who did not see the Men's Program committed sexual assault during their freshman year. Fraternity men who saw the Men's Program had this cut almost in half, down to 6%. The severity of the sexual assaults they committed was even more affected. Guys who missed seeing the Men's Program committed acts of sexual assaults that were eight times worse on a scale of sexual assault severity than guys who saw the Men's Program (Foubert, Newberry, & Tatum, 2007).

■ Two years after seeing the Men's Program, 79% of men reported that either their attitudes or their behavior had changed due to the program's effects, or that the program reinforced their beliefs (Foubert, Godin, & Tatum, in press).

Comments these men made include the following:

■ There was one time when a friend was going to engage in sexual activity with a girl who was really drunk. Me and a couple of other guys intervened because the girl seemed out of it (also, she was another friend's sister). They ended up not having sex.

■ Mostly as a result of the One in Four program I am very cautious about initiating any kind of sexual activity while under the influence of alcohol.

■ My attitude is pretty much to avoid mixing alcohol with sex and One in Four definitely helped me commit to that idea.

■ I have helped a girl friend get out of a potentially scary situation.

■ Yes. Drunk girl asked me to take her home, then tried to hook up with me and I said no.

■ Yes, I have refused sex with a girl who was asking for it, but was more drunk that I was.

■ I have been more aware not only of my own sobriety, but of the sobriety of the girl and acted accordingly by suggesting that we're both too drunk.

■ Yes—A woman had consumed alcohol, and although she wasn't passing out drunk and seemed coherent, we refrained from sexual activity. Regardless of my personal views of rape and alcohol, I'm aware that situations can easily be misconstrued and get out of control, and I don't want to risk having that happen to a woman, or me.

■ Yes, I turned down sex because the girl was very intoxicated. She thanked me afterward and things progressed how I wanted them to.

# Module 6

## *The Male Box**

**Time needed: 60 minutes**
**Intended audience: Men (could also be used to help women understand men)**

State: I am going to ask that you share your ideas about several things. I will lead you through a discussion of several topics including

1. Some of the stereotypical ways society tells men they need to act.
2. Words used to describe those who do not conform.
3. Commonalities of those words.
4. Damaging behaviors men sometimes do to themselves to conform.
5. And finally, we'll work together to connect this to sexual assault.

Ask: So who here knows the difference between sex and gender?
Note: *People are born with a biological, anatomical sex, male or female. Gender roles, masculine and feminine, are a way people behave according to societal standards. "Male" refers to sex, "masculine" refers to gender. Likewise "female" refers to sex, "feminine" refers to gender.*
Ask: How do we learn to be men in today's society? *Who* teaches us?
Note: *Media, parents, professors/officers, teachers, coaches, peers—all parts of "society"*

State: I'm going to draw a box up here on the board and label it at the top "To Be a Man." I want us to fill this box with words and phrases that answer this very important question:

Ask: What does society *stereotypically* say it means "to be a man?"
Note: *Make sure that all the categories below are covered; if they use curse words, that is okay for this exercise.*

- Relationships with women (dominant, player, in charge)
- Attitude (tough, unemotional, hard)
- Possessions (car, money, job, women)
- Sexuality (heterosexual, experienced, definitely not gay)
- Behaviors (drinking, playing sports, having sex, fighting)

---

* Original printed with permission from the Mentors in Violence Prevention (MVP) Program. Copyright 1994, Northeastern University's Center for the Study of Sport in Society. Substantial modifications made.

State: Okay. You did a great job filling that box.

Ask: Let's take an initial look at what you put in the box. What do you notice about the characteristics that you put in the box?

Prompt: Do you think that the characteristics are mostly positive, mostly negative, or a mix of both?

Note: *At some point you should be able to lead the group to agree that at least some of the characteristics are harmful under some circumstances.*

State: So it looks like we're saying that there is a lot in this box that is just natural stuff about being male and there is nothing wrong with that. So particularly when these things are the result of our own choices and not of conformity to what society tells us we have to be like, and they aren't harmful to ourselves or others, no big deal. There is also some stuff in the box that especially when carried to an extreme is not very healthy.

Ask: Do we agree on that?

Note: *Most guys will be able to admit that at least one thing in the box when carried to an extreme is harmful. If you have a guy who won't admit this, he is being overly difficult. Just move on.*

State: Now let's see if we can fill the space around the outside of the box.

Ask: What names would a guy be called if he steps outside of the box, if he does something that doesn't fit that stereotypical mode?

Note: *Guys are likely to come up with about 20 words or so, including words such as fag, pussy, weak, woman, bitch....*

State: This is interesting. Let's look at the words we used for men who step outside the box.

Ask: Is there anything they seem to have in common?

Note: *Most are either negative words about women or gay men.*

State: Really? Let's count them to be sure.

Ask: So how many are negative words about women? About men who are gay?

Ask: So why do you think these words outside the box are used to refer to men who step outside the box?

Note: *To insult, imply weakness.*

Ask: What message does this send to men?

Note: *Girls and women (and gay men) are inferior to men.*

State: So isn't that interesting. When men want to put each other down, one of the most common types of words they use are slang terms for a woman.

Ask: Based on your observations of others historically, culturally, or sociologically, as you studied groups who are at war, or as you've observed people around you, how does a group that believes another group is inferior typically treat that group?

Note: *Poorly, with no respect.*

State: Right. So when people use words like "bitch" to refer to a man who doesn't live up to an absolute masculine standard, on the one hand you could just say, who cares, they don't mean anything by it. On the other hand, if you think about it, when we use words like (insert words here that the group used that refer to women), words meant as derogatory words about women, with the intent to demean men who have stepped outside of social norms for men, what are we implying?

Note: *That women don't deserve any respect and neither does the man who stepped out of the box.*

Ask: So what kinds of things do men do to women who they think don't deserve any respect?

Note: *Ridicule, treat as inferior, abuse, ignore, treat as an object not a person,* rape.

State: Yes, all of these things are possible. Does this mean that every man who calls a guy "bitch" as an insult is a rapist? Of course not. However, when we use words that are demeaning toward women as a put down for other men, first of all we are being highly insulting to women. Second, we are saying that women are "less than" men and they don't deserve respect. This lack of respect, much like the lack of respect shown for other groups mentioned throughout history, can justify hurting them. And that is something I don't think any of us wants to be part of in our lives.

State: So let's take this in a slightly different direction.

Ask: Can you think of a time when it is healthy for a man to make a personal choice to be outside the box?

Note: *A man might choose to cry at a funeral, he might make a personal choice not to have sex before marriage, he could be a nurturing father to his children, he might say "no" to a dare that he doesn't want to take. Numerous other great examples exist.*

Ask: If a guy realizes he has stepped outside the box and wants to get back inside, what kinds of things will he do to get back in?
  – Unnecessarily risky verbal and physical challenges
  – Suppression of emotions (It's no big deal that Dad died, I can handle it)
  – Risk-taking behavior (I bet I can jump off this 40-foot building with no gear)
  – Oppression of underprivileged groups (Let's go beat up some immigrants)
  – Have unprotected sex with many women they don't know
  – Have sex (unprotected or not) when intoxicated
  – Drink and drive
  – Get into fights (I don't care if all 10 of you are pro boxers; I'll crush you)
  – Rape (to prove his virility at all costs no matter what the woman wants)

Ask: To what extent should we be encouraging guys to do these things to get back inside the box?

Note: *We shouldn't.*

Ask: What can we do to make guys feel less compelled to do these things to stay in or try to get back into the box?

Note: *We can support men who step outside the box by not making fun of them, by saying "that's okay" or "that's cool" if they act differently than the norm.*

State: One thing we hope you can take away from this is that being worried all the time about doing only what is inside the male box limits our potential. As human beings we all exhibit a full range of emotions and it can be harmful to suppress them. It is healthier to define your own identity without having to confine yourself to that box that society puts there. A question we hope that this raised is whether you want to be a leader who decides on your own standards for expectations of masculinity, or if you want to be controlled by the media and other outside forces that have one view of what it means to be a man that doesn't always fit with your own best interests. Of course, ultimately what I hope none of us wants to do is dehumanize another group of people and justify violence against them.

State: So, the main points of our exercise were these:

- Using words like "bitch" to make fun of men is dehumanizing to both men and women.
- Historically, when people dehumanize others, it justifies violence against them.
- If we normalize using words that refer to women as put downs, it justifies violence against women.
- When we call guys "bitches" or "pussies" or other such words that demean women we are supporting a culture that justifies rape.

# Module 7

## *The Female Circle**

**Time needed: 60 minutes**
**Intended audience: Women (can be used with men to help them understand women)**

State: Today, we are going to talk about several things.

First and foremost, we are going to talk about some of the stereotypical ways society tells women that they need to act.

We will also discuss some words used to describe those who do not conform.

We'll discuss some commonalities of those words.

We'll talk about some damaging behaviors women do to conform.

We'll then talk about how society would be different if the standards for femininity were changed.

And finally, we'll explore how this all relates to sexual assault.

Ask: So who here knows the difference between sex and gender?

Note: *People are born with a biological, anatomical sex, male or female. Gender roles, masculine and feminine, are a way people behave according to societal standards. "Male" refers to sex, "masculine" refers to gender. Likewise "female" refers to sex, "feminine" refers to gender.*

Ask: How do we learn to be women in today's society? Who teaches us?

Note: *Media, parents, professors/officers, teachers, coaches, peers—all parts of "society"*

State: I'm going to draw a large circle up here on the board and label it at the top "To Be a Woman." I want us to fill it with words and phrases that answer this very important question:

Ask: What does society *stereotypically* say it means "to be a woman?"

Note: *Make sure that all the categories below are covered; if they use curse words, it is okay for this exercise.*

- Body image/beauty (thin, big-chested, beautiful)
- Relationships with men (monogamous, submissive, nurturer)
- Relationships with children/family (nurturer, caretaker, in the home)
- Jobs (low level, nurses, teachers, low pay, glass ceiling)
- Sexuality (heterosexual, innocent, virgin)
- Activities (no sports, cheerleading)

---

* Original printed with permission from the Mentors in Violence Prevention (MVP) Program. Copyright 1994, Northeastern University's Center for the Study of Sport in Society. Substantial modifications made.

State: Okay. You did a great job filling that circle. Now let's see if we can fill the space around the outside of the circle. This time though I want us to fill it with something different.

Ask: What names would a woman be called if she steps outside of the circle? If she does something that doesn't fit that stereotypical mode?

Note: *Words are likely to include dyke, bitch, ho, slut....*

State: This is interesting. Let's look at the words we used for women who step outside the circle.

Ask: Is there anything they seem to have in common?

Note: *Most are negative words and are degrading to women.*

Ask rhetorically: Really? So most of them are negative and degrading to women?

Ask: So why do you think these words are used?

Note: *To silence women, to police women's behavior, to keep women inside this restrictive circle.*

State: So when we use these words, we silence them, police them, and keep them inside this restrictive circle.

Ask: What message does this send to women?

Note: *Women must conform in order to be accepted by others.*

State: So what this all says is that women must conform to be accepted by others.

State: So don't you think this is all very interesting? We live in a society in which men have set the standards for what our bodies should look like, what are relationships with them should be like, how we should relate to them and to our children, what jobs we should be allowed to have, how we should express our sexuality, and what activities we should take part in. This system creates all of these stereotypes represented in this circle that we all came up with. And what happens when one of us steps outside this circle? One of us makes sure she steps right back in that circle by calling her a slut or a bitch.

Ask: Can you now see how when you call a woman a slut or a bitch for stepping outside this circle that you are reinforcing a system men created to keep you, yourself, restricted in what you are "allowed" to do?

Ask: So what is the only logical alternative?

Note (to presenter): *Work to change these social norms, break the barriers of the female circle.*

State: Right. We as women need to start changing these social norms. We as women need to break the barriers of this women's circle.

Ask: Let's get to one final point before we wrap this up. What harmful things to women do to stay in or get back into the circle?

Note (to presenter): *Diet, eating disorders, plastic surgery, not play sports, not speak up in class or in relationships, remain in harmful relationships....*

State: Right, so there are many ways in which women hurt themselves to either get back in the circle or stay in that circle.

State: In the end, we hope that you will take away the following points:

1. Women should define their own identities.
2. It is okay to have some of the qualities and characteristics that are inside the box as long as it is a personal decision and not a response to conform to a socially prescribed norm.
3. As leaders, it is our responsibility to support other women who may choose to be outside the circle.

# Module 8

## *Alcohol and Sexual Assault*

### Time needed = 1 hour
### Intended audience = Men or women

Ask: Before we start this session, I want to ask you a couple of questions. How many senators are in the U.S. Senate?

Do: *Pause to take responses from people in the room. The answer is, of course, 100 (as of the publication of this book).*

Ask: Okay, next question. What is the best form of government?

Do: *Take responses. Request that people state reasons why their form of government is the best. Continue asking "what is the best form of government." Continue to note that you can't seem to get "the right answer" and how frustrating it is for you because you just want an easy answer, an absolute right or wrong answer, and why don't they just tell you what the answer is? Continue until you receive several different answers.*

State: Okay. Well, we've just identified the basic issue of why it can be so frustrating to try to educate people about the intersections between alcohol and sexual assault. It boils down to this: your peers will want you to state rules that relate to how much alcohol someone can drink and still be able to consent. They will want a rule that is as simple as answering the question "how many senators are in the U.S. Senate?" The reality is that in many cases, an answer like that just doesn't exist. In many cases, the answer is much more like that of the second question, "What is the best form of government?" There is no simple, right answer.

Write: *1, 2, 3, 4, 5, 6, 7, 8, 9, 10, 11, 12, 13, 14, 15, 16.*

Ask: How much does someone's blood alcohol content (BAC) level increase for every 12 ounces of beer, 5 ounces of wine, or 1.5 ounces of 80-proof liquor the person consumes?

State: Yes, you are correct, about .02—a bit more really depending on several factors, but at least .02. So let's write underneath these numbers of drinks how much someone's BAC would be after consuming that many drinks.

Write: *Directly beneath each of the numbers 1 to 16, write the corresponding BAC: .02, .04, .06, .08, .10, .12, .14, .16, .18, .20, .22, .24, .26, .28, .30, .32*

State: The basic problem with educating people about the issue of alcohol and sexual assault is that people try to force an issue of infinite complexity into one that can be summed up into a simple rule. In particular, men want to know "How many beers can she have and still consent." "How can I tell if things are still okay?" The problem is that in many situations a person cannot tell. It is impossible to tell if a person is too drunk to consent if that person does not show many visible signs of drunkenness. It can also be paticularly hard to determine the level of drunkenness of another, when you are drunk and sexually aroused.

State: Some situations are clear. A person who has had nothing to drink and is otherwise able to consent (free from coercion, legal age, etc.) can consent. In nearly every case imaginable, a person with one drink can also consent. A person who has had 16 drinks in an hour, leading to a BAC of at least .32, cannot consent. That person is dangerously intoxicated and in need of medical attention. What about a woman who weighs 120 pounds, has had a normal amount of food for her that day, and has had 5 drinks in 2 hours. Can she consent? If someone has intercourse with her, is that rape? Legally, that is a question for a jury.

State: The law includes rape statues that are vague on purpose, so that juries have to figure out whether something is rape or not. The same thing often goes for campus judicial boards and administrative hearings. They have to interpret. Is it rape? That is up to a board or administrators to decide. It is not always clear.

State: Most toxicologists will say that if someone is vomiting or passing out, she is definitely too drunk to consent. But you don't have to be vomiting or passing out to be too drunk to consent. Most juries will say if a man can have and maintain an erection he is capable of giving consent.

State: If you want to be safe, if you don't want to rape, the best thing to do is to make low-risk decisions. Low-risk decisions involve not having intercourse with someone who has consumed increasingly higher quantities of alcohol, or quantities of alcohol that you don't know.

State: An important thing to remember in all of this is that it is the responsibility of the person who initiates physical activity with another person to obtain proper consent before proceeding with that behavior. If that person is so intoxicated that she doesn't know what is going on, she might even say yes—but only because she is so drunk that she would say yes to anything like buying a new car, signing a contract, things she would not otherwise do if she were sober. The burden lies with the person initiating the behavior to obtain proper consent—whether that is the man or the woman.

Ask: What are some reasons men seek a specific answer about when it is okay to have sex with alcohol?

Ask: Are all men going to be satisfied by hearing that "it is a jury question, make low-risk decisions, and the initiator has to get consent?" Why?

Ask: What are some other possible strategies we can use in addressing the concerns of these men?

Ask: Why is it frustrating for alcohol to be an unclear issue? Can it be a clear issue?

Ask: How would you personally answer questions about alcohol if they come up at the end of a program, for example, "If they are both drunk, why is the guy at fault?" or "How drunk can she be before it is rape?"

## Module 9

### *Rape Myths and the Importance of Bystander Intervention*

**Time needed: 1 hour**
**Intended audience: Men or women**

This session helps accomplish several goals:

- To help peer educators develop a deeper understanding of what rape is like.
- To help peer educators notice the opportunities different people have to intervene as bystanders, why they choose to do so, and why they choose not to do so.
- To educate peer educators about rape myths. In particular, one can address the rape myth that a woman who dresses in a certain way and "leads men on" deserves to be raped.

This session can also be used as a motivational tool for peer educators who are just starting out. They are likely to feel powerless when they see the movie clip of a rape scene. The processing of this scene allows you to transfer that feeling of powerlessness into a feeling of empowerment that they can do something about rape when they see a potential rape situation about to occur.

**Very important:** The day before, morning of, and just before the session, be sure to issue a disclaimer that the movie clip you will be using will show a Hollywood depiction of a rape scene. State that the movie is rated R, so it will not show penetration, but it will show a rape from the side and there will be some partial nudity. State that it will be graphically violent and very disturbing, especially to those who are survivors or those who are friends of survivors. People can choose to leave or opt out entirely. Offer support resources and have a counselor on hand or on call.

Before you begin the session, set up and test your video clip so you don't fumble with it when it is time to show. To find (before you present this session!), go to scene selection, then go to the scene that starts with view of a prison on an island. Fast forward through the scene of two guys talking on either side of a plastic wall in a prison visitors room. Fast forward through the scene of Sara, her lawyer, a witness, and his lawyer in a lawyer's office.

> State: In this session we are going to learn more about several issues including the reality of how awful rape is, why some people decide to intervene and others don't, and how some people can be influenced by others to make certain choices. We will also talk about some beliefs about rape that permeate our culture.

> State: What we're going to do today is start this session by viewing a 12-minute portion of the movie *The Accused*. In this movie, Jodi Foster won an academy award for best actress for playing the role of Sara—a woman who

survived rape in a bar. It is based on a true story. This clip shows a graphic rape scene. The movie is rated R, so it will not show penetration, but it will show a rape from the side and there will be some partial nudity. It is graphically violent and very disturbing, especially to survivors or those who are friends of survivors. Seriously, you can choose to sit this one out and you can leave during if you'd like.

Do: *Begin movie clip.*

*Start the clip just as Sara's lawyer calls her witness to the stand.*

*End the clip just as Sara's lawyer asks her witness whether he thinks Sara Tobias was responsible for the rape, and he says "No."*

Do: *Turn on the lights after the clip is over. Pause for 15 seconds or so.*

Ask: How did it feel to watch that scene?

Ask: How do you feel right now?

State: For those of you who felt helpless in watching that scene, or angry, or (insert appropriate words here), the good news is that you can do something to help prevent something like that—the real-life story you just saw depicted on that screen—from happening. There are many different ways to intervene as a bystander that could have prevented that rape from happening. There are many choices people made in that scene that were missed opportunities. There were also many choices people made that were just awful, even evil.

Ask: Who are some of the characters you saw in the clip, the major ones (make sure you write Sara's name at the end, or at least don't discuss her until the end)?

1. Rapist 1
2. Rapist 2
3. Rapist 3
4. Waitress/Sara's friend (same person)
5. Ring leader/instigator
6. Red-haired guy who came/left
7. Videogame guy
8. Sara

Ask: How responsible do you think (insert character name here) was for what happened?

Note: *When you get to Sara state the following as the "devil's advocate" position and look for the group to refute it.*

State: Well, then there was Sara. Clearly *she* deserved to be raped in this situation, didn't she! I mean come on. She walked into the bar, lit up a cigarette, and scoped out the room just looking for who she'd hook up with. She sat down with a friend and drank like a lush. She gave "the look" to Bob and said she should take him home and f*ck him right in front of her husband. She took the drink from Danny, let him touch her ass. Pffft. She then followed him back into the back room. What was she expecting? Then she made sure she was the only woman in the room by chasing away the other one there. She then smoked a joint and started dancing around like an exotic dancer and pulled Danny right over to her. I mean, what was Danny supposed to think? Of course he was going to do her right there! It was all her fault! Right? The whole thing was all her fault.

Note: *Peer educators are likely to disagree with you (thankfully). If some seem hesitant, ask them to make their point. Others in the group are likely to confront them.*

Ask: When does a bystander have an obligation to do something?

Ask: What are some potential ways that the guy at the video game could have intervened in this situation?

Note: *Be sure to emphasize that one needs to balance personal safety with intervention, but there is almost always a way to do something without putting oneself in immediate danger.*

# Module 10

## *Rape-Trauma Syndrome*

**Time needed: 1 hour**
   **Intended audience: Men or women**

State: This session will focus on understanding rape-trauma syndrome. It
   relates to something identified by the military. Back in the Vietnam War
   when the vets came home, they had a lot of psychological symptoms that
   seemed to proceed in a predictable fashion.

Ask: What was that disorder called?

Note: *Post-traumatic stress disorder, also known as PTSD.*

State: Yes, the physical and psychological reactions they had in response to the
   war became known as post-traumatic stress disorder, or PTSD.

State: Interestingly, soon after, counselors who worked in rape crisis centers
   noticed that women who survived rape experienced a lot of these same
   symptoms. The physical and psychological reactions women experienced after
   rape became known as rape-trauma syndrome—a process much like PTSD.

State: During today's session, we are going to go through an interactive learning experience that will help you to discover the typical phases of recovery
   experienced by sexual assault survivors. As part of this exercise, we will
   discuss why survivors' descriptions of their rape experiences are likely to be
   different during different stages of their recovery.

Ask: Have you ever heard a rumor about a sexual assault having occurred?

State: Of course, it is likely that at some point you will hear a rumor about a
   sexual assault taking place. Given that, we want you to better understand
   some of the issues of judgment and responsibility about the people who
   might have been involved. Of course there is always the chance that one day
   you might even be on a jury deciding a rape case. This exercise will help you
   to evaluate what you hear about incidents of rape in many different contexts.

State: In the last session we watched a clip from *The Accused* where three men
   raped the character Sara.

Ask: Do you believe that Sara used good judgment in this situation?

Ask: Do you believe that Sara is responsible for the gang rape?

Ask: Why?

Ask: Ultimately, who is responsible for what happened?

State: Now, we want you to divide into four groups. Please count off (1, 2, 3, 4,
   1, 2, 3, 4, etc.).

State: Using the handout provided about rape-trauma syndrome (at the end
   of this training module, in *The Men's Program: Peer Educator's Manual and
   The Women's Program: A Peer Educator's Manual*) I want each group to
   write a statement that you think Sara Tobias would write if she were sitting in
   a police station reporting the rape that happened to her that you saw in the

movie *The Accused*. Based on your group number, I want you to assume that she is in that stage of rape-trauma syndrome. Assume she is writing out what happened to her and how she feels about it in that stage, whether it is soon after, a few months later, or up to a year later depending upon her stage of rape-trauma syndrome. You'll have 15 minutes to write these as a group.

## Instructions:

### Group 1

Think back to the rape situation experienced by Sara in *The Accused*. Assume that it is a few days after the rape and she is stage 1 of rape-trauma syndrome. With your group, write a paragraph or two about how Sara is likely to describe what happened to her and how she feels now.

### Group 2

Think back to the rape situation experienced by Sara in *The Accused*. Assume that it is a few months after the rape and she is in stage 2 of rape-trauma syndrome. With your group, write a paragraph or two about how Sara is likely to describe what happened to her and how she feels now.

### Group 3

Think back to the rape situation experienced by Sara in *The Accused*. Assume that it is about 6 months after the rape and she is in stage 3 of rape-trauma syndrome. With your group, write a paragraph or two about how Sara is likely to describe what happened to her and how she feels now.

### Group 4

Think back to the rape situation experienced by Sara in *The Accused*. Assume that it is about 2 years after the rape and she is in stage 4 of rape-trauma syndrome. With your group, write a paragraph or two about how Sara is likely to describe what happened to her and how she feels now.

Note: *Give each group 15 minutes. They may end up needing more.*
State: Now I want each group to read its statement.
Note: *As each group is reading its monologue, take personal notes about the key points they mention.*
Do:
   – *Have group 1 read its monologue.*
   – *Summarize the points the group members made and note points that relate to their stage of rape-trauma syndrome.*
   – *Mention things about rape-trauma syndrome in that stage that they didn't include in their monologue based on your handout.*

Do:

- *Have group 2 read its monologue.*
- *Summarize the points the group members made and note points that relate to their stage of rape-trauma syndrome.*
- *Mention things about rape-trauma syndrome in that stage that they didn't include in their monologue based on your handout.*

Do:

- *Have group 3 read its monologue.*
- *Summarize the points the group members made and note points that relate to their stage of rape-trauma syndrome.*
- *Mention things about rape-trauma syndrome in that stage that they didn't include in their monologue based on your handout.*

Do:

- *Have group 4 read its monologue.*
- *Summarize the points the group members made and note points that relate to their stage of rape-trauma syndrome.*
- *Mention things about rape-trauma syndrome in that stage that they didn't include in their monologue based on your handout.*

Ask: What do you notice that is different about how Sara tells her story in the different stages of rape-trauma syndrome?

State: Isn't it interesting how Sara's story differed so markedly depending on which stage of rape-trauma syndrome she was in at the time she made her report.

State: Here in stage 1 she reported about the rape in one way (summarize what group 1 said based on your notes), in stage 2 another way (brief summary of group 2), in stage 3 yet another (brief summary of group 3), and in stage 4 a different way (brief summary of group 4).

Ask: Have any of you ever heard someone say, "Oh, she changed her story, she must have made the whole thing up; she's lying!"

State: What *you* just proved by the monologues *you* wrote based on the *exact* same account of rape is that if a survivor's story changes during different stages of her recovery, it is actually a sign that she is telling the truth (pause for impact). It is a sign that she is proceeding through the stages of rape-trauma syndrome *exactly* as expected. A changing story is all part of the body's reaction to trauma and is a natural part of the recovery process to rape. So if you hear about a case of rape and you hear that a survivor's story changed at different times during the investigation, remember, this is *completely* consistent with rape-trauma syndrome. Most people believe that a changing story means the survivor is lying. This is not the case with rape and other forms of trauma. A changing story is *completely* consistent with rape-trauma syndrome, and the stories *you* just wrote are completely consistent with that. (Pause again for impact.)

Ask: Okay. Now what questions do you have?

## Handout on Rape-Trauma Syndrome*

Rape-trauma syndrome (RTS) is a form of post-traumatic stress disorder (PTSD) that is often experienced by survivors of rape and attempted rape. Not all survivors will experience RTS in the same way. Rather, this handout outlines possible reactions.

### STAGE 1: ACUTE DISORGANIZATION (DAYS TO WEEKS; 3 MONTHS COMMON)

A. Immediate reactions
  1. Shock "Did it really happen?" "Why me?"
  2. One of two coping styles is usually used
     a. Controlled—Talks about assault in a flat voice, shows no emotion, numb
     b. Expressed—Visibly upset, angry, fearful, anxious

B. Physical reactions
  1. Shock—(Unable to concentrate, blood pressure change, rapid pulse)
  2. Sleeping or eating changes
  3. Symptoms in the area of the body that was attacked
  4. Loss of sex drive, other sex disturbances
  5. Fatigue

C. Emotional reactions
  1. Fear (of retaliation, of meeting the attacker, of being alone, of opinions of others, of dying, of further injury)
  2. Helplessness, loss of control
  3. Repression, denial
  4. Minimizing the incident ("He didn't really hurt me")
  5. Shame, self-blame, guilt, humiliation, embarrassment, degradation
  6. Unwillingness to talk about all or part of the incident
  7. Anger, revenge, retaliation
  8. Inability to cope with own rage and hostility
  9. Irritation
  10. Mood swings, overreactive
  11. Overprotective
  12. Depression
  13. Lowered self-esteem
  14. Anxiety
  15. Can't concentrate
  16. Can't care for self, perform on job/in school, impacts on interpersonal relationships

---

* Adapted with permission from "Rape-Trauma Syndrome." Paper presented at the meeting of Virginians Aligned Against Sexual Assault, November 1992, Richmond, Va.

## STAGE 2: DENIAL PHASE (1 TO 3 MONTHS)

A. Avoids discussion and thoughts of the rape
    1. Does not express own anger
    2. Attempts to forget the whole thing
    3. Puts the rape "in the past"
    4. Stops thinking of the assault every day

## STAGE 3: LONG-TERM REORGANIZATION (6 TO 12 MONTHS)

A. Physical changes
    1. Vaginal problems
    2. Menstrual changes
    3. Headaches, stomach cramps
    4. Eating/sleeping disturbances
    5. Easily startled

B. Psychological changes
    1. Nightmares about the rape
    2. Flashbacks
    3. Fear of crowds, being alone, sleeping, similar locations to rape scene
    4. Lowered self-esteem

C. Social changes
    1. Trades freedom for security
    2. Changes daily routine
    3. Stays home more
    4. Drops out of school/work
    5. Changes in frequency of time spent with family
    6. Moves, changes jobs, phone number
    7. Lacks or loses support from significant others

D. Sexual Changes
    1. Fear of sex
    2. Lack of sexual desire or may greatly increase frequency of having sex

## STAGE 4: INTEGRATION/RECOVERY (AFTER REORGANIZATION)

A. Resolution
    1. Feels safe and in control
    2. Can trust people again
    3. No longer fearful
    4. Blames the rapist
    5. Pursues legal action
    6. Believes self to be normal
    7. Expresses and resolves anger

8. Integrates assault into personal history
9. Shows compassion and advocacy for survivors

**Note:** Timeframes listed throughout the handout are approximate and assume the survivor discusses her emotions soon after the assault, and receives appropriate support. Without support, several years or decades may pass without progression; regression to a previous stage can be triggered by situational events.

# Module 11

## *Consent*

**Time needed: 1 hour**
   **Intended audience: Men or women**

State: We're going to do an exercise to help develop a deeper understanding of the meaning of consent.

State: Please divide up into smaller groups. To do so, count off. 1, 2, 3, 4, 1, 2….

State: The person with the longest hair will facilitate the discussion. The person with the shortest hair will take notes.

State: Once you are in your groups, your task will be to develop a definition of consent. You will have 10 to 15 minutes. Begin.

Note: *When the groups are finished, have the note takers write the definitions on a chalkboard, dry erase board, or newsprint.*

Do: *Compare and discuss the definitions.*

Ask: How can someone tell when someone else is uncomfortable in an intimate situation?

Ask: When is it unclear whether consent exits?

Ask: When is consent no longer present?

Ask: Must a person say "no" for an act to be rape? (If training a group that has seen the Men's Program, ask "Did the police officer in the police rape training video ever say no?")

Ask: What can a person do to make sure consent is present?

Ask: If you were talking with someone who resists obtaining verbal consent, what are some arguments you could use to convince that person otherwise?

## Module 12

### *Male-on-Male Rape and the Men's Program*

**Time needed: 30 minutes**
**Intended audience: Men**

Do: *Have students turn to the corresponding handout in* The Men's Program: A Peer Educator's Manual.

Do: *Work through the handout below, discussing its logic and reasoning. Discuss issues that peer educators have questions about as they come up.*

### *Using a Male-on-Male Rape Scenario to Educate Men About Sexual Assault*

#### *How Do the Police Rape Training Video and the Men's Program Describe a Male-on-Male Rape Scenario?*

The video refers to one attacker as married and the other as having a girlfriend—suggesting that their sexual orientation is presumably heterosexual. Of course, one's partner does not establish an orientation, but is a fairly reliable predictor. In the context of the video, casting these characters as presumably heterosexual allows us to emphasize the violence of the attack and puts the emphasis on what many male-on-male rape situations involve: a heterosexual perpetrator.

The script for "The Men's Program" reinforces the presumed heterosexuality of the rapists, and uses this to reinforce male-on-male rape as an act of violence where many perpetrators are presumably heterosexual.

#### *How Are Other Stimulus Tools Used?*

Many programs show or describe a male-on-female rape situation. Does this practice promote violence against women and/or misogyny? Of course not. Would we show a male-on-female rape scenario without framing, disclaiming, and processing? No. Why not? It doesn't warn people; there is no context set for why we show it; it could reinforce people's perceptions. Also, what if we showed another kind of video that described something painful and/or hurtful—for example a speech that was anti-Semitic. Are there contexts within an institution where this could be useful as a teaching tool? Yes, to teach people about the effects of hate and what it can lead to as evidenced by the Holocaust. Would we just show an anti-Semitic video without framing, disclaiming, and processing? Of course not.

#### *What Is Homophobia?*

Homophobia is described in many ways. Most often the definition involves an irrational fear of activity and/or people who are gay, lesbian, bisexual, or transgender. It is rational to fear something like a gun being held to your head. It is not rational to *fear* a group of people simply because of their sexual orientation.

### Why and How Should We Process a Male-on-Male Scenario?

Stimulus tools are all in how we as educators use them to teach others. We know (through 10 studies reported by Schewe, 2007) that the only technique so far that has been shown to affect men's sexual assault behavior is to show and discuss a male-on-male rape scenario combined with bystander intervention training. Some men in our audience are probably homophobic. Do we then not discuss this scenario because some might be homophobic? No. Talking about male-on-male rape is not something that is homophobic by nature. Discussing our scenario appropriately can both reduce sexual assault and give us the chance to educate men in a way that confronts a common homophobic misperception—that male-on-male rape is motivated by sexual desire and is most commonly done by a homosexual man. We confront this perception with the Men's Program. If we did not make the sexual orientation of the men in the video clear, this could be problematic. We also make sure that it is described (in the video and in processing) as a violent act by nature committed by presumably heterosexual men. Thus, we use the male-on-male rape scenario as a teaching tool to help men understand rape more fully, empathize with survivors, and identify rape as an act of violence.

### What Is One Possible Way to Answer the Question "Is There Any Concern That Describing a Male-on-Male Scenario Might Bring up Any Issues of Homophobia?"

We have to remember that rape is primarily an act of violence. What is depicted on the video is clearly a violent act. One of the things we do in our program is combat any preexisting homophobic attitudes among members of the audience. A common manner in which homophobia manifests is assuming that if a man is raped, his attacker must be a homosexual man. The video we use describes a situation in which a man is raped by presumably heterosexual men, thus helping debunk the myth that men who rape men are necessarily homosexual. In addition, we hit this point home immediately after the video concludes by noting that the perpetrators were presumably heterosexual, as with many male-on-male rape situations. Thus, we work to attenuate homophobia, not perpetuate it. Also, think about this for a second. Many programs for women have focused on describing women being raped and the effects rape has on them, but these programs surely don't perpetuate misogyny and violence against women just because they talk about women who are raped. In the same way, our program does not perpetuate homophobia, we actually do the opposite.

# Module 13

## *The Voice of a Survivor*

**Time needed: 60 to 90 minutes**
**Intended audience: Men or women**

Do: *Prior to this session, carefully screen potential visitors to come to class to speak about their experience as survivors. It can be a very powerful experience, particularly for men, to hear a survivor talk about her experience in person. This should come toward the end of a training experience when peer educators have become more sensitive to issues of sexual violence. Scheduling this toward the end of training will also provide the benefit of having the survivor's experience reinforce the concepts you have discussed.*

Do: *As you consider whom to invite to tell her story, be careful to invite someone who is emotionally prepared to speak to a room full of people about what happened to her. Someone who has been in therapy for a long time, or has been through therapy is highly recommended. I also recommend that you seek someone whose experience occurred in an environment similar to the environment in which your peer educators live. For example, if you are training a group that will educate students on a particular college campus, getting a survivor from that campus to talk about her experience can be particularly powerful. This brings the issue home to them.*

Do: *If you are training a group of women, I also recommend that you bring a survivor in to talk about her experience. It is extremely likely that you will have several survivors in your group. Many of them may choose to share parts of their experience with the group at some point in time. Having a survivor who is not part of the group in to share her experience will help provide the group with a detailed survivor experience from the beginning to learn from and process. It also provides group members the opportunity to discuss a particular survivor experience for educational reasons, without having the survivor present at every group meeting.*

State: Today (first name of survivor) has agreed to come in to talk about what she has experienced. So that she knows who is here, let's all introduce ourselves.

State: To begin the discussion, let's remember that what is said in the room stays in the room. Even (first name of survivor) should always be kept a secret to maintain her confidentiality. She will start by sharing with us what happened to her so that we can learn from her experience. She and I have talked beforehand about how this is a way for her to find something positive to gain from her awful experience. As with anyone who agrees to be a speaker for this part of training, she said that she wants to be here to share her experience to help you all be in a better position to educate your peers about sexual assault. So she's going to talk about what happened to her.

Next, she's going to open things up for questions. I've told her that each of you has one question ready. If she doesn't want to answer the question, she'll say so or she'll just say pass.

Do: *Open the floor for the survivor to share her experience.*

Do: *End by thanking her for the tremendous contribution she made to the training of the group. Let her know that nothing you could say to them could ever match the impact of the words she spoke to them.*

Ask: What did you learn from the survivor's experience?

Ask: How does the survivor's experience teach us about the ways in which rape-trauma syndrome manifests itself?

Note: *If for whatever reason you are unable to bring a survivor in to tell her story to your group, an alternative is to order a copy of the CD Voices of Courage and play the story of "Barb." To order, go to www.VoicesOfCourage. com.*

## Module 14

### *Starting Points for Difficult Questions and Difficult Audience Members*

**Time needed: 60 minutes**
**Intended audience: Men or women**

Do: *During this class session, spend time preparing peer educators to handle difficult questions and audience members. The information that follows, also included in the peer education guides, will help you structure your time.*

Do: *Take the class members through the information. Encourage questions throughout. Ask them for alternative ways of answering the questions and/or dealing with the challenges. Ask them for personal experiences of how they may have dealt with questions and/or presenting situations that are similar to this.*

### *Suggested Techniques for Difficult People*

When handling questions from difficult audiences, two basic steps tend to help:

■ First, try to empathize with the questioner. Oftentimes, people are asking questions because they are genuinely confused or frustrated with a concept they don't fully understand. It's *critical* that they not feel alone in this. Give a few examples from your personal experience prior to your understanding of sexual assault issues that could help validate the questioner's concern, without saying that what the person is saying is actually true.
  – "I definitely see where you're coming from …"
  – "Yeah, I used to feel that way too, but …"
  – "I know when you hear it at first it doesn't seem that clear cut, but maybe I can clarify that a little …"

■ Then, try to answer their question as frankly as possible, emphasizing the broader themes of the program: rape is more common and more painful than most people think, and there are a lot of things we can do to prevent it. A few examples of what you could say.:
  – "But what about girls who get drunk, wake up and call it rape? That happened to my friend, roommate, etc."
    • "I'm sorry to hear about your friend, and without knowing more it's hard to say, but FBI statistics show that 96 to 98% of the time …"
  – "Girls lie about it all the time, and there's nothing guys can do."
    • "I used to think that too, but then I thought about what survivors go through, and realized that it's rarely worth it to lie …"
  – "But why should it be the guy's fault when he is really drunk too?"
  – "I know where you're coming from. Physically speaking, because men are the ones who usually initiate sex, responsibility for getting consent falls on them in these kinds of situations."

**Two Important Points to Remember:**

1. Don't think of this as an exhaustive list. These are just a few examples to guide you. If you remember the basic strategy (*empathize,* then *answer* as best as you can), you don't have to know the perfect answer or the perfect statistic every time. If you do this, the questioner will sense that you identify with him, and will be more likely to be receptive to the broader message you convey.
2. While empathy is important, remember that you don't have to agree with questioners every time. Sometimes, you have to tell them that they're wrong, or that what they are saying is offensive (especially if they use language that is degrading to women).

Additional advice:

Ask that questions wait until the end of the program. Call first on people who raised their hands during the program, if applicable.

Unless the person is so out of control that dialogue is clearly not possible, make sure you understand the question and convince the person that you hear his or her concern.

Use a combination of logic, your experience, your knowledge of facts, and affirmation of the individual's right to have an opinion on the matter.

Use your fellow presenters; step in and support each other.

Find a place of agreement and move on when necessary.

Offer to talk with the person further after the program is over.

Offer to get the person more information or discuss the matter more thoroughly at a later time.

Use others in the audience to confront the difficult person.

## *Suggested Answers for a Variety of Questions*

**Question 1: You said one in four women has survived rape or attempted rape? You can make statistics say anything you want. I don't know anybody who has been raped. There is no way that one quarter of girls have been raped. You really think that there are that many rapists here? We'd hear about it all the time. Your statistic is full of crap.**

**Response:** You are absolutely right that there are people who manipulate statistics to support biased conclusions. If I were to stand outside a meeting of rape survivors and then take a poll as they left, asking whether women had ever experienced rape I could easily come up with a statistic much higher than one in four. However, the one in four statistic was found through rigorous scientific studies.

In these surveys of thousands of college women on hundreds of college campuses nationwide; one in four has consistently reported surviving rape or attempted rape.

These women answered anonymous surveys about their experiences and had no reason to do anything but report their experiences accurately—they were just answering anonymous surveys and turning them into researchers. The one in four statistic has been found ever since the 1980s (Koss et al., 1987). The same results were found in the 1990s (Douglas et al., 1997) and again in a study (Fisher et al.) published in 2006.

A lot of people don't think they know someone who has been raped. It may be that no individual you know has told you that she has experienced rape. Research also shows that almost half of those who experience rape tell absolutely nobody about their experience. The most common person they tell is a friend. If they do tell you, I hope you will support your friend.

> ### *Research on the One in Four Statistic*
>
> Koss, Gidycz, & Wisniewski published a study in 1987 in which they interviewed approximately 6,000 college students on 32 college campuses nationwide. They asked several questions covering a wide range of behaviors. From this study 15% of college women answered "yes" to questions about whether they had experienced something that met the definition of rape. An additional 12% of women answered "yes" to questions about whether they had experienced something that met the definition of attempted rape, thus the statistic one in four.
>
> In 1995 the Centers for Disease Control (CDC) replicated part of this study. It didn't look at attempted rape, only rape. It found that 20% of approximately 5,000 women on 138 college campuses experienced rape during the course of their lifetime (Douglas et al., 1997). Had they asked about attempted rape, it is surely likely that they would have reached the one in four proportion.
>
> In 2000 and again in 2006, the U.S. Department of Justice published a study called The Sexual Victimization of College Women. To see this study for yourself, enter "The Sexual Victimization of College Women" into Google. The study will come up as a .pdf. The authors are Fisher, Cullen, and Turner (2006). If you look at page 11, you will see that 3.1% of undergraduate women reported surviving rape or attempted rape during a 6- to 7-month academic year. If you look at Exhibit 7, page 18 of the report, you will see that 10.1% of college women reported experiencing rape prior to entering college. Another 10.9% reported attempted rape prior to college. Note by reading the report that there is no overlap between these numbers. Add 3%, 10%, and 11% and you get 24% or the proportion one in four. That is a main source of the one in four statistic.
>
> When you look at other studies of the annual incidence of rape, others find it to be closer to 5%. For example, Mohler-Kuo, Dowdall, Koss, & Weschler (2004) found in a study of approximately 25,000 college women nationwide that 4.7% experienced rape or attempted rape during a single academic year. This study did not measure lifetime incidence of rape or attempted rape. Similarly, Kilpatrick, Resnick, Ruggiero, Conoscenti, & McCauley (2007) found in a study of 2,000 college women nationwide that every year 5.2% experienced rape.

**Question 2: If the girl was drunk and can't remember anything, how can she say it was sexual assault? She could have wanted it and shown the guy that she did. Giving the girl free reign to cry rape isn't fair to guys.**

**Response:** If a woman was so drunk that she was blacked out, there was *no way* that she was sober enough to consent to intercourse. That makes it sexual assault for sure. If she woke up and found signs in or on her body that someone had intercourse with her, she is likely to try to figure out who did. She might look to see who is around her when she wakes up, what others tell her about who she was around the night before, or what her last memory was. But if she can't remember anything, there is no way she could meet the legal standard for consent necessary in most if not all states.

As for whether she wanted it, if you think about it, people can't want something that is forced upon them. Stop and think about it. The meaning of *force* includes being pushed into doing something you *do not* want to do. How can somebody on the one hand *want* to be sexually assaulted when part of sexual assault involves *force*—a word that involves something, by definition, which is not wanted? Do you see what I mean?

As for giving an accuser a blank slate to cry rape and that not being fair to guys, at first blush I can understand why you might feel that way; I can remember when I thought that way too. But after I learned what survivors go through, I realized that it's just not worth it to lie in their situation. It is also extremely rare. A study released in 2007 (Lonsway, Archambault, & Berkowitz) found that 2 to 4% of rapes reported to the police were false reports. That's *really* low. Also, in order to prove a rape allegation, a survivor has to endure many things that could include rejection by some of her friends or family; a hospital visit that is extremely thorough, long, and painful; telling many different investigators and others involved with the judicial process about what happened over and over and over again; having to have contact with the accused on multiple occasions; facing people who blame her for what happened; and having people who ostracize her for being too naïve, saying she was too slutty, or too clueless to know what was going to happen in her future. Not many women I know would choose to go through that kind of revictimization unless something really awful happened to them.

**Question 3: How does someone know what a reasonable amount of alcohol is before the other person can't consent? It's a guessing game and it's too easy to use that as a way to cry rape falsely afterwards.**

**Response:** You can't know precisely how much a reasonable amount of alcohol is for another person to consent. There are too many factors to consider. You can be fairly sure that one drink, the other person can consent. You can also be certain that if the other person has had a dozen drinks, the person cannot consent. Guys tend to want to hear an absolute rule about how much alcohol is okay before a woman can no longer consent to sex. Stop and think about what you are asking. How many drinks can she have before I am raping her? How many drinks can she have before I risk hurting someone? Before I'm taking advantage of her vulnerability?

The truth is we can't tell you an exact quantity of alcohol for every person in every situation that is a "reasonable" amount before the other person can't consent, because there are too many factors to consider. The best advice we can give you is to make low-risk decisions. The lowest-risk decision to make is not to have intercourse after consuming alcohol. Every drink you or the other person has raises your risk that consent is not clear or not there.

**Question 4: Why are there laws and policies in place that prohibit initiating sexual contact with someone who has consumed a large quantity of alcohol?**

**Response:** Essentially, laws are in place to protect the vulnerable from those who might take advantage of them. So if a person takes advantage of another person's weakness due to intoxication, the law provides recourse to hold perpetrators accountable for taking advantage of another person's temporary or permanent inability to fully consent. The law is not in place to help those who exploit the weak. If it were, having intercourse with someone whose state of mind was impaired by alcohol or drug intoxication would be perfectly legal. Ultimately, if you have to ask about the legal definition of rape to figure out if you have consent or not, there is a very good chance that you don't have consent.

**Question 5: If both people are drunk, did they rape each other?**

**Response:** One of the things that must be considered is the context of each case. First, each person is responsible for obtaining proper consent to do something with another person's body before doing so. Research on sexual assault has shown (Lisak & Miller, 2002) that men's use of alcohol is often geared toward encouraging women to be more open to sexual advances, in some cases to be defenseless against them. When alcohol is used by an individual to make another individual defenseless, even when both are drinking, the responsibility falls in the hands of the one using the alcohol to take advantage.

**Question 6: Why do you present the program in a single-sex environment?**

**Response:** Everything about our program is based on what has been shown by the research literature to be most effective. The research is conclusive that when talking to college students about rape, the most effective way is to speak to single-sex audiences. One of the things you often find in coeducational programs is that men try to impress the women in the room, try to antagonize them, or shut down and don't talk for fear of having their opinions attacked. None of these reactions promotes learning for anyone. What we aim for is to follow the research on what works best. Everything about our program is based on what has been shown by the research literature to be most effective.

**Question 7: "You keep using the term 'survivor' instead of victim. Why do you do that?"**

**Response:** There are different people who have different opinions about this topic. Generally speaking, many people who educate others about sexual assault use the word "survivor" to refer to someone who has experienced rape after the rape is over. Many people who experience rape believe that during the rape that the rapist may kill them, and that they are fortunate to have survived the experience. They also feel empowered to use the term "survivor" to say that they lived through this and are now a stronger person from it, even though they wish it never happened. "Victim" is a term that has connotations that one really never pulls out of. It is used by many in the field, particularly when referring to someone during the act of rape, and in some cases immediately after a rape. There are some people who experience rape who say that we need to let people who experience rape have their time being a victim and allow them that space.

# Module 15

## *Practice Answering Difficult Questions*

**Time needed—90 minutes**
**Intended audience—Men or women**

1. Assign each trainee a number—this is easily done by writing numbers on participant name tags before the day starts.
2. Have pairs of peer educators walk to the front of the room. Fire questions at peer educators one by one. The partner is there for moral support, but in this exercise cannot help answer the question. Once both people in the pair have successfully answered a question, they can sit back down.
3. Process their answers with the group to talk about what was effective about their responses and what could have been improved.

## *Questions for Male Audiences*

1. I have a family member who is survivor, where can I go to find help for her?
2. My girlfriend told me she was raped and I don't know what to do to help her. Do you have any suggestions?
3. I think I might have committed rape. What can I do about it now?
4. The video you use for the Men's Program is very different from most rapes. Why do you use it?
5. You talk about survivors as women but how often are men raped?
6. Do women rape men?
7. If two people are drunk and hook up, why is the guy automatically labeled as the rapist? That happened to my friend.
8. From the news and stories I've heard it seems like women lie a lot about rape. Since it's so easy for them to lie, why should we automatically believe them?
9. I understand that rape is wrong, but what about when a guy and a girl are hooking up and a girl gets a guy so excited that he can't stop? You can't really blame him for finishing up, right?
10. What about all those girls who wear clothes that just advertise the fact that they want it. Aren't they at least a little bit responsible for what happens next if a guy loses control?
11. Isn't rape just bad communication?
12. Why is the man always the one at fault if they are both drunk and they have sex? Isn't the whole justice system set up against men?
13. I think my friend was raped but she won't admit it to me. What should I do?
14. People who have been dating for a while don't have to ask before they have sex, right?

15. Don't you understand that if a girl goes back to a guy's room after a party, she knows they are going to hook up? It's not like they are going back just to hang out. She wouldn't have gone back to his room if she didn't want to be there. If she claims rape later, she's just ashamed of what she did the next morning?

16. What are some good ways to intervene if you think, but definitely aren't sure, that an assault might take place?

17. How drunk is too drunk to hook up?

18. You said one in four women has survived rape or attempted rape? You can make statistics say anything you want. I don't know anybody who has been raped. There is no way that one quarter of girls have been raped. You really think that there are that many rapists here? We'd hear about it all the time. Your statistic is full of crap.

19. Okay, maybe rape is a problem, but what about all those men who get falsely accused. I know this girl back home who falsely accused three different guys. No one cares about those guys. They just get shafted. What about them?

20. If the girl was drunk and can't remember anything, how can she say it was sexual assault? She could have wanted it and shown the guy that she did. Giving the girl free reign to cry rape isn't fair to guys.

21. How does someone know what a reasonable amount of alcohol is before the other person can't consent? It's a guessing game and it's too easy to use that as a way to cry rape falsely afterwards.

22. What if I know that my female friend really likes this guy (she's always talking about him, she went to this party because he was going to be there, etc.). So, we're at this party together, everyone's drinking, they're talking and dancing a fair amount, and then I notice them going home together. This happens all the time here, and many times that is how people meet/hook up the first time and they may still be dating months later. Should I stop her from going home with him?

23. Why do you present the program in a single-sex environment?

24. How do you know the Men's Program works?

## Questions for Female Audiences

1. I have a family member who is survivor, where can I go to find help for her?

2. My friend told me she was raped and I don't know what to do to help her. Do you have any suggestions?

3. This guy I know told me that he thinks he committed rape. What should I tell him?

4. You talk about survivors as women but how often are men raped?

5. Do women rape men?

6. If two people are drunk and hook up, why is the guy automatically labeled as the rapist? That happened to my friend.

7. I can say this because I'm a woman, and we're all women. I just think that women need to stop dressing up like sluts and drinking like lushes, and then they wouldn't be getting themselves raped. Then you all could stop wasting your time presenting this program, too. Right?

8. From the news and stories I've heard it seems like women lie a lot about rape. Since it's so easy for them to lie, why should we automatically believe them?

9. I understand that rape is wrong, but what about when a guy and a girl are hooking up and a girl gets a guy so excited that he can't stop? You can't really blame him for finishing up, right? I mean, my roommate totally got her panties in a wad about this really nice guy who she got all worked up like that and I just don't think she understood what she was doing.

10. What about all those girls who wear clothes that just advertise the fact that they want it. Aren't they at least a little bit responsible for what happens next if a guy loses control?

11. Isn't rape just bad communication?

12. Why is the man always the one at fault if they are both drunk and they have sex? Isn't the whole justice system set up against men? I feel sorry for them.

13. I think my friend was raped but she won't admit it to me. What should I do?

14. How can I tell my boyfriend that people who have been dating for a while still have to ask before they have sex?

15. I don't understand why guys think that when a girl goes back to a guy's room after a party, they are going to hook up. Sometimes we just want to hang out. It is so frustrating when the guy automatically assumes there is going to be sex. How do you tell a guy you just want to hang out and not have sex with him?

16. What are some good ways to intervene if you think, but definitely aren't sure, that an assault might take place?

17. One in four? You can make statistics say anything you want. I don't know anybody who has been raped. There is no way that one quarter of girls here have been raped. You really think that there are that many rapists around here? It would be on the news every day. You're full of crap.

18. Okay, maybe rape is a problem, but what about all those men who get falsely accused. No one cares about them. I know this girl back home who accused three different guys of rape. All those men who get falsely accused just get shafted. What about them?

19. Yeah, but if a girl dresses like a slut and gets drunk, she's asking for it. Don't you think?

20. If the girl was drunk and can't remember anything, how can she say it was sexual assault? She could have wanted it and shown the guy that she did. Giving the girl free reign to cry rape isn't fair to guys.

21. How does someone know what a reasonable amount of alcohol is before the other person can't consent? It's a guessing game and it's too easy to use that as a way to cry rape falsely afterwards.

22. What if I know that my female friend really likes this guy (she's always talking about him, she went to this party because he was going to be there, etc.). So, we're at this party together, everyone's drinking, they're talking and dancing a fair amount, and then I notice them going home together. This happens all the time here, and many times that is how people meet/hook up the first time and they may still be dating months later. Should I stop her from going home with him?

23. Why do you present the program in a single-sex environment?

24. How do you know the Women's Program works?

## Module 16

### *Recognizing Rape Myths*

**Time needed: 30 minutes**
**Intended audience: Men or women**

Note: *This exercise is designed to help people better understand some of the attitudes others commonly have about rape, rape victims, and rapists. These attitudes are often referred to as "rape myths" because of their false nature.*

Do: *Have two people act out this brief scene. Afterward, facilitate a discussion about the different issues that the dialogue raises about sexual assault. The handout immediately following identifies the different rape myths raised by the scene. The script for this scene is in both peer education guides.*

### The Legal Bias Against Rape Victims

Narrator: Imagine how it might sound if a robbery victim were subjected to the kind of cross examination a rape victim usually must undergo.

*Attorney:* Mr. Smith, you were held up at gunpoint on the corner of First and Main?

*Victim:* Yes.

A: Did you struggle with the robber?

V: No.

A: Why not?

V: He was armed.

A: Then you made a conscious decision to comply with his demands rather than resist?

V: Yes.

A: Did you scream? Yell for help?

V: No. I was scared.

A: Oh. I see. Have you ever been held up before?

V: No.

A: Have you ever *given* money away?

V: Yes, of course.

A: And you did so *willingly?*

V: What are you implying?

A: Well, let's put it this way, Mr. Smith. You've admitted giving money away in the past. In fact, you have quite a reputation for philanthropy. How can we be sure that you didn't really want to have your money taken away from you by force?

V: Listen, if I *wanted* ...

A: Never mind. What time do you allege that this "robbery" took place, Mr. Smith?

V: Oh, about 11:00 p.m.

*A:* You were out on the street at 11:00 p.m. Doing what?!?!

*V:* Just walking.

*A:* Just walking!?! You know it is dangerous being out on the street late at night! Weren't you aware that you could be robbed?

*V:* I didn't really think about it that night when I decided to go for a walk.

*A:* Well, what were you wearing that night, Mr. Smith.

*V:* Let's see … a suit. Yes, a suit.

*A:* An *expensive* suit?

*V:* Well, yes. I own a successful business and I like wearing nice suits, so what?

*A:* Well, Mr. Smith, you were walking around the streets late at night in a suit that practically advertised the fact that you were a good target for some easy money, isn't that right? I mean, really Mr. Smith, we can easily come to the conclusion that you really were asking for this to happen. Can't we?

## *Rape Myths Addressed by Mr. Smith Dialogue*

1. **If she didn't kick him in the balls or fight to the death, obviously it wasn't rape.** Mr. Smith did not struggle with the robber because he was afraid, a natural reaction to an armed robber. Many rape survivors are intimidated by the physical strength of the attacker.

2. **If she didn't scream or call for help, it wasn't rape.** Mr. Smith did not call 911 on his cell phone, scream, or say "help me!" Doing so could have gotten him shot or beaten up further. He chose the path that would cause him the least injury in the long run.

3. **If she's had sex before, is known to have sex frequently, it wasn't rape and/or she probably deserved it or asked for it.** Mr. Smith was known for giving money away and enjoyed giving money away, but only when he decided whom to give his money to, not when it was forcibly stolen from him at gunpoint. Who likes to have something stolen from him?

4. **Maybe she wanted to be raped.** Mr. Smith was out taking a walk. He wasn't out hoping that someone would rob him and take his money away. It isn't logical to think that someone hopes to be robbed; it also isn't logical that someone would hope to be raped. Some women may go out wanting to have sex. Rape is defined as sexual intercourse without consent and by force. By definition, someone cannot desire something without consent— that is contradictory.

5. **Women deserve rape if they are in risky situations.** If Mr. Smith was walking alone at 11 p.m. he might have been in a risky situation, who knows. But being in a risky situation doesn't make someone at fault for the choices of others. Mr. Smith did not choose to be robbed. The robber chose to rob him. Women don't choose to be raped. Rapists choose to rape them. Either way, there is a difference between judgment and responsibility.

6. **Women who wear attractive clothes should expect to be raped because they are just advertising the fact that they are a good target.** Mr. Smith was wearing a nice suit. Does this mean he was advertising his wealth in order to be robbed? No. If you see a great advertisement for a car does that make you say, "Well, I guess that means I can steal it!"? Of course not, that is just as ridiculous as saying that women who dress nicely are advertising themselves for rape.

### Using the Mr. Smith Dialogue to Answer Difficult Questions

If you, as a peer educator, are ever asked a question along the lines of "Is it really rape if she didn't struggle?" or "What if you know she really wants it but is just being a tease?" or "She should have known better than to wear what she was wearing given the place she was in," you might recite a shortened version of this dialogue. For example, you might say something like this:

"I'd like to answer your question with another question. What if you were wearing a nice suit, were out walking alone at night on your way back from a semiformal, and you got held up. The robber had a gun, you thought you might get killed, and you didn't struggle. You were dressed up, so he thought you'd have money on you; in fact, he'd seen you giving money to a local homeless shelter before so he assumed you must like giving money away. Is it your fault, then, for being robbed, or were you the victim of a violent crime you did not ask for?"

# Chapter 4

## Advanced Training for Peer Educators

This chapter provides helpful advanced training exercises for peer educators to go through either before or during their service as peer educators.

Some training modules here are intended for male audiences, some for female audiences, and some can be used with either group. Some include special wording for military audiences. Ultimately, it is up to you whether you decide to present any of these modules to your peer educators and which you use. As with everything, the choice is yours!

The size of your training group should be around 12 to 16 people. More than 20 people in a training class can make the climate prohibitive for small group discussion.

You may find that some of these advanced training modules make excellent follow-up programs to present to students or members of the military some time after presenting either the Men's Program or the Women's Program.

# Module 17

## *Exploring Privilege*

**Time needed: 45 minutes**
**Intended audience: Men or women**

Do: *Have participants complete the "Experience in Society Scale" as printed below and also found in* The Men's Program: Peer Educator's Manual *and* The Women's Program: Peer Educator's Manual.

Ask: To what extent can you see yourselves as having some of the privileges this scale identifies?

Ask: If you can see yourself as having some of these privileges, which ones?

Ask: With this knowledge of privilege, what do you think you should do about it?

Ask: How does this relate to our work in sexual-assault prevention?

## *Experience in Society Scale\**

**Please put a T or an F (true or false) to the left of each item.**

1. I can, if I wish, arrange to be in the company of people of my race most of the time.
2. If I should need to move, I can be pretty sure of renting or purchasing housing in an area which I can afford and in which I would want to live.
3. I can be reasonably sure that my neighbors in such a location will be neutral or pleasant to me.
4. I can go shopping alone most of the time, fairly well assured that I will not be followed or harassed by store detectives.
5. I can turn on the television or open to the front page of the paper and see people of my race widely and positively represented.
6. When I am told about our national heritage or about "civilization," I am shown that people of my race made it what it is.
7. I can be sure that my children will be given curricular materials that testify to the existence of their race.
8. I can be fairly sure of having my voice heard in a group in which I am the only member of my race.
9. I can go into a bookshop and count on finding writings of my race represented, into a supermarket and find the staple foods that fit with my cultural traditions, into a hairdresser's shop and find someone who can deal with my hair.

---

\* Based on article by Peggy McIntosh (1998), White privilege and male privilege: A personal account of coming to see correspondences through work in women's studies.

10. Whether I use checks, credit cards, or cash, I can count on my skin color not to work against the appearance that I am financially reliable.
11. I could arrange to protect our young children most of the time from people who might not like them.
12. I did not have to educate our children to be aware of systemic racism for their own daily physical protection.
13. I can be pretty sure that my children's teachers and employers will tolerate them if they fit school and workplace norms; my chief worries about them do not concern others' attitudes toward their race.
14. I can talk with my mouth full and not have people put this down to my color.
15. I can swear, or dress in secondhand clothes, or not answer letters, without having people attribute these choices to the bad morals, the poverty, or the illiteracy of my race.
16. I can speak in public to a powerful male group without putting my race on trial.
17. I can do well in a challenging situation without being called a credit to my race.
18. I am never asked to speak for all the people of my racial group.
19. I can remain oblivious to the language and customs of persons of color who constitute the world's majority without feeling in my culture any penalty for such oblivion.
20. I can be reasonably sure that if I ask to talk to "the person in charge," I will be facing a person of my race.
21. If a traffic cop pulls me over or if the IRS audits my tax return, I can be sure I haven't been singled out because of my race.
22. I can easily buy posters, postcards, picture books, greeting cards, dolls, toys, and children's magazines featuring people of my race.
23. I can go home from most meetings of organizations I belong to feeling somewhat tied in, rather than isolated, out of place, outnumbered, unheard, held at a distance, or feared.
24. If I declare there is a racial issue at hand, or there isn't a racial issue at hand, my race will lend me more credibility for either position.
25. I am not made acutely aware that my shape, bearing, or body odor will be taken as a reflection on my race.
26. I can worry about racism without being seen as self-interested or self-seeking.
27. I can take a job with an affirmative action employer without having my co-workers on the job suspect that I got it because of my race.
28. If my day, week, or year is going badly, I need not ask of each negative episode or situation whether it has racial overtones.
29. I can be pretty sure of finding people who would be willing to talk with me and advise me about my next steps, professionally.
30. I can be late to a meeting without having the lateness reflect on my race.
31. If I have low credibility as a leader, I can be sure that my race is not the problem.

## Module 18

### *Identifying Characteristics of Dangerous Men*

**Time needed: 30 minutes**
**Intended audience: Men or women**

Do: *Have two men (current peer educators or others as available) lead an exercise in which one role-plays the part of a man not likely to rape and one who role-plays the part of a man likely to rape. Have role players use the handout for the Women's Program included in Chapter 2 of this book and in* The Women's Program: A Peer Educator's Manual *to determine what characteristics and behaviors they should portray.*

Do: *Have each role player introduce himself (in character) to the audience and give a speech about his relationships with women and how he thinks men and women should relate to one another.*

Do: *Allow the role players to engage in dialogue together, confronting each other's beliefs.*

Do: *Next, allow the audience to engage in this dialogue. Allow the audience to ask the role players questions, which should be answered in character.*

Do: *After the role play is over, give role players a chance to convey their true beliefs, particularly the role player who took the part of the potential rapist.*

## Module 19

### *Follow-up to the Men's Program*

**Time needed: 60 minutes**
**Intended audience: Men—Special features for military audiences**

*Team 1*

State: Today we are going to talk more about the concepts that were discussed in the program you saw that included the DVD with the male police officer who described the situation where two men chose to rape him.

*Team 2*

Ask: So let's talk about the suggestions made during the program, about how you could intervene, and how you could support a woman whom a man chose to rape. What do you think you could do right now that was suggested in the program? (Write down responses on board.)

#### For Military Only

Ask: So when you think about all of the suggestions made in the Men's Program, how do these suggestions help us do our job in the military?

Examples:

A military without rape makes us more mission ready.
Helping fellow members of the military fits with our core values.
Doing something if we see a potential safety violation is our duty.
A member of the military should never have to fear "friendly fire" or other violence from another member of our military.

Ask: What in the program do you believe you'd need to know more about before you could do something?

*Team 1*

Note: *Clear a large area, point to one direction or a wall, and mark one end with a sign that says "I will intervene," and the other end with "I won't intervene."*
State: One of the messages of the Men's Program is that there are certain things we can all do as bystanders to help prevent others from becoming survivors in the first place—by stepping up as leaders and preventing a rape from happening. This was probably some of the toughest stuff that was presented. To get a sense for everyone's opinions of this, we're going to do an exercise where everyone will need to move around, so please get up.

State: Okay, please stand along this imaginary line to indicate how strongly you agree or disagree with a few statements we will read to you.

State: You go to a party that a friend of yours is having. You see two people there you don't know, who are your age. The woman is so drunk that she can't stand on her own and you know for sure that she is extremely drunk. You can see that she is much too intoxicated to give consent. You overhear the guy ask his friend for a room so the two of them can go have sex. The man then drags her by the hand and heads to a private room.

Ask: How likely are you personally to intervene in this situation in which you can see that the female is much too intoxicated to give consent?

State: If you are very likely to intervene, stand by the "I will intervene" side of the room. If you are not at all likely, stand to the other side of the room. If you are somewhere in the middle, stand along the line based on where you think your willingness to intervene might fall.

Do: *Choose people from extremes and various parts of the middle to discuss their opinions and to explain why they are standing where they are. Point out differences in their reasoning. Remain neutral, yet feel free to use those people who would intervene to counteract comments of those who would do nothing.*

Ask: What are the potential consequences if you intervene?

Ask: What are the potential consequences if you don't intervene?

Ask: Has anyone here ever intervened in a situation like this? Are you willing to talk about it?

## Team 2

State: Okay, here is the second situation.

State: You are in a small apartment over the summer and the guy you share a room with brings a woman home who is so drunk that she can't stand on her own and you know for sure that she is extremely drunk. You can see that she is much too intoxicated to give consent. Your roommate asks you to crash on the couch for the night so that the two of them can have sex.

Ask: How likely are you to actually act in some manner to try to prevent them from having intercourse when she is too intoxicated to consent. Stand to that side of the room if you are very likely to do something, to the other side if you are very unlikely and somewhere in the middle depending on the strength of your opinion.

Do: *Choose people from extremes and various parts of the middle to discuss their opinions and to explain why they are standing where they are. Point out differences in their reasoning. Remain neutral, yet feel free to use those people who would intervene to counteract comments of those who would do nothing.*

Ask: What are the potential consequences if you intervene?

Ask: What are the potential consequences if you don't intervene?

Ask: Has anyone here ever intervened in a situation like this? Are you willing to talk about it?

Do: *Return to classroom setting.*

## Team 1

State: Some of you suggested that you didn't want to intervene to do something to prevent a rape from happening.

Ask: Why?

Ask: Let's take the example of your roommate coming home with a woman who is too drunk to consent to intercourse.

- What action on your part would make it most likely that a rape would not happen?
- What action on your part would make it least likely that someone would get hurt?

### For Military Only

- What action on your part would lead to a more effective military?
- Assume that your roommate, the woman, and you are all in the same unit. What action would lead to the most effective unit cohesion?

Ask: Do any of these questions make you think any differently about what you might do in this situation? How?

## Team 2

Ask: Let's think about this a little differently. Do you have any responsibility to intervene in other party situations that involve a risk of something bad happening?

### For Military Only

Ask: To what extent is this like observing a safety violation (e.g., not wearing a seatbelt, standing on an unstable object instead of a ladder) and either doing, or not doing something about it?

Ask: If a leader stands by and watches something happen and does nothing about it, what message does this send to subordinates?

Ask: So if you, as a leader in whatever capacity, stand by and do nothing when a potential rape situation occurs, what message does this send?

## Team 1

Ask: What are some of the most important things to do to help a sexual assault survivor?

State: Today we have mentioned several different ways to intervene as a bystander. I would like to hear if any of you is willing to commit today to using any of the methods that were described to intervene as a bystander. If any of you is willing to intervene in that way, I will ask you to state that method. If others are willing to do the same thing I will ask you to raise your hand to commit to intervening in the same way.

Ask: Who here is willing to name a specific way he is willing to intervene as an active bystander, and can name something specific that he is willing to do?

State: Thank you. Please raise your hand if you are also willing to commit to doing that as well.

Do: *Repeat the previous question and follow up until there are no more suggestions raised.*

State: Thank you for your willingness to be part of the solution to end sexual assault.

# Module 20

## Advanced Bystander Intervention Training

**Time needed: 60 minutes**
   **Intended audience: Men or women—Special features for military audiences**

Note: *This training module can be used for many purposes. It is useful for training peer educators who have seen the Men's Program to help them process the material on a deeper level. This module could also be used as a follow-up program to be presented by peer educators to students or soldiers who have seen the Men's Program. This session includes specific applications for military audiences. Additional discussion questions are labeled and provided for this purpose.*

## Team 1

State: Today we are going to conduct some advanced training on how to intervene as a bystander when you see a situation that could turn into a sexual assault.

Ask: How many of you believe that you have leadership potential?

State: Good, because stepping up and intervening as a bystander is all about being a leader. It is specifically about how we step up and be leaders when we notice something isn't quite right.

Ask: Here is a simple question. As a leader, do you desire to be an active or a passive leader?

State: Okay. Not surprisingly, you want to be active leaders. The bystander intervention model fits right in with that.

State: Today we'll talk about some ways to intervene, and ask for your help in identifying things to say to someone who might make a mistake.

## Making It Relevant

### Team 2

Ask: How many of you think it is possible that during your college (*or military*) career you will be around a situation that could turn into a sexual assault?

State: Okay. For those of you who don't think so, here is some information to consider.

### For College Audiences

Two separate nationwide studies found that 5% of college women experience rape every single year. If you know 20 women, odds are that one will experience rape this year.

### For Military Audiences

Several studies have shown that over one quarter of women who serve in the military experience rape during their military service. This proportion of women does not include incidents that happened before these women came into the military, just the cases that happened while they were serving. Studies also show that almost all of the perpetrators are men in our own military. Moreover, studies have shown that men who enlist in the U.S. military are up to twice as likely as men in the general population to have committed rape before they enlisted. Thus, their risk for continuing this behavior while in the military is very high.

Ask: Given that, how many of you think it is possible that you might encounter a situation this year that could turn into a rape at some point in your college (or military) career?

Note: *At this point, most people are likely to raise their hands in agreement.*

State: By the time this session is over, we hope that all of you will make a commitment to step up and intervene when you either see a situation that could turn into a sexual assault or hear others make comments that are consistent with this kind of behavior.

## Team 1

State: We believe that all of us share a responsibility for helping to end sexual assault (at our college/*in our military*). Through bystander intervention, we can all share in the efforts to end it. By thinking through ways to intervene and by practicing an intervention conversation, we hope that you will feel a more developed sense of confidence to do something if the situation presents itself.

State: If you consider yourself a leader (in college/*in the military*), stepping up and doing something is important. If we choose to stand by and let bad things happen, we choose not to lead. Bystander intervention is all about stepping up and doing something. It is about doing something to help out others right here in our midst—our fellow (students/*members of the military*).

## Scenario 1

### Team 2

Let's consider this scenario for a minute. You are out at a bar sitting at a table with some of your friends. You haven't had anything to drink yet; you think you might later, but for now you are just hanging out. It's a bar where they don't closely monitor the drinking age. At the next table is a guy you know named Mike. You can hear the other guys sitting with Mike saying things like "She totally wants you." "Didn't you see the way she ordered that drink and then looked right at you?" "You know she wants to have sex with you."

You can tell that Mike is being encouraged to go hit on someone. Initially, that seems fairly harmless. You also know that Mike is one of those guys who is a little bit clueless. He just doesn't quite get it when a woman says, "I have to go home to get some reading done." He thinks that means "Come home with me so we can have sex" not "go away, dumb ass." Later in the evening, you notice that the woman Mike's friends were trying to get him to go after is completely trashed. Her friends are having trouble holding her up. Mike has had a lot to drink as well; probably about three pitchers by himself. At this point, Mike has been hanging all over this woman for about a half an hour and she seems to be annoyed with him. Mike, as oblivious as usual, doesn't seem to get it or care. The woman seems annoyed, but is so drunk that she can't seem to fend him off. You then see that one of the woman's friends leaves. Mike puts his arm around the drunk woman's shoulder, and he is getting ready to walk her out of the bar.

Ask: First of all, how many of you have seen something like this happen? (Pause while many people raise hands to indicate whether they have.)
State: So it looks like we have at least a reasonably realistic scenario.
State: Okay. That is the scene. Think for a minute about what you would actually do.

## Team 1

Ask: What would you do? Let's hear some responses. (Write them down on newsprint or a board for later reference.)
Note: *The responses should generally fall into three categories: Do nothing, get someone else to do something (police, bartender, etc.), and intervene in person. Try to get several brief responses from people and write them on the board. The following exercises will focus on "doing nothing" and "doing something."*
State: So clearly some of you would not intervene. Others would do something.

## Team 2

Ask: What are some of the possible consequences of doing nothing in this scenario?
Ask: Okay, let's go back to the ideas people had about intervening in this scenario. What on this list do you think would work best to help prevent a rape from occurring?

Ask: I'd like some volunteers to come up and act that out.

Do: *Get a volunteer to play Mike, Mike's male friend, and the woman Mike is hitting on. Have the three people act out the scene and have Mike's friend use the techniques brainstormed by the group that they think would work best to help prevent a rape from occurring.*

### Team 1

State: Obviously what we're talking about is stuff that's hard to do. How do you step in and intervene without feeling like a "cock blocker" or risking your friendship? There were some really great ideas that came out of this exercise. If you look at the board, some of the great ideas you came up with were (note great ideas here).

State: In addition, some other ideas about how to intervene in a situation in which a guy like Mike is about to engage in dangerous behavior include:

**Distract him.** For example, go up with a couple friends, insist that his favorite song is playing, and move him back into the bar so quickly that he doesn't know what happened. Meanwhile have another person make sure the woman gets home safely.

**Use humor.** For example, walk up to him, pretend to be oblivious about what he is trying to do, get him to laugh at himself and the situation, and convince him to go home with you. You might remind him that he just tested positive for genital warts and it wouldn't be nice of him to share that with someone else. Make sure the woman gets home safely.

**Get him alone.** For example, talk with him privately, remind him that he is your friend, that he needs to respect your sober judgment that he is drunk and that the woman he is with can't give consent to him and that he needs to do the right thing and stay away from her the rest of the night. While you are talking with him, have someone else take her home safely so that he is unable to continue to put himself and the woman in jeopardy.

**Offer him help.** For example, walk up and say, "Oh Mike, you are so nice, you are taking care of her!" When he says he doesn't need help, don't take no for an answer. Get a cab or other transportation for her to get home and take him home in a separate vehicle. Continuously praise him for how helpful he was being to make sure that she got home safely.

## Scenario 2

### Team 2

State: Now we are going to go through the second of two scenarios. In this scenario, we want you to imagine that you hanging out with a bunch of your friends eating dinner. During dinner one of your friends, Steve, says,

"I'm sick and tired of all those bitches around here getting in my way. They are always out there leading some guy on and then not putting out or crying rape the next morning. They just need to shut the heck up. I mean seriously, just find me a good piece of ass for the weekend and that's all I need and then kick that bitch out the door when I'm finished. Girls. They're nice to look at and screw but all those pussies are good for is a nice lay."

State: Okay. That is the scene. At this point we want you to get into pairs and talk about what you would do at this point in the conversation and why. Remember, talk about what you would really do, not just what you think you should do.

## Team 1

Ask: By a show of hands, how many of you would intervene in some way?
Ask: Let's hear from some of you who would say something, after that we'll hear from some who wouldn't.
Ask: Why would some of you say something?
Ask: Why would some of you not say something?

## Team 2

State: For now, regardless of whether you think you should intervene, we want you to develop some practice on what it is like to intervene. So we are going to ask a few of you to come forward to get some practice.
Do: *First call on someone who would intervene to practice in front of the group. Next, call on someone who originally would not intervene to practice in front of the group.*
State: I will be playing the role of Steve. You will play the role of someone who is talking to Steve later on about what he said. The rest of you will be observing and watching what you think is realistic, what is not, and what you think could be said differently.
Do: *Invite people to come up one at a time to practice confronting you in your role as "Steve." Respond as if you think a person like Steve would. Be real, not overly difficult nor overly easy. If you think Steve would be convinced, respond as he would. If you think Steve would blow them off, blow them off. After a few minutes, stop the role play with that person, process the dialogue with the whole group, and bring up someone else.*
Ask: Now that we have been through different people confronting Steve, what are some of the techniques you found were most helpful in having a discussion with Steve about his comments?

*Team 1*

State: In addition to the ones you mentioned, here are several more techniques for confronting a man who makes derogatory comments about women:
- Approach him as someone who is **concerned about his choices** and how they affect him.
- **Confront the behavior,** don't clobber the individual.
- Ask him to **restate his words,** and discuss them part by part. Note your concern that he might not mean to hurt anyone but the words indicate that he could.
- Ask him to **explain the meaning** behind what he said.
- (*Military. Ask the person if he thinks everyone in his company should be able to count on him, including the women.*)

*Team 2*

State: So we've just gone through a number of strategies for how to confront people. One thing we haven't talked about yet is what you as the person who does the confronting has to gain. Think about it this way. Do you want to live with (*for military audiences, serve with*) a guy who would be such a loose cannon? Do you want to have someone like that hurt someone you know?

State: When you intervene in these kinds of situations, you can help prevent someone from not only hurting someone else but also facing the possibility of guilt, frustration, and potential consequences that could alter his future. Would you let a guy like Steve act on his ideas like this that could be so damaging? The time to talk with him is now, not after he acts on these ideas.

*Team 1*

State: Approaching a friend (*for military audiences, fellow service-member*) in this situation can be awkward and difficult.
*For military audiences: Of course if you stop and think about it, how many of us joined the military because we thought things would be easy?*

State: Okay, leadership is difficult. It is also where we show our integrity as mature individuals. When we intervene as bystanders with a guy who is about to make a big mistake, we do him a favor by confronting him, not to mention the harm we save a potential victim.

State: Through our efforts intervening as bystanders we can work together to make the rape statistics go down. And that is something worth fighting for.

(End of program for college audiences)

## Additional Material for Military Audiences

State: As we said at the beginning of this program, a national study found that 28% of U.S. women veterans experience rape during their military service. Almost all of those women, 96%, are raped by members of the military (Sadler, Booth, & Doebbeling, 2005). That's over one in four women in the U.S. military who experiences rape during her military service.

### Team 1

State: That is one of the things that makes it so important that we intervene as bystanders when we see a situation that might turn into a rape. That is what makes it so important that we say something when a guy says "They're nice to look at and screw—all those pussies are good for is a nice lay." It is time that we took control of our one in four statistic and obliterated it. If we decide to stand up and intervene when things look like they might get out of hand, we can. We hope you will join us.

State: Thank you.

## Module 21

### *Advanced Training on Consent*

**Time needed: 60 minutes**
**Intended audience: Men or women**

Note: *This training module can be used for many purposes. It is useful for training peer educators to help them learn more about sexual assault. This module could also be used as a follow-up program to be presented by peer educators to students or military personnel who have seen either the Men's Program or the Women's Program.*

State: This session is going to go into depth on the topic of consent.

Ask: To start off, based on what you've learned so far, what is the basic definition of rape?

State: So basically, rape is sexual intercourse without consent. It happens when someone doesn't give consent

1. Because she doesn't want to give consent
2. Because she is unable to give consent
3. Because she isn't given the chance to consent

Ask: So what's the common theme here?

Note: *Consent.*

State: Right, it's the idea of consent.

Ask: So what is consent?

Do: *Take a couple of responses.*

State: Alright, you all had a lot of different opinions about what consent is. That makes sense. One of the things about consent is that it is a complex idea. Some people are really confused about what it is. Here is one basic definition of consent:

> The act of willingly agreeing to engage in specific sexual contact by a competent, unimpaired individual.

State: It's important to add that if sexual contact is not mutually and simultaneously initiated, the person who initiates sexual contact is responsible for getting the consent of the other individual(s) involved.

### *The Importance of Verbal Consent*

Ask: Now, how many of you, the last time you hooked up, however you define that, actually had a long conversation outlining exactly what you were going to do with each other before you started getting into it?

State: Okay. Safe to say, that's usually not how things happen.

State: If two people are hooking up, and not just making out but really hooking up, what often happens is that there's very rarely a serious discussion taking place. Most often people just try to read one another, test each other out. You try one thing and the other seems to like it. You try something more, but how do you really know? (rhetorical question)

State: Well, just because someone is going along with something doesn't mean that person is cool with it. But still, we know that can be confusing.

Ask: Who here is ever confused by what someone you are trying to hook up with is thinking, sexually or otherwise? (If hands are not raised, repeat "*ever* confused.")

State: Some of the most common cases when people don't understand each other happen when people just guess what someone else has in mind and they don't talk about it.

State: The only way you can really know what another person wants, and more importantly avoid what the other person doesn't want, is to actually ask, and that's part of the idea of consent.

## Alcohol/Peer Influence

Ask: Who here likes to drink? (raise hands)

State: Well, we're not here to lecture you about drinking. However, we do need to talk about alcohol. We just talked about how confusing it can be to try to read another person's mind. I know for a lot of people if they are trying to understand what someone else is thinking and they have been drinking, then it's a whole new ballgame—they understand even less. It's very easy to misinterpret the other person, but even more so when you yourself have been drinking. Do you agree?

State: Now what if that person has been drinking? If someone has 16 drinks, is puking in the bathroom, and then stumbles back into the party, it's pretty obvious that person shouldn't be hooking up with anyone later that night. Kissing someone who's been vomiting can leave you with more than just a bad taste in your mouth. On the other hand if that person hasn't been drinking at all and is otherwise competent, that person can certainly consent to sexual activity.

State: In between these two places is a very large area of uncertainty that poses a lot of problems (of course, someone who has had 15 drinks is still clearly too drunk to consent).

State: So we'd like you to consider two differing principles you might choose to follow about when you think it's okay to hook up when alcohol is involved.

State: The first principle is "It's better to err on the side of caution and not hook up when the other person might be too drunk to consent." The second principle is "It's better to err on the side of hooking up when you have the chance."

Ask: Which one do you prefer and why?

Ask: What circumstances would affect your decision?

Ask: What do you think should be done?

Ask: What would you actually do?

Ask: Why?

State: The point here is that if there's ever any doubt in your mind, it's always better to wait until you're sure the person you are with can consent to what you are doing.

Intoxication = Confusion (at best)

State: I don't know about you, but one thing I've noticed when I'm hanging around at a party is that when people drink, especially guys, they tend to feel a lot braver about approaching a woman they want to hook up with. In talking with a bunch of people and hearing about the stuff that goes on, I've also noticed that there are some guys who are really clueless when it comes to reading women. Are you with me on that?

State: Not only do some guys feel a lot braver about approaching women when they themselves are drunk, these guys also have basically no chance of reading the woman's body language. Now sure, if she's sober and rips all his clothes off and says "put your penis in my vagina," it's pretty obvious, but that usually isn't the case.

State: What I worry about sometimes is the guys who really want to hook up, who get drunk, who get a woman alone, who have no clue what her body language means, who have no idea what consent is, and then push ahead when they see the first sign they interpret as a yes—"She smiled at me. Yes! she wants me. Let's do it." They also just don't even get it when a woman pushes him away or says "I want to go home" when she means "get the hell away from me" or "yeah, kiss me but keep your hands off my butt."

State: It's those guys that really need some help—from their friends who don't want to see them getting into trouble, not to mention seeing women getting hurt. It's those guys and those times when they need their friends to say "Dude, slow down, she's wasted and so are you, give it a try next time."

State: Let's try a different exercise. I'm going to start a list on the board and label it "signs a person is trashed." Give me some ways you know that a person is trashed, just obliterated from alcohol. (Take responses.)

State: Now I'm going to relabel this list.

Do: *Write "warning signs that a person can't consent."*

Ask: To what extent do you think this label is valid?

Do: *Ask participants about some of the individual warning signs and ask them if each is a sign that a person can't consent to sex.*

State: Before we start to wrap up today, we'd like you to think about this question and then share some of your thoughts about it:

Ask: What advice would you give to someone who is a few years younger than you who has asked you for your advice about how to make sure to always have consent during intimate encounters?

## *Verbal Consent*

State: A lot of people have a fear that if they ask to do something intimate with another person, it will be over. They think the other person will be offended. We're not suggesting you just walk up to a person at the party and say "I think you're hot, lets get naked and have wild passionate sex." But we do suggest that as you begin getting physical, and during physical activity, you say something about what you two are doing and make sure both of you agree to what is going on.

State: So why is consent so important? It is important because two women experience rape in the United States during every minute that goes by. Every 30 seconds another woman experiences rape. We think if we talk about consent more and more, we might be able to change that number. We hope you do too.

State: Thank you for coming.

# Module 22

## *Pornography and Men's Violence Against Women*

**Time needed: 45 minutes**
**Intended audience: Men or women**

State: When we use the phrase "the pornography industry" it includes a large variety of media, people, and behaviors. A common thread includes some element used to increase sexual arousal. Such elements include sexually explicit media, erotica, online sexual activity/Internet porn, stripping, prostitution, and other live performances (Carroll, Padilla-Walker, Nelson, Olson, Barry, & Medsen, 2008).

State: The reach of the pornography industry is extensive: 93% of boys, 62% of girls have seen online porn before turning 18. Most exposure begins between ages 11 and 14. Not surprisingly, boys view online porn more frequently and view a wider variety of images than girls (Malarek, 2009; Sabina, Wolack, & Finkelhor, 2008).

## *What Are Porn Executives Trying to Do? Just Ask*

State: Dr. Robert Jensen, after attending a convention for the pornography industry observed:

"I had listened to a pornography producer tell me that he thinks anal sex is popular in pornography because men like to think about f*cking their wives and girlfriends in the ass to pay them back for being bitchy." (Jensen, 2007, p. 44)

State: Jensen continued, "I interviewed the producer who takes great pride that his 'Gag Factor' series was the first to feature exclusively aggressive 'throat f*cking'" (Jensen, 2007, p. 44). This involves violent oral sex until the woman vomits.

State: This producer was not the only one to brag about what he filmed. Another porn industry executive spoke of the appeal of anal sex in this way:

"Essentially it comes from every man who is unhappily married, and he looks at his wife who just nagged at him about this or that or whatnot and he says, 'I'd like to f*ck you in the ass.' He's angry at her, right? And he can't, so he would rather watch some girl taking it up the ass and fantasize at that point he's doing whatever girl happened to be mean to him that particular day, and *that* is the attraction, because when people watch anal, *nobody* wants to watch a girl *enjoying* anal." (Jensen, 2007, p. 58)

## *A Case in Point: Stripping the Kelly Holsopple Study*

State:  Kelly Holsopple (1999b) is a woman who escaped the pornography industry. Her involvement included performing in strip clubs and being prostituted. She has conducted research on the experiences of women in the industry and has spoken to a wide variety of audiences on this issue.

State:  Holsopple notes that strippers receive pressure to shave all of their pubic hair to produce a childlike appearance and receive breast implants to please the men who frequent strip clubs. In stark contrast to the perception that being a stripper is a fun job, Holsopple's research found that *all* of the strippers reported physical and sexual abuse while working; three out of four were stalked. In addition, all of the strippers in her study reported that the following beliefs about stripping and strippers are completely false:

- "That no one touches you, women enjoy it."
- "That we get sexually aroused doing this."
- "That men are there to have harmless fun, when they are really there to abuse women."
- "That it is a big party and that the women want to be there for some reason other than money, like sex or to meet men or because they are nudists or exhibitionists."
- "That you are doing things you want to be doing."
- "That they are not degrading us because girls always are justifying it with college."
- "That it is not prostitution."
- "That it is glamorous, fast money, easy work, way to get ahead" (Holsopple, 1999b, p. 15).

## *Prostitution*

State:  Prostitution is often called a victimless crime. Consider these statistics and see if you come to the same conclusion.

State:  Internationally the average age for the entrance of girls into prostitution is 14 (Ekberg, 2002). One of the consequences of prostitution is that it creates an international sex trade driven by men's desire for "new merchandise" from different countries, cultures, and backgrounds.

State:  If men did not buy and sexually exploit women and girls, the sex trade would not exist. Do these men care? Not really. Three of four men who rent women for sex state that they know prostitution leads to the international trafficking of sex slaves. (Malarek, 2009)

### Violence Is Intrinsic to Prostitution

State: Research has shown that prostitution includes slashing the woman with razor blades; tying women to bedposts and lashing them until they bleed; biting women's breasts; burning the women with cigarettes; cutting her arms, legs and genital areas; and urinating and defecating on women (Raymond, d'Cunha, Ruhaini Dzuhayatin, Hynes, Ramirez Rodriguez, & Santos, 2002). If this is called victimless, we basically state that the woman being prostituted is not a person.

### Legalization

State: Legalized or overlooked prostitution actually creates a greater demand for human trafficking. In cases where there has been legalization of prostitution, there is nearly always a resulting increase in the number of women and children trafficked into commercial sex slavery (O'Connor & Healy, 2006).

State: This is easy to imagine if you think about it. Once you make it legal, it becomes easier for people who want to rent people's bodies to do so. In the mind of a pimp, madam, filmmaker, or other pornography purveyor, there needs to be as much supply as possible to maximize profit. People in the home state or country often cannot meet the demands of the population, so the pornography purveyor works with sex traffickers to ship in more people to use.

State: When speaking to the National Women's Studies Association, as later printed in the *Women's Studies Quarterly* (Holsopple, 1999a), Kelly Holsopple expressed her outrage that some in the feminist movement were promoting prostitution as a means of sexual empowerment and liberation. Holsopple invited women at the conference to abandon their academic careers for a job where people:

> …pay to penetrate you orally, anally, and vaginally with penises, fists, animals, bottles, guns, and garden hoses. They can and will bind and gag you, tie you with ropes and chains, and burn you with cigarettes. They can photograph and tape you doing your job…. Your manager reserves the right to seize all your earnings. You will have no benefits. You will have no legal restitution for job hazards of sexually transmitted diseases, pregnancy, lacerations, broken bones, mutilation, dismemberment, or death. Do you want this job? Do you want your daughter to take this job? If not your daughter than whose daughter? (Holsopple, 1999a, p. 48)

State: Holsopple pulled no punches when talking about feminists who promote prostitution:

> "I was devastated to learn that some feminist books recommending prostitution for women and upholding the lies that pimps and tricks

used.… [T]his is what feminists do when they promote prostitution: they pimp other women. They consign women and children to the profit and use of pimps and tricks … just like pimps and tricks, feminist proponents of prostitution keep women on their backs and on their knees." (Holsopple, 1999b, pp. 49–50)

State:  It is no surprise then that 89% of prostituted women stated in a survey that they want to escape (Farley, Cotton, Lynne, Zumbeck, & Spiwak, 2003).

## Sex Trafficking

Ask:  What do you guess are the top three countries in the world into which women and children are trafficked for purposes of sexual exploitation?
1.  Germany
2.  The United States (18,000 to 50,000 per year)
3.  Italy

State:  The next countries on the list are the Netherlands, Japan, Greece, India, Thailand, and Australia.
State:  Of these people, 96% are female and one half are children (Mizus, Moody, Privado, & Douglas, 2003). In total, 700,000 people are trafficked worldwide every year (Office of Violence Against Women, 2000).

## The Undeniable Harms

State:  Men who view pornographic magazines, Web sites, videos, or go to strip clubs are more likely to commit sexual violence than those who do not (Carr & VanDeusen, 2004). More specifically, men who use pornography have a:
–  20% increase in the risk of experiencing difficulty in intimate relationships
–  31% increase in the risk of accepting attitudes that condone rape and other false beliefs about rape
–  22% increase in the risk of committing sexual assault (Oddone-Paolucci, Genuis, & Violato, 2000)

State:  A review of 16 experimental studies with 2,000 participants found that there is a cause-and-effect relationship between men's use of pornography—particularly movies—and their sexually aggressive attitudes. This held true for consensual, nonviolent, and violent pornography. All types of pornography caused increases in men's support for sexual aggression (Malamuth, Addison, & Koss, 2000). An additional analysis by researchers on the available nonexperimental studies (those that find correlations but not causes) also found the same trend—that there was a positive correlation between

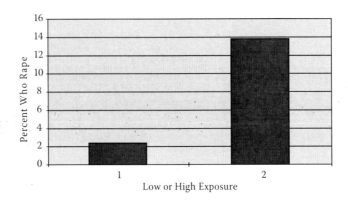

**Percent of men who rape by frequency of porn use.**

pornography use and attitudes supporting violence against women for both violent and nonviolent pornography (Hald, Malamuth, & Yuen, 2009).

State: Pornography exposure has also been shown to cause aggressive behavior in 33 experimental studies involving several thousand men. This effect was shown for both violent and nonviolent pornography as well (Malamuth et al., 2000).

*State:* Men who use porn more frequently and who use more violent porn commit more rape (Malamuth et al., 2000). Approximately 2% of men who are infrequent porn users have committed rape. Approximately 14% of men who are frequent porn users have committed rape (Boeringer, 1994).

## *Wives and Significant Others*

State: When men use pornography, their wives and girlfriends often experience profound effects as well. Not surprisingly, research has shown that when partners discover pornography use or addiction it is often a traumatic experience. Emotions commonly reported include devastation, confusion, finding it incomprehensible, and being at a loss for how to deal with the situation. Women also report that it affects their view of their desirability and their view of the character of their partner (Bergner & Bridges, 2002). Such women report feeling unloved and that they no longer have a place in the world of their partner. The vast majority report that the pornography use feels like a betrayal and use terms to describe it that are synonymous with infidelity such as "cheating" and "affair." Comments from women in this study that were representative of the reactions of others included

– "I am no longer sexually attractive or desirable to him."
– "He's more attracted to the women depicted in his movies, magazines, and websites than he is to me, and I feel completely unable to compete with these women."

– "I am no longer a sexual person or partner to him, but a sexual object. He is not really with me, not really making love to me when we have intercourse. He seems to be thinking about something or someone else— likely those porn women—or he is just inserting me to play a role in some novel sexual scenario that he saw somewhere. He is just using me as a warm body." (Bergner & Bridges, 2002, p. 196–197)

State: Where children are involved, the user often comes to be seen as a failure in his crucial role as a father. Additional research on the partners of men with online porn addiction has shown that:
  – 68% experienced decreased sexual intimacy with their partner
  – These difficulties coincided with the beginning of the cybersex activities
  – 52% of the cybersex users had lost interest in relational sex, as had one-third of the partners. (Schneider, 2000)

## Online Porn and Affairs

State: It is prophetic that women with husbands who use online pornography often use words describing infidelity to describe how they feel about what their husbands are doing. Research has shown that said behavior isn't always limited to that which is online. For example,
  – Internet users who have extramarital affairs are over three times more likely to have used online porn.
  – People who paid for sex (with prostitutes) were nearly four times more likely to have used online porn. (Stack, Wasserman, & Kern, 2004)

## *Erotica*

State: Some argue that exposure to "erotica," seen by some as pornography's less severe cousin, isn't at all problematic. Research suggests otherwise. Specifically, frequent exposure to erotica yields the following effects:
  – Developing tolerance toward sexually explicit material, requiring more novel or bizarre material to achieve the same level of arousal or interest
  – Overestimating the prevalence of less common sexual practices (e.g., group sex, bestiality, sadomasochism)
  – Diminished trust in intimate partners
  – Abandoning the goal of sexual exclusivity with a partner
  – Perceiving promiscuity as a normal state of interaction
  – Developing cynical attitudes about love
  – Believing superior sexual satisfaction is attainable without having affection for a partner
  – Believing marriage is sexually confining
  – Believing that raising children and having a family is unattractive
  – Developing a negative body image, especially for women (Zillmann, 2000)

### *Youth*

State: Despite the fact that it is illegal for minors to access pornography, it is extremely easy to do. Youth are commonly being solicited, tricked, misled, or "mouse-trapped" into viewing sexually explicit content online. And those who do experience:
- Earlier onset of sexual intercourse
- Increased likelihood of engaging in anal sex
- Sexual relations with people they are not romantically engaged with (Manning, 2006)

Ask: If you knew that you were financially supporting a group that was hurting other people, would you continue to give them your money?

Ask: What is PTSD?
- "Flashbacks" about trauma
- Feelings of estrangement or detachment
- Nightmares
- Sleep disturbances
- Impaired functioning
- Occupational instability
- Memory disturbances
- Family discord
- Parenting or marital difficulties

State: Just under one third of Vietnam Veterans suffered from PTSD after serving in the war (Weiss, Marmar, Schlenger, Fairbank, Jordan, Hough, & Kulka, 1992).

Ask: When one out of three people has the same set of symptoms after they have a common experience, what do you conclude?

State: Two thirds of the women in the sex industry suffer from post-traumatic stress disorder (Farley et al., 2003).

Ask: When two out of three women in the porn industry experience post-traumatic stress disorder—a level double the rate of veterans of a war—what do you conclude about how their line of work affects them?

Ask: Can we really conclude that guys who go to strip clubs, buy porn magazines, visit porn sites, and thus create the demand for online porn, and pay prostituted women for sex are just having harmless fun? Is it just a victimless crime? Or is it dangerous?

### *Another Porn Movie Producer*

State: One final word about the intent of porn producers comes from another porn movie producer interviewed by Dr. Robert Jensen. The intent of his mainstream pornographic movies can be summed up like this:

"I'd like to show what I believe the men want to see: violence against women. I firmly believe that we serve a purpose by showing that. The most violent we can get is the cum shot in the face. Men get off behind that, because they get even with the women they can't have. We try to inundate the world with orgasms in the face." (Jensen, 2007, p. 70)

State:  Every time people buy a pornographic magazine, pay a cover charge to enter a strip club, visit a porn website, they financially support a business in which research shows that two of three employees suffer from post-traumatic stress disorder. A choice to use pornography is a choice to support violence against women and to contribute to keeping women in PTSD.

## *What Can We All Do?*

State:
- Refuse to do business with any company or store that sells or supports the pornography industry.
- Speak out against any effort by the porn industry to push the envelope toward greater acceptance of pornography and the resulting violence against women.
- On college campuses, support a ban on showing naked pictures of children such as those shown in the Century Project and a ban on showing porn movies using university funds or facilities.
- If your campus bookstore sells pornography, ask it to stop. Appeal to its corporate values and relate these to the research on pornography.
- Support a ban on nude dancing and support regulations such as employee background checks, HIV tests, and keeping clubs 2,000 feet from churches, schools, and homes wherever you live.
- Support the Clean Hotel Initiative. This initiative encourages that meetings and conferences be held in facilities that do not offer in-room adult pay-per-view pornography, see: www.menaspeacemakers.org.
- Share research on the effects of pornography with everyone you know.
- Don't use porn or tolerate its use by someone with whom you have a romantic relationship. Discourage its use among your friends.

## *Resources*

- www.settingcaptivesfree.com
- http://pureloveclub.net/
- http://www.urbanministry.org/wiki/what-i-wish-i-would-have-known-about-sex-addiction-20-years-ago

- www.sexandmoneyfilm.com
- http://pornharms.com
- http://photogenx.net
- http://antipornactivist.com
- http://stoppornculture.org/home
- http://www.sctnow.com

# Chapter 5

## Recruiting Peer Educators

This chapter describes a process for recruiting and selecting members for a peer education group. You can tailor these ideas to fit an all-male or all-female peer education group. The process is written assuming that you are starting from scratch, with no peer educators. If you have a group in place already, you will likely want to adapt this material slightly in acknowledgment of your established group. Still, most of the process written herein can still prove useful once you get past the first section on selection of new members.

Whether you are recruiting men for an all-male sexual assault peer education group or women for an all-female sexual assault peer education group, I recommend that you use a personal approach to recruitment. The model suggested below has been used successfully for these purposes.

## Guiding Philosophical Principles

When selecting your candidates, I suggest that you look for the following:

1. Good instincts: Does the person you are interviewing seem to have his wits about him? Can the person reason well through an argument? Can he or she empathize with another person? Remember that specific knowledge is not important for a selection process—you can provide that during training. But good instincts are tough to train into a person.
2. Presenting skill: If a person can't present well to a group of people, that person should never, ever be selected as a peer educator. There are many places for people to be in the sexual assault prevention movement. One of them is as a peer educator. Peer educators must be able to effectively educate. A huge responsibility of education is presentation. If the individual cannot present effectively and well, it is your ethical responsibility not to select that person. Selecting a person who is unable to effectively present to his or her peers sets the stage for the failure of your program.

3. Charisma: People you select as peer educators should be the type of people who have influence over their peers. If your goal is to change the culture of your campus, military organization, or community, you need to engage people with influence over others to lead the way to that change. This doesn't mean that you will want to have all people of the same type in your group. To the contrary, you should search for diversity in your group so that your peer educators represent the diversity of the audiences to whom they will present. To be successful, your peer educators should be members of your community who have the power of persuasion over their peers so that you can meet your objectives.

4. Screen out troublesome behavior: It will be up to you where you will want to draw the line about what kind of behavior disqualifies someone from the group, and under what kind of circumstances you would accept such behavior. My recommendation is that you do not allow people into your group who have committed rape. There is some difference of opinion on this issue within the field; however, I do not see enough value in admitting someone who has perpetrated rape into this kind of group, particularly with the risks of re-perpetration. Your college, military unit, or organization may also have other disciplinary records to check and consider.

5. Survivors as peer educators: One should also carefully consider whether the peer educator candidate has experienced a recent trauma. Often people who have personally experienced sexual assault or have known of the sexual assault of someone close to them will seek to be peer educators. People with such experiences can be some of the most powerful members of any group. You should be sure that people with such experiences are emotionally ready to go through intense training experiences, be challenged by rude questions from audience members, and to be otherwise challenged by the peer education experience before proceeding with the selections process. Meeting with a counselor to assess this could be advisable under some circumstances.

6. Diversity: To have the greatest impact on the population you seek to change, it is important that your group of peer educators reflect in as many ways as possible the diversity of the population to whom they will be presenting. It is also particularly advisable to seek members from populations found by research to be of higher risk than the normal population for perpetration. This will help you to have a greater impact on populations most likely to be the source of the problem within your community.

## Stage 1: Recruiting Founding Members

Getting your first new members can seem daunting, but it isn't as difficult as it seems. It takes effort, and most of all you must be proactive and use proactive techniques that go beyond the ordinary to be successful.

## *Letters*

Send a letter (see copy later in this chapter) requesting nominations to administrators, faculty members, and student organization leaders on campus, including fraternity presidents and athletic team captains. Include residence-life staff, health center staff, athletic coaches, student union and campus program staff, career center staff, multicultural center staff, select faculty, etc. Also solicit nominations from student groups and organizations on your campus including student council, other sexual assault and health education groups, and activist organizations. When possible avoid means that can easily be ignored (i.e., e-mail). Let people know that you are organizing a new sexual assault, peer education group and that you are inviting them to nominate students who might qualify as peer educators. Note in your letter that you seek candidates with good public speaking skills, leaders who relate well to their peers, and those who are or could be sensitive to issues of violence against women.

## *Talking to Groups*

Visit groups (residence life student staff, interfraternity/intersorority council, athletic coaches) and pitch the idea of a new sexual assault peer education group (all-male, all-female, or both). The content of your "presentation" should be similar to that of the form letter you send out. Other groups you might visit include athletic council meetings, service organizations, residence hall meetings, and of course, other peer education groups on campus.

## *Collecting as Many Nominations as Possible*

Even though you are likely to get great members through the nomination process, I recommend that you also allow self-nominations. I mentioned how many people don't intend on becoming involved in the issue of rape and sexual assault, but some will respond to a table at an activity fair. Publicize around campus, attend events that will allow you to set up a table and talk to interested people who walk by. Another great recruiting tool is to present the program you will be using (the Men's Program and/or the Women's Program). Usually several potential peer educators will come forward afterward and ask how they can get involved.

## Stage 2: Converting Nominees to Interviewees

Call, visit in person, or send a letter (samples later in this chapter) to every student nominated to be in your group. If you call or visit, tell each of them that you are forming a peer education group that will educate others about sexual assault.

Investing time in your nominees plays a huge role in how successful your recruitment efforts will be. As you continue to develop your list of possible members, it will become time to convince these nominees to come in for an interview. The thing to realize here is that many candidates who are ideal members have never even considered becoming involved in something like sexual assault prevention. A key is to empower them by stressing in letters/e-mails/phone messages that they have been nominated, that someone feels good enough about them to suggest that they have what it takes to do this important work, and that you very much want to talk with them further. Each nominee should know that someone he or she interacts with—a professor, coach, chapter president, or residence life director—believes he or she possesses the qualities necessary to be a part of something like this.

Stress to nominees that they have the ability to make a difference, and that if they decide to become part of the group, they will surely improve their public speaking skills as well as a variety of other tools necessary for life after college.

A very common first concern of many nominees is the time commitment required by the group. Many sexual assault peer education groups thrive on active, busy, very involved student leaders. As long as you maintain a core group of officers to handle day-to-day business of the organization, you can still thrive as an organization with members who are willing to put in an initial commitment for training (at least 15 hours depending on how long you structure it) and 3 hours per week for the group (1 hour per week for a meeting and just over an hour per week on average for a presentation plus setup and hanging out afterward with anyone who has questions).

## Stage 3: Interviews

### *Why You Can't Accept Everyone*

It's difficult sometimes to turn away people who apply for a position to help end rape when it's such an overwhelming task just trying to motivate people to get involved. But it's a necessary process. Some people have good intentions, but are simply not the right fit to be peer educators. Either the person is not a good public speaker or isn't effective at connecting with peers well enough to be convincing.

In the case of men, some will simply have ulterior motives for interviewing to become part of the group. Some men are looking to pad their resumes, to make up for what in their minds was behavior that hurt women in their past, or even to use their membership in your group to make them appear like a safe man to hook up with when, in reality, they are dangerous. These concerns point to the need for a discerning selections process. Women who apply to sexual assault peer education groups may have resume padding motives as well, but in my experience, their intentions tend to be more universally pure.

However, they still require careful screening for public speaking and connecting with an audience.

When screening candidates, there are a variety of things to look for during interviews. An openness to learn more and modify preconceptions is one of the most desirable traits in a candidate. Most people who interview are there because they want to help end rape and sexual assault; so if you believe they will make a solid contribution and have the other skills and traits necessary, it's probably a good idea to admit them.

## How to Sign Candidates Up for Interviews

Coordinating all of the different interview times can be difficult. One effective method is to set aside large blocks of time on a limited number of days and post these times on an office door or on a website. Tell candidates that each interview will last 30 minutes and that they can come by and sign up for interview time slots on a first come, first served basis. If you're not comfortable doing this, you can try to sign them up yourself by coordinating schedules over e-mail, but if you have a large pool of candidates, it's a better idea to allow them to come by and sign up. When candidates sign up for interviews, send them a portion of the script from the program that the group will use. Explain to each candidate that the interview will include a presentation of that brief portion of the script to assess presentation skills.

## Conducting the Interviews

Explain why the group is being formed, what training will take place, and the time commitment involved. This information should have been shared with the candidate when you called or wrote, but you can present it in a little more detail. Ask if the candidate has any questions, and whether there is still interest in participating. If so, ask these questions (see also the suggested evaluation scale):

Select from the questions below according to what you believe is most appropriate for your group's needs.

1. Our group will be (insert planned activities); we anticipate that it will take (x) hours per week for the average member. Is this something you can commit to?
2. Our training dates are (insert here). Are you able to make all of the times for these dates?
3. What other organizations are you a part of?
4. Do you have any leadership roles in these organizations, if so what?
5. Have you had other experiences that would help you be successful in this group?
6. What is your GPA?
7. Why are you interested in being part of our organization?

8. Why do you think sexual assault happens?

9. Is rape anyone's fault?

10. Do you think that women are more responsible for experiencing rape in some circumstances and less in others?

11. How often do you think women falsely report rape? Why would a woman falsely report rape?

12. What are some skills you are working on improving? How are you trying to improve them?

13. As a peer educator, you would be expected to uphold what we talk about in our programs. This includes your behavior in intimate encounters and your behavior intervening as a bystander if you hear people speak negatively about women or if you see a situation that could turn into a rape. What challenges might this pose for you? To what extent do you believe that you can live up to all these challenges?

14. It will be important for members of this new group to be role models for others in what they say and in what they do—particularly with regard to their intimate behavior. Talk to me (or us) about how you would feel being in the spotlight as a role model on these issues. How comfortable would you be? Why do you feel this way?

15. Help us to get to know your personality a little better. Like for example, if we asked your best friend what you are like when you are around other people, what would he or she say?

16. One of the responsibilities that peer educators take on is placing themselves in a position of visibility and leadership on campus on the issue of sexual assault. To an extent, this really involves being a role model. This means representing the best of what the group is capable in what you say and in what you do. Talk to me about how you think it might feel for you personally to be looked at by people you know and don't know as a role model for this cause? What parts of this might make you feel uncomfortable? Is this still something that you can commit to?

17. Tell me about a time in your life when your behavior came the closest to meeting the legal definition of sexual assault? Follow up if candidate says never: We recognize that there is nobody in our group who has always behaved perfectly. We also talk about consent occurring on a continuum with rape at one end, let's say a continuum of 1 to 100 with rape being 100, and let's say a 1 is a written contract where you decide ahead of time verbally and in writing everything you are going to do, sign it with witnesses, and have it on file in the Court Clerk's office. So with 1 being that, and 100 being rape, if you think about your whole life and any intimate activity in which you have engaged—anything from kissing to intercourse—think about that one time in your life when your behavior came closest to 100 on that scale, that one time you wish you could do things over, where it came closest to 100. Talk with us about that time and describe to us in detail what happened.

18. Why should we admit you to the group?

## Stage 4: Making Admissions Decisions

The idea for the preceding questions is not to test the interviewee's knowledge (the candidate hasn't been through training yet), but rather to probe opinions, determine teachability, and learn attitudes toward rape. If the candidate states things that cause you concern, particularly if the candidate does not indicate an openness to learn, you may have someone who is a bad fit. In my experience, most people who interview for such groups are workable. At some institutions, you can reach the point where you end up interviewing up to 50 candidates for 15 open spots per year.

# Candidate Evaluation Scale

## Public Speaking

1 = Avoids eye contact, voice irregularities, mumbles

2 = Fidgets, restless, difficult to follow

3 = Tries for eye contact, projection/clarity lacking

4 = Good eye contact, clear, cogent, coherent

5 = Well-polished speaker, smooth, confident

6 = Stellar, this person could debate with Socrates

## Passion for the Cause

1 = Candidate would rather be somewhere else; honestly, I wish I had been as well

2 = Questionable; a resume builder or not applying for good reasons

3 = Ready to help given the right circumstances

4 = Clearly wants to get involved

5 = Enthusiastic and ready to get started

6 = Five-alarm fire!

## Contribution to the Group

1 = No distinguishable talents or distinguishing factors that could benefit the group

2 = Might have some less common traits, not sure how much will be contributed

3 = Seems to be someone who would add something to the group

4 = Would add to the group in a measurable way

5 = We need this person; adds elements that we seek and can clearly benefit from

6 = Adds unique element to the group we don't have and will definitely make group top priority—land this person or else!

## Demeanor/Relationship to Others

1 = I wouldn't look forward to working with this person at all (negative, rude, etc.)

2 = Either awkward, cocky, or self-absorbed

3 = Polite, interested

4 = Friendly, optimistic, pleasant

5 = Great person, would look forward to seeing at meetings

6 = I think I just met my new best friend

## Letter to Send to Nominators for an All-Male Group

Dear Colleague,

I am writing to ask for your assistance in identifying candidates for an all-male, sexual assault, peer education group that is being created here at (your institution).

Based on research showing the efficacy of single-sex peer education programs, this new group will present a program called "How to Help a Sexual Assault Survivor: What Men Can Do" to men in residence halls, fraternities, athletic teams, and any other group who will listen.

The 1-hour workshop these men will learn to present is designed to help men learn how to help a woman recover from a rape experience and how to intervene to prevent a rape from occurring. The tone of the program is empowering, not blaming in nature. As this new group teaches men how to help their women friends recover from rape, audience members also become significantly less likely to rape in the first place. A recently published study found that men who see the program commit less sexual assault than men who don't. In short, it is the most effective rape prevention program evaluated in the research literature today. An added benefit is that men who see it learn how to help a friend recover from a rape experience. This new group will be selected, trained, and advised by (name or names of people).

Ideal candidates are men who (a) are strong public speakers, (b) relate well to their male peers, and (c) are or could be sensitive to issues of violence against women. On the back of this letter, in an email, or on a sheet of paper, would you please write down the names of students you think would be good for this group? If you have their addresses and phone numbers, that would be great too, but I can look them up if needed.

Please send your nominations to (name, address, email, phone). Please send these names by (date).

Please call anytime with any questions. Thank you in advance for your assistance.

Sincerely,

Your name

## Letter to Send to Nominators for an All-Female Group

Dear Colleague,

I am writing to ask for your assistance in identifying candidates for an all-female, sexual assault, peer education group that is being created here at (your institution).

Based on research showing the efficacy of single-sex peer education programs, this new group will present a program called "Empowering Women: Learning About Dangerous Men and Helping Rape Survivors" to women in residence halls, sororities, athletic teams, and any other group who will listen.

The workshop these women will learn to present is designed to help women learn how to help a woman recover from a rape experience and how to intervene to prevent a rape from occurring. A recent study found that women who see the program are significantly more willing to intervene as bystanders if they see a potential rape situation occurring than women who haven't seen the program. The program also significantly improves women's attitudes toward rape and rape survivors. This new group will be selected, trained, and advised by (name or names of people).

Ideal candidates are women who (a) are strong public speakers, (b) relate well to their female peers, and (c) are or could be sensitive to issues of violence against women. On the back of this letter, in an email, or on a sheet of paper, would you please write down the names of students you think would be good for this group? If you have their addresses and phone numbers, that would be great too, but I can look them up if needed.

Please send your nominations to (name, address, email, phone). Please send these names by (date).

Please call anytime with any questions. Thank you in advance for your assistance.

Sincerely,

Your name

## Letter to Candidates of an All-Male Group Encouraging Them to Sign Up for an Interview

Dear,

I am writing you with news of an opportunity for you to make a tangible difference in the lives of many people, including your own. I am creating a new all-male sexual assault peer education group at (name of your institution). I'm writing you because you have been nominated by (x) to be interviewed to be a founding member of this new student organization. I hope you will take the time to read further about what this opportunity may mean for you.

Back in 1993, the first version of a program was written with one basic goal in mind: to empower men to take a positive role in ending the suffering caused by rape. Too many programs dealing with rape treated men as potential rapists. Not surprisingly, none of them really worked. The program we will use treats men as potential helpers. It is called "How to Help a Sexual Assault Survivor: What Men Can Do," also known as the Men's Program. The Men's Program is a training workshop for men designed to teach them how awful rape feels, how they can help their women friends recover from rape, and how they as men can become part of the solution. The program itself is most effective when men present it to men. That's where you may fit into this picture.

I would like to interview you, and many other nominees, as a part of a selective process to choose the best men at (name of your institution) to be founding members of this new peer education group. This group will present the program all over campus, and I hope to surrounding campuses, high schools, and the local community.

There are a few details that may interest you. The Men's Program has been proven to do many things. First, it significantly improves men's ability to help women recover from rape. Second, recently published research found that it is the most effective rape prevention program published in the research literature today. In short, men who see the program commit less sexual assault than men who don't. No other program for college men has ever been shown to do this.

Few things in life are guaranteed. I am fairly sure that I can guarantee you a few things. One is that if you are selected to be in this group, your life will be different from what it was before. I can also guarantee you beyond any reasonable doubt that if you present this program, every time you do so, you will change the lives of the men who see it and, indirectly, the lives of many women too. I hope to be able to tell you more about this. More importantly, I hope you discover this for yourself.

I will be interviewing nominees throughout (insert time frame here). If you know that you would like to be interviewed, please (e-mail me/sign up on my door/etc.) If you want more information, please (call me/e-mail me/etc.) and we can talk further. I hope you do, and I hope we meet soon.

Sincerely,

Your name

## Letter to Candidates of an All-Female Group Encouraging Them to Sign Up for an Interview

Dear,

I am writing you with news of an opportunity for you to make a tangible difference in the lives of many people, including your own. I am creating a new all-female sexual assault peer education group at (name of your institution). I'm writing you because you have been nominated by (x) to be interviewed to be a founding member of this new student organization. I hope you will take the time to read further about what this opportunity may mean for you.

For too long, rape awareness programs for women have focused only on how women can avoid sexual assault. While that is important, I believe we can do better. I believe that we can empower women not only to reduce their own risk for being sexually assaulted; I believe that women can also be part of the solution to help prevent the rape of other women. That is why I'm creating a group that will use the Women's Program. This program, also called "Empowering Women: Learning About Dangerous Men and Helping Rape Survivors," is a training workshop for women designed to teach them about characteristics of men who are likely to rape, how to help their friends avoid these men, how to help friends recover from rape when it happens, and how to intervene if they see that a friend might be getting into a rape situation. We suspect that the program will be highly effective if women present it to women. That's where you may fit into this picture.

I would like to interview you, and many other nominees, as a part of a selective process to choose the best women at (name of your institution) to be founding members of this new peer education group. This group will present the program all over campus, and I hope to surrounding campuses, high schools, and the local community.

There are a few details that may interest you. The Women's Program has been proven to do many things. First, it significantly improves women's attitudes toward rape and rape survivors. Second, a recent study showed that women who see the program are significantly more willing to intervene in situations where a rape is about to occur. Women who see it also feel more knowledgeable about how to intervene. In short, you can know that by presenting that you will have made a significant difference.

Few things in life are guaranteed. I am fairly sure that I can guarantee you a few things. One is that if you are selected to be in this group, your life will be different from what it was before. I can also guarantee you beyond any reasonable doubt that if you present this program, every time you do so, you will change the lives of the women who see it.

I will be interviewing nominees throughout (insert time frame here). If you know that you would like to be interviewed, please (e-mail me/sign up on my door/etc.) If you want more information, please (call me/e-mail me/etc.) and we can talk further. I hope you do, and I hope we meet soon.

Sincerely,

Your name

## Sample of Letter to Send Candidates Who Agree to Interview

Dear (name of interviewee),

I am glad that you are interested in interviewing to be a founding member of (name of your peer education group). The experience promises to be fun, challenging, meaningful, and a lot of hard work. If you're up to it, please read on.

During your interview, you will be asked to talk about your interest in being a peer educator. You will also be asked to give a very brief presentation using the attached handout as a guide. Please be as familiar as you can with it so that I can fairly assess your presentation style. It's okay to refer to this script from time to time during your presentation if you need to do so.

I hope to conclude the selection process on (insert appropriate date here), and I hope to notify people around (insert appropriate date here) about their status. If you become part of this group, I assure you that you will make a difference in the lives of others. I can think of few other experiences that offer you the same opportunity. I will pledge myself to the group to challenge and support each member throughout their experience—an experience that will make a profound impact on all those involved.

I look forward to our interview time. See you then.

Sincerely,

Your name

**Note:** Remember to attach a page of the script from the appropriate program!

## Letter Rejecting Candidates Who Interviewed

Dear,

Thank you so much for meeting with me to interview for membership in our peer education group. I deeply regret that at the present time I am unable to offer you a spot in the group. With over (x) students nominated and a high volume of interviews, it was very difficult to make final decisions. While I would have liked to have taken everyone, we simply can't train that many people at the same time. These were among the toughest decisions I've made in a long time.

I do appreciate your interest, very much. I hope that you will be a supporter of the issue of sexual assault prevention in any other way that you can. Please let me know if you would like to talk about this, or any other matter, further.

Thank you once again.

Sincerely,

Your name

# Chapter 6

## Advice for Peer Educators From Peer Educators

Thomas Broeker and Aaron Kraus

### Part 1: Thoughts for New Members
*Thomas Broeker\**

Like many guys I worked with in One in Four, I would never have guessed that I would spend so much of my time in college working on this issue. I was not the kind to put myself out for anything I perceived as an offshoot of "political correctness." Beyond that this was not the type of issue that I ever thought I would care about. I remember hearing about the group my first semester. At the time, I shared the same mistrust many undergraduates have for anyone who seems like they are preaching to you during orientation, and I did not see how this had anything to do with me.

That changed quickly the next year when a close friend of mine in college was raped. She told me the day after it happened. I was one of the few people she ever told and I would have probably never found out if I hadn't happened to call her and then bother her about why she had not called me the night before. She was upset about something, and I probed thoughtlessly for details, thinking she just had an embarrassing story. When she finally spoke about the incident, she told me that someone had physically forced himself on her. She never used the words *rape* or *sexual assault*, not in that first conversation at least. For my part, I was confused, furious, and even a little skeptical. I was shocked that someone in our community could do this to someone I cared about. The more

---

\* Captain, U.S. Army; President, One in Four, University of Virginia, 2004–2005. Thomas Broeker is a captain in the Army. He has served overseas as a platoon leader for both mechanized infantry and Ranger platoons. He is currently serving as an executive officer in 3rd Battalion, 75th Ranger Regiment. His views are his alone and do not necessarily represent the views of the Army or the Department of Defense.

I talked to her, the more I thought about it, and the more I realized that this guy would probably get away with it, the angrier I became.

What stopped me from doing something stupid was seeing how fragile my friend was. Since I was the one person she had accidentally ended up confiding in, I spent far more time with her than I could have imagined. I quickly learned how hard it was for her to move past this, and how it would have hurt her if I did something rash that might have made things public. So eventually, after causing her a lot of pain by forcing her to keep talking me down, I finally focused on trying to help her.

That's when I was introduced to One in Four, again. I was still simmering inside, but I had decided to focus any conversation with my friend on whatever she wanted to talk about—panic attacks, sleepless nights, her feelings of helplessness. However, I didn't know how to help her, and I didn't know anyone to ask for advice, so I spent a lot of time online researching the subject. This managed to both divert and intensify my rage. Fortunately, I did find some concrete advice on how to help her. I also found this group, One in Four, which seemed, frankly, like it might be a way to address my feelings of futility and actually do something.

## Notes on Joining the Group

When I entered the group, I still really knew only my friend's story, and my primary reason for joining the group was anger over the injustice that had been done to her. After you join, though, you are quickly introduced to the stories of many, many other survivors, and you start to accept the statistical fact of how often sexual assault occurs. Eventually, I realized that the problem was much worse than I first thought. The only thing I could hope to do would be to change the conditions that foster rape, and maybe improve the treatment of survivors. It's a lesson I would repeat for men starting or just entering into One in Four: Don't confuse your work with some form of revenge or even justice. Not only will you be disappointed with the outcome, but your misplaced focus will hinder the progress that is possible.

And it is a considerable impact that you can have. At the very least, most of the men you speak to will learn the basics of what to do when, inevitably, sadly, some of them are faced with a friend who has been raped. No, you cannot convince every man you present to that sexual assault is a repugnant but prevalent affliction that our society faces, and you won't even be able to persuade some of your friends who ask why you care so much about this. But don't be discouraged by setbacks like these. Consider carefully your goals for yourself and the group. I submit that with a problem of this magnitude, just as in a civil rights movement, a war, or a political struggle, you cannot expect to win everyone to your side, and you don't need to. It is about building foundations and accumulating momentum. You just need a majority on your campus, and eventually in society, to understand the dynamics of rape, the trauma it causes, and the need to treat it as a serious crime, and we will have begun to turn the tide. Obviously, as the program says, we want to end rape and the suffering it causes, but realistically, I would define success for any One in Four group this way: as being able to make it legally and socially impossible for someone to commit sexual assault and to remain in that particular community, whether it is a social group or branch of the military or a college. It may seem like a small, limited victory, but not if you consider the number of assaults that occur without any real punishment. Discouraging sexual assault by ensuring those offenders are no longer welcome in that group would be a huge step forward. Furthermore, the men you influence in your community or your college will spread across society.

Whether you consider this task daunting or achievable (or both), it can easily become all-consuming. I know it was for me during college. Just as with my service in the military, the chance to serve with other dedicated individuals on a worthwhile cause is something I could never regret, no matter the ordeals involved. However, the challenges are formidable, and not just because of the time you spend. It can be demoralizing to present to men and feel as if you're having no effect. It can also be frustrating explaining the problem to your friends or family. Hardest of all, though, is the emotional drain from getting to know all the survivors you will certainly encounter. They will motivate you and teach you more than anyone else, but it will also overwhelm you with the scope of this and the pain it has caused in each of their lives.

For me, the other men in the group were essential to deal with all of it, to share some of the pain, and still stay motivated. Appreciate this group of friends you make. I would rather share a beer with the men who are willing to make common cause on this issue, however unlike we might be, than many of the friends I have made throughout my life. And please learn from the women working on this issue, too, as well as the individual survivors you know. I have found the women who devote themselves to fighting rape and sexual assault to be as dedicated, talented, and courageous as anyone I have ever met. Though you might address the issue in very different ways, there is no limit to what you can gain from working as closely with them as possible.

As part of that willingness to work with allies, make sure you leave out the rest of your politics when you present for One in Four. You will have a wide spectrum of political and social views in the group, and guys will be passionate about a variety of other issues; some of these will even seem closely connected to your mission of ending sexual assault. However, I argue that outside a narrowly defined set of related positions (mainly opposition to domestic violence and to sexual violence against women and men in general, and a recognition of sexism's role in enabling sexual assault), it is critical to forgo taking a stand on a wider array of political issues, wherever they fall on the ideological spectrum. Not only do you risk diluting the focus of the group, you risk losing important allies inside and outside the movement against sexual assault, alienating great men in your group who do not share your beliefs, and losing your credibility with your audiences. I'm not saying that you cannot advocate for other things you believe in, only that you need to separate it from your work in the group.

The last thing I would urge on you is discretion. Throughout your time in the group, you will likely have survivors come up and share their stories with you. As you present more, you will be tempted to use these stories as anonymous examples to illustrate the dilemmas survivors face when you are presenting to other men. Just remember, even when you strip these anecdotes of identifying details, campuses are incredibly small places, and they are interconnected to many of the other places you might visit. It's not worth destroying one survivor's trust to try to reach more men.

## *Practical Advice on Presentating to the Military*

I've been in the military nearly 5 years now. I led a large-scale discussion about sexual assault a couple years back with my old platoon. I've had hundreds of other informal, one-on-one talks with men I've worked with, and to be honest, many have gone badly. A friend of mine in the Army even had a girlfriend who was drugged and raped at a bar, while we were both off training, several states away. Even though he tried to help her in that specific situation, the incident did not compel him to change his backward views on sexual assault.

I don't think the resistance you will see is significantly more than you would get presenting to your average group of undergraduates, though. In fact, you should have an advantage because most members of the military respect notions of honor and loyalty, and will quickly grasp their duty to help survivors they know, and they understand that sexual assault violates those same standards of behavior. Still, many men in our country simply have wrong, preconceived notions about the dynamics behind rape and sexual assault, and that is no different in the military. However, there are some pertinent differences in working with your average military and college groups, and some strategies I recommend.

For instance, your audience will probably have already sat through more mandatory briefs on sexual harassment or assault, suicide awareness, post-traumatic stress disorder, motorcycle safety, etc., than you can imagine, even more than your average college student. There's a good chance that a lot of the classes will even be on that same day. All of this makes most service members jaded when it comes to classes on public health or related issues, especially when you roll them into the busy schedule of training and deployments that most of the military is operating on. In the middle of all this, you will have to overcome their cynicism toward more mandated training in order to gain their attention. The Men's Program is a great tool to do this, but you will have to adapt it to make it work.

One way is to work twice as hard at knowing your audience and establishing a rapport with it. Most outside presenters to the military that I have seen are extremely poor at this. Having other veterans or service members to help you present would be ideal, but even if that is not possible, try to find the common denominators with your audience, whether it is geographic or whatever. Try to talk to a few of the guys you're presenting to beforehand and feel them out. Some members of the military will be skeptical of civilian speakers, so if you are a civilian, you will have to find a way to get around that. Consider the specific unit or group you're addressing and the best way to reach them. For instance, what is their branch of service and what do they do? Is it all one unit or a selection of leaders from a professional course? Have they deployed? Many men in the military, like myself, are serving now and may have served in only all-male units. This doesn't mean that they have no interactions with women in the military, but that these interactions might be different from what you would expect in a unit where many or most of the personnel are female. So, as an example, when you're talking about helping out a survivor, many male service members won't relate if you illustrate your point by talking about assisting a colleague. Instead, since many of the men might be old enough to have adolescent daughters, while for others their closest female friends might be a thousand miles away, back wherever home is. You might have more effect if you use those situations to make your case.

I would also advise engaging leaders in the unit in your efforts, at all levels of leadership. Most operational units have some form of unit victim advocate who is a normal member of the unit trained to provide that assistance. That person, who is often double tapped as the equal opportunity officer and might be the unit chaplain or work in the personnel (S-1) office, should probably be able to point you in the right direction, and inform you of the kind of training the unit has received before about sexual assault. However, I would urge you to consider that person as your initial contact, and try to work directly with the unit leadership to tailor your presentations. Leaders in the military can make changes in their ranks that are disproportionate to the capability of leaders in other organizations. Non-commissioned officers (NCOs), especially, are the "backbone of the Army" and other branches. Oftentimes, it will be higher-level leaders who will sponsor a presentation like One in Four for a unit, but it is critical to target the NCOs as front-line leaders. NCOs can have a tremendous impact on their soldiers, not only at work but in their personal lives as well.

## Final Thoughts

I don't regret a minute of the time I spent working on One in Four. Once I was in the group and saw how important and widespread the issue is, I could not imagine spending my time and energy otherwise. I would encourage you to set realistic goals, to tirelessly focus on breaking down the cycle of sexual assault wherever you go, and to rely on the men and women working with you to sustain your commitment. Finally, as someone who wishes he could have done more himself, I extend my deep appreciation to you for your courage and commitment to work on this cause.

## Part 2: Building a Chapter

*Aaron Kraus**

The transition from high school to college is tumultuous, multifaceted, and full of the unexpected. When a student moves from high school to college, academic, social, and independence issues are consistently identified as the most significant changes that affect the freshmen population. Where do students learn that Wikipedia is not an acceptable resource for an academic paper? Where does an only child learn how to share a small space with a roommate? Where does an 18-year-old with his first credit card learn how to manage his money? How do you respond when your friend becomes part of the one in four college women who have survived rape or attempted rape?

There are no simple answers to those questions; yet they are all common issues, typically addressed once a problem arises. Once someone submits a paper with Wikipedia on the references page, points are deducted and the professor may make a perturbed comment to the class about what is and is not an acceptable source. When roommates have problems, they are asked to sign a contract or go their separate ways. When a student mismanages finances, it can have serious and lasting consequences. But most significantly of all, when a friend comes to you after experiencing rape and her recovery is partially dependent on your response, can either of you afford a mistake?

I was in high school the first time a friend told me she was raped. At the time, I had no idea how to react, what to say, or how to respond. It was not until 2 years later, well into my freshmen year at Western New England College, that I learned how to help a friend who survived rape. This early exposure to the issue, as well as a negative experience with another sexual assault prevention program that visited my college campus, prompted me to join One in Four. These experiences changed my life.

### Getting Started

Within the first 2 weeks of my undergraduate career, my entire freshman class attended a presentation about rape and sexual assault. While I watched the various skits being performed and scenarios being acted out, I was shocked by the accusatory tone of the entire production and was, to be honest, offended by many of the assumptions the presenters made regarding the intentions of men. I was not surprised in the least by the lack of impact this had on my peers. The following week, as an assignment for a course, I wrote a response describing how I felt there was a need for a discussion on the topic of sexual assault, but how I thought it needed to be done in a completely different way. A professor who read it approached me about joining a team of guys starting a One in Four chapter on campus.

---

* President, One in Four, Western New England College, 2009–2010.

I joined a sophomore, two juniors, and a senior in starting our chapter. Our group of five included two student athletes, a resident advisor, a peer advisor, and the president of the Psychology Club. The fact that our chapter was, and still is, composed almost solely of prominent student leaders on campus has had a tremendous impact on our continued success.

Our first obstacle was securing funding for the initial costs. Given the rules at our institution, our chapter was not eligible for funding from our student senate due to the selective nature of our group, but fortunately it did not take us long to discover grants from the Alumni Association. Armed with an undeniable cause and a touch of eloquence, we were awarded enough money to get off the ground.

## Making Presentations

In our first full year as an official chapter we took many crucial steps. We developed an application process and added two new members who would prove to be two of the most influential members our group had to date. With membership increased to six, we sponsored a benefit concert to support the local YWCA, raising well over a thousand dollars. In the spring, we were contacted by a local high school and were asked to deliver a presentation as part of their sexual assault and violence awareness week. We delivered three 30-minute presentations, which were essentially edited and compressed versions of the Men's Program, to groups of juniors and seniors. By giving these mini-presentations in such close succession to three very different audiences, we were able to test different approaches and learn to adapt our styles and responses to questions more effectively. Although it was a very rudimentary setting, it proved to be a tremendous learning experience for our chapter, and the lessons we learned that afternoon by speaking with high school students translated directly to many of the stereotypes that we would face on our own college campus.

The questions we received after the presentations were extremely ignorant and outlandish. One student said he wanted to join our cause, but felt that rape was always the victim's fault. Another said that almost all women are lying when they claim rape. A third said that rape was an appropriate means of disciplining a spouse. The four of us were appalled by the questions and comments we received, but were able to remain calm and give fact-based rational answers that some seemed to comprehend.

It has proved helpful that our first question-and-answer session was so trying. The questions that are the most absurd are the ones that deserve the most attention because the audience members who posed them are more likely to commit acts of sexual assault based on their rape myth acceptance. These difficult questions deserve a careful and calm response that is based on facts and delivered with kindness, because it is imperative that the person understands and accepts your answer. Even a trace of hostility or anger in your voice may make the person defensive, and less inclined to believe what you are saying. Remember, the person who asks a brash question is misinformed and not necessarily trying to get a rise out of you. Asking a question about rape and sexual assault is not easy, especially among a group of people. So this person wants to learn more about what you are discussing, has the courage to ask the question, and deserves a good answer. So now when our chapter receives questions like that, we pause, formulate a complete and logical answer, and deliver it with kindness. I encourage you to do the same.

We did not present the Men's Program in its entirety to the high school. In retrospect, we should have. The information conveyed in the presentation is composed in a way that many of the questions the audience might otherwise ask, however ridiculous, are answered by the program already. This means that every section of the presentation is vital to the full understanding of rape, how to prevent it, and how to help a survivor. That was the first and last time we did not deliver the presentation in its entirety.

While I firmly believe that the Men's Program should be delivered in its entirety, I do believe you should adapt it to your school. I encourage emerging chapters to reference local landmarks in your presentation, and use language applicable to your region and school. Additionally, I strongly encourage you to look up the laws surrounding rape in your state and school and use those for your definition poster or PowerPoint™ slides (depending on what you use). Give the audience the resources available to them at your institution in your presentation by mentioning your counseling or health services offices. Try to make the presentation as personal as possible for the audience members and inserting information and terminology relevant to them will only aid in that mission. The Men's Program should be presented naturally, so changing diction and phrasing to suit your personality and presentation is advisable. If there is a word you always trip on, or a phrase that does not come off your tongue well, change it, but be sure to maintain the integrity of the passage.

In the fall of 2008 we booked our first official presentation for a class called "Sex and Sexual Assault in Our Society." Our presentation group conducted script practices four to five times a week for a month to memorize the script, tone, and body language indicative of an effective presentation. We wanted to nail it! We were able to bond and get to know each other well during these sessions, and became better presenters just by knowing each other so well. It is not easy to present on the topic of sexual assault, and we were all anxious about presenting in front of a class studying the very subject on which we were presenting. The presentation itself was a great success as the presentation has since been incorporated into the class curriculum; however, it was not until our second or third presentation when we began to find our rhythm and lose our nerves.

## *Our Impact*

Since then we have increased membership to 16 and had three groups of presenters deliver 13 presentations on campus to more than 400 people, including populations from every first- and second-year dorm. Most recently, we delivered a presentation to faculty, staff, and administration. We were fortunate to have many deans in attendance in addition to the president, provost, athletic directors, director of health services, and professors. They came to understand exactly what our message is, and how we affect the campus community. The presentation went well and the question-and-answer section lasted about 45 minutes. We answered questions about how we started our chapter, what our impact on campus has been, and the prevalence of rape on our campus. The question-and-answer section took an unexpected turn when members of the audience started having a discussion on how best to incorporate the One in Four presentation into the college's curriculum. Members of our senior administration felt that the presentation was so effective that it was not a matter of *if* all should see the presentation, but *how* all should see it.

As a result of that presentation, Western New England College will be adding the Men's and Women's Programs into the mandatory freshmen Personal Health and Wellness class. This move will ensure that all freshmen students receive the presentation in their first year on campus with 60% seeing it in the first semester and 40% in the second. One administrator even went so far as to say it was imperative that all freshmen receive the presentation within the first 2 weeks of coming to campus.

Audience members also felt that the presentation would be beneficial for faculty members. Many stated that professors often have students come to them to describe a rape situation they have endured, and many do not completely know how to handle those situations. To help educate our faculty, we have been asked to conduct a presentation and training seminar for them so they too can be better equipped when a survivor comes to them after experiencing rape.

I believe there are several reasons the program is so effective. One of the most significant factors in the program's effectiveness is the presenters. If it is delivered by a group of approachable and identifiable men on campus with whom having a conversation would be a pleasant experience, the audience will be more engaged and more apt to listen.

Another factor is how it is presented. I was immediately taken by the fact the presentation portrays men as part of the solution, and not necessarily part of the problem. The program identifies with men based on the natural responses that men have to rape, validates them, and then shows them better ways to accomplish their overall goal of helping their friend. The presentation does not overtly state "do not rape women"; rather, it provides the audience with abundant information on what rape is, how it affects survivors, and how to avoid potentially dangerous situations, which allows men and women to deduce what aspects of their behaviors, if any, need to be altered.

Since I have become a member of One in Four and identified myself as a resource and advocate, I have had countless women approach me and describe rape situations they have been through. Had it not been for the training I received from the Men's Program and One in Four, I could not have helped those women nearly as effectively. Obviously, one of the goals of our chapter is to educate others on how to assist in the recovery process and to be a resource to survivors.

The members of One in Four have become my best friends and the people I trust more than anyone else. I am very thankful that I have them to talk to and use as resources. After hearing a survivor describe what has happened to her, I oftentimes need to talk it over with someone, and there are no better people to talk to than fellow One in Four members. Of course I make sure to maintain the survivor's confidentiality and never reveal her name or identifying information to them if I seek support on how best to help her.

Since you will be identifying yourself as an advocate and resource for people who have survived rape and sexual assault, you will hear stories that will be emotionally difficult to handle and it is important you seek support so you can remain a good advocate. I would suggest seeking out an older member of the group or someone else that you can talk to about your feelings and reactions. You will find that once you talk about it, you will feel better and be less likely to experience burnout.

The keys to our success have rested in a few crucial mind-sets. The first is that we do make a difference. Once you start hearing stories from survivors, you can understand just what you are preventing. Even more impactful are the stories of people whom the presentation has helped. I was fortunate to come across a journal entry written by a freshman student as part of a class for which I am a teacher's assistant:

> One of my friends who is like a little sister to me felt comfortable enough to tell me she had been raped. I used the techniques I learned at the One in Four presentation to help her. I found that it is very effective to listen more than talk. I had to hold back my anger because I wanted to go find the guy that did this to her and make sure he never tried to do anything like it again. Instead I expressed my willingness to help her in whatever way she needed. I let her recall what happened and keep telling her that no matter what happened it was not her fault. It hurt me so much to know that there was nothing I could do to prevent what happened. This is the first time I am mentioning it since she told me because it is her story, and if nothing else, she should have control of that.

I was very proud of our group and the work we have accomplished when I came across this entry in the student's personal weekly journal. Without the presentation he might not have been able to help his friend, and would have probably exacerbated the situation by confronting his friend's attacker. The difference One in Four makes extends far beyond just those who see the presentation.

The other significant impact we make is on survivors. On more than one occasion I have had a survivor come to me saying how she always felt the rape was her fault until she saw the presentation. These are some of the most heart-wrenching stories I have ever heard. Some of these survivors have endured seeing their rapist every day in the community and were living with unfounded guilt that what happened was their fault. So when a survivor comes forward and describes how the program has helped her, there is no greater motivator to continue the work One in Four does.

One trait that has served us well has been an ambitious, resourceful, and indomitable attitude. Our chapter has overcome a great deal of adversity on our way to success. It is important for chapters to remember there is always support for our cause, although it may not always be easy to find. Colleges appreciate initiatives that make the community safer and more secure, so I encourage you to have the confidence to set up a meeting with your dean of students, college president, director of residence life, and director of counseling services. Let those individuals know who you are and what you are hoping to accomplish, and most importantly, ask for their advice. Many will have experience dealing with this issue and can be wonderful resources and allies.

Additionally, I credit much of our success over the past few years to the cohesiveness of our group. We are a diverse group of people with different skills that complement each other extremely well. We work well as a team, and one group member summed it fittingly when he said, "We have a president but we make decisions as a group, we have a treasurer but no money, and a secretary but we don't take meeting minutes." We trusted each other to lead, fulfill deadlines, complete tasks, and present well. We had an excellent combination of motivation, ambition, and rationale, which means we set high and attainable goals that we worked hard and successfully to complete.

When you start selecting members, make sure you have the people you want. Pick the guys who you think would represent you and the group well and whom you can get along with well. Being a member of One in Four should be a fun experience, and much of that is dependent on the group members. Be social together, spend time together outside of meetings, get to know the guys you are working with beyond what you see when they are presenting. Learning the script can be a long and arduous process, so if you are going to spend hours upon hours with other guys memorizing a long script, it is important you guys have fun with it along the way. The issue we deal with is extremely serious, and the topics we cover should be treated with reverence, but that does not mean you cannot have fun and enjoy making a positive impact in others' lives.

As a member of One in Four please live what you say in the presentation. We hold our members to the highest standards and expect them to intervene effectively in potentially bad situations, confront others about saying the word *rape* casually, and demonstrate exceptional morals in their daily lives. Understand that as a member of One in Four you will be expected to set an example around others. Take the information that has been delivered to you through the Men's Program and implement it into your daily lives. Use the techniques when talking to survivors, and never be afraid to intervene because it could save somebody a lot of pain and suffering.

My last suggestion is to set goals for your chapter. Make a strategic plan with goals and objectives for multiple semesters at a time and then follow through with them. I encourage you to set lofty yet realistic goals. Do not be dissuaded by the phrases "that will be difficult" or "that may not work" because if you believe you can accomplish a goal, and are persistent and dedicated enough, you most certainly will. The feeling of repeatedly accomplishing goals that others were skeptical of is fantastic, especially when it is for a cause as great as One in Four. So as you go about starting a chapter, or work toward strengthening your chapter, be motivated by the impact you are making on people's lives to set high goals and be the men that help to change the statistic we all know too well.

## Chapter 7

# Resources for Advisors

This chapter provides you, the advisor of a One in Four chapter, with ideas about how to lead the organizational side, as opposed to the educational side, of your peer education group. Your role as an advisor is critical even before creating the organization. This chapter provides you with ideas, materials, and resources that will pave the way to success for your new peer education group.

## Your Role as Advisor

Among many other things, you are the consistency factor in the group. If you are going to be an advisor, be prepared to be committed. It is highly beneficial for you to be at every group meeting. Also, plan to have a weekly meeting with the president to make sure everything is up to par. Be there for the members, as entering the world of sexual assault education can be very difficult. An advisor's commitment to the group can set the stage for the commitment for group members, so set the bar high!

**If you are not willing to structure your time to make that kind of commitment:**

You might think that you don't have time to make this a priority. It is better to realize that before you start the group than afterwards. There are two things you can do:

1. Coadvise the group with somebody else. It could be a colleague or a grad student, but doing this will take some of the time commitment off of your hands.
2. If you don't feel that you have the time for this, find somebody else who does. Even if the person is not fully trained in this issue, if you can find a dedicated person, sensitive to this issue, willing to learn, and who is somebody the members can rally around, then that person can do a great job. You may need to coach the person, but the group will be stronger for it. Commitment is essential to a group like this.

**I have the commitment, but:**

Many administrators will say that they have time for the group, are committed to it, but feel that they are not the kind of person either men or women (as the case may be) will rally around.

This is another place where you might want to consider a coadvisor. Find somebody who is trainable and sensitive to this issue, but will also be somebody that the group members can rally around. You can offer the message; your coadvisor can offer the morale.

Being an effective advisor requires being dedicated to and being able to connect well with the peer educators in your group. There is no requirement that the advisor be the same sex as the group being advised! There are great success stories of advisors of the other sex advising single-sex peer education groups.

## Getting Commitment From Stakeholders

Before you even begin recruiting members for a sexual assault peer education group, it is important to gather information about the context of a sexual assault awareness program in the environment where you are located. Who has done work in this area before, who is around, who has done so in the past, what players were involved, who (if anyone) feels ownership over the issue, are there political dynamics you should be concerned with, who should be made aware of and could be an ally in your efforts? All these issues should be delicately handled as you begin your efforts. Note that not everyone has to agree with 100% of what you want to do and how you want to do it. However, the more allies you have on your side, and the more people you have knowing what you are doing, the better.

## Conducting Regular Team Building

Throughout your efforts to advise your chapter, remember that the strength of your peer educators' commitment to the cause will be strongly affected by the strength of the bonds among members of the group. Work hard to create the most cohesive, open, and vigorous group that you can. Continually push them to grow. Empower them to make changes in their peers, each other, and in themselves. To accomplish these goals, it will be important for you to conduct frequent team-building exercises. Educating one's peers about sexual assault can be draining. Peer educators need their motivational batteries constantly recharged. The more you can foster a sense of community within the group, the more supported they will feel in their efforts and the better their performance will be. A wide variety of traditional and alternative team-building ideas can work, depending on the nature of your group and the culture of your community. Movie nights, self-disclosure activities, playing or watching athletic events, road trips to conferences or recreational locations, and eating meals together are all things to do on a regular basis to hold your group together.

## Building Group Identity

Another way to help build group cohesion and promote your educational mission is to have t-shirts and/or polo shirts with the name and logo of your group on them. Particularly if your group name is a statistic about sexual assault, such as the One in Four logo, by wearing clothing with this information on it, peer educators spread awareness about the issue simply by wearing their shirt. You can also suggest that your group all wear their shirts on the same day of the week, perhaps the day of your group meeting, to have a consistent presence on campus. T-shirts and polo shirts with the One in Four logo can be ordered directly from www.atlanticembroidery.com.

## After Training, What Now?

So you have an interested group and they are all trained and ready go. Where do you go from here? How do you go from the excitement and enthusiasm of training to presentation of programs? Here are a few things that you can do:

### *Generate Buzz*

An important part of the vitality of your group is going to be its recognition on campus and the respect and credibility that it has in the eyes of the students, faculty, and administration. One goal you should have is for every student on campus to know who the group is and what it does.

You basically want to explode onto campus. Have an advertising campaign across your campus to let everybody know that this group has formed. Use social networking sites and paper flyers that explain (1) what the group does, (2) who the founding members of the organization are, (3) with what other organizations they are involved. This should help people on campus to notice the mission of the organization and that someone in the organization is part of a group or organization that they are also a member of on campus.

### *Debut Presentations*

One way to get your chapter off to a great start is to plan "debut presentations" in a popular venue on your campus or other work setting. If at a university, invite faculty, staff, and students—focus on those who are leaders of groups who can preview your program for their organizations. Encourage resident assistants (RAs) to come, and say to them that if they like the program, you'll come present it to their residents. Encourage fraternity leaders, sorority leaders, and athletic team captains to come preview it for their chapters and teams. If you started a men's group, encourage women to come to the debut so that they can see what it is that your chapter will be presenting to the men on your campus. If you started a women's group, invite male leaders on campus to come and demonstrate their support for women's education.

If you put a lot of work into publicity, it can really pay off. With some very minor additional effort, you can get a lot of attention and get off to a great start. For example, work with the press office of your university to issue a press release about the debut. That might sound a bit overboard at first, but you'll be surprised at how much response you might get. This helps spread awareness about the cause to the public.

Advertise these debut presentations like it is a sneak preview to a new movie. Advertise like crazy through word of mouth, social networking sites, flyers, handwritten invitations, advertisements, and letters. Asking people in person to attend will be most effective. Let the university newspapers, as well as local community newspapers and television stations, know that your group is taking a stance on sexual assault and see if you can get some articles written or broadcast about it. Make this a big deal—because it is. See the sample press release later in this chapter.

At the debut presentations, make sure that every group member gets a chance to speak even if it requires breaking up the script into small parts. This will give everyone experience speaking to audiences and will do so with a more manageable portion of the script.

Finally, at that presentation, introduce this group to the audience. Explain what the group does, how it was assembled, that the members were selected and trained for as many hours and what their goals are. Then, as is the case with every presentation, let the members introduce themselves and talk about some of the things that they are involved in on campus.

### After This Initial Push

Once the ball is rolling with the debut performances, it is time to find groups where you can make presentations. This is when the diversity of the members of your group will be really important. Use the network of activities and contacts that they have to book presentations. Also, there are always RAs out there looking for hall programs to do, Greek organizations looking for risk management programs, and athletic teams looking to meet NCAA requirements.

## Structure Within the Group

Your group must have an organizational structure within it to survive. The advisor must play a very active role. However, if the advisor does everything, the group is likely to fall apart. What happens if the group starts to fizzle? What happens if the number of presentations is starting to slow down? What happens if you are having difficulty finding new members to replace those who graduate? The group's chances of not only surviving but thriving are going to be much stronger if there are individual members whose task it is to answer these questions.

This chapter includes a constitution for your group. Use it. You may find that you want to make modifications to certain sections, switch out a few officer positions, etc. Either way, you are likely to find that having a group structure is a vital part of the group's survival. For example, you will need an officer whose job it is to organize the group to bring in a new class of diverse and dedicated members for the next year. You will need to have a vice president who is in charge of making sure that presentations are booked and new audiences are always being sought. You will need a president, one person, whose job it is to motivate the members and make sure everybody is working to accomplish the goals of the group.

## How to Boost Attendance at Programs

There are some places that have no problem getting students to come to their programs. Others struggle. Here are some ideas for how to make sure you are in the former category.

1. Make the program mandatory. There is no substitute for this suggestion and no acceptable excuse for your institution not to do so. The programs in this book are introductory programs about sexual assault and they take about 1 hour to present. Every college and university in the nation is required by federal law to provide sexual assault prevention programming to its students. The introductory programs in this book provide you with material to meet those requirements. Of course, presenting more than one program is preferable! Not presenting rape prevention programs is illegal, unethical, and immoral, and in all likelihood runs counter to the mission of most every higher education institution in the nation. Show me a school that doesn't have time for a 1-hour rape prevention program in the week prior to the start of classes and I'll show you a calendar with 168 hours in it during that week from which it can choose.

2. Make the program part of a life skills initiative; for example, students must attend 6 of 15 events that will take place over the course of a semester to receive credit toward meeting a goal (preferred course registration, preferred housing, $10 off books for the following semester), preferred seating at a university event (graduation, an athletic event), or some other institutional incentive.

3. Talk with administrators in your fraternity and sorority life office about having their chapters receive program credit to fulfill risk management quotas.

Alternatively, have program attendance of a certain percentage of their chapter (70 to 80%) count toward philanthropy or some other requirement their chapters must meet on your campus. If a chapter is on probation or on some other disciplinary status, offer a small reduction in the sanction for 70 to 80% program attendance.

4. When a student organization or residence hall floor/unit invites your organization in to do a presentation, ask it to have at least 80% of its members at the presentation.

## Sample Press Release for Debut of an All-Male Peer Education Group

**Contact: (Name and phone number)**
**For Immediate Release**

### *Male Student Leaders at (Name of College) Unite to Educate Peers About Rape*

Your City, State.—A group of (number) male student leaders at (your university) has founded an all-male sexual assault, peer education group. Their name, "One in Four," comes from the statistic that one in four college women has survived rape or attempted rape at some point in her lifetime. The group seeks to change that statistic at (your university) through use of the only program shown by research on college students to reduce sexual assault.

One in Four will present "How to Help a Sexual Assault Survivor: What Men Can Do" to men in residence halls, athletic teams, fraternities, and other groups of men throughout the year.

One in Four will hold two debut presentations to kick off their effort. During these presentations, they will present their program and take questions. Members of the group and their advisor(s) will be available afterward for media questions. Presentations will be held on (date, time, place).

\* \* \*

## Sample Press Release for Debut of an All-Female Peer Education Group

**Contact: (Name and phone number)**
**For Immediate Release**

### Female Student Leaders at (Name of College) Unite to Educate Peers About Rape

Your City, State.—A group of (number) female student leaders at (your university) has founded an all-female sexual assault, peer education group. The group plans to present an innovative, research-based program emphasizing how women can recognize and avoid dangerous men and how women can help each other if they experience rape. Research shows the program improves women's willingness to intervene when they see dangerous situations and that it leads to desired attitude changes.

The group will present its program to women in residence halls, athletic teams, sororities, and other groups of women throughout the year. Two debut presentations will kick off the effort. During these presentations, they will present their program and take questions. Members of the group and their advisor(s) will be available afterward for media questions. Presentations will be held on (date, time, and place).

* * *

## Sample Statement

The following sample statement is for the president of your organization to give at the beginning of your debut presentation, assuming a mixed sex audience. It is important for people in your audience to know who your members are, what their mission is, and about their desire to present to various groups. It is also important that audience members recognize their roles as people who can help spread the word of your availability to make presentations. In addition, it is important to note how pleased you are that everyone is there, women and men, to see the efforts that peer educators will normally make to single-sex audiences.

## Sample Statement for a President to Make at a Debut Performance

Welcome! My name is (name) and I am president of (One in Four/group name). We are a new sexual assault, peer education group that presents a program called (How to Help a Sexual Assault Survivor: What Men Can Do/ Empowering Women: Learning About Dangerous Men and Helping Rape Survivors). We hope to present this program all over campus—in residence halls, to fraternities/sororities, sports teams, classes, and to any other group that will listen.

As we start off, I'd like to ask the other members of One in Four/group name to introduce themselves to you. (State name, major, and two activities.)

And as I said, I am (insert name, state major, and two activities).

We are a group that is united, passionately, behind a cause that is very meaningful to all of us, to work toward ending men's violence against women and all of the suffering it causes. Based on research demonstrating that the best way to educate college students about sexual assault is in a single-sex environment, we usually present to single-sex audiences. However, today we are presenting to both men and women so that everyone can see what it is that we do. We hope that all of you will support us by encouraging people to invite us in to speak to your organizations.

As we present today, we will do so as though you are a typical college-age audience to whom we would usually present. We want you to see our program in its purest form, so you will know exactly what it is that we do. Thank you all very much for coming. Now, we will begin.

## Retreat!

After your chapter has been around for at least a semester, and you start off a new year, it is time for a retreat to get things off on the right foot. The sample agenda below is for such a retreat. The main activity of this retreat is to have the group write its own mission statement. Who are they? What will they be about? How will they accomplish their goals? Suggestions about how to guide this discussion are included in the agenda. Immediately after the agenda is one sample mission statement. It is suggested that you take a look at this and use it as a way to guide the discussion of your peer educators. If they are missing a point you think is important, ask an open-ended question to determine if they think they've left something out (suggest what that might be).

## Sample Agenda for a Beginning of the Year (or Mid-Year) Retreat

(After your group has been active at least one semester; this is designed to take a day.)

1. Ice Breaker
Go around the room and have each member answer the following questions.
   A. If you could change one thing, *anything*, about our group what would you change? It could be something about how we relate to one another, what we do as a group, anything at all.
   B. Now that you've been in our group for a while, what motivates you personally to continue our work in our group?

2. Team Builder
Distribute blank sheets of white paper to each person. Give the following instructions:

> *Draw your own personal coat of arms. It is up to your creativity and imagination and, if applicable, artistic skills to come up with your personal rendition. The drawing should include symbols that represent some personal values, how our group fits into your life, and significant influences in your life.*

Give the group time to finish—about 10 minutes or so.

Ask members to share their coat of arms with the group. Give time for people to ask questions about it.

At the end, ask the group as a whole the following questions:

Who did you learn the most about?
What surprised you the most?
What is the most significant thing you learned about someone else?

3. Old Business
Discuss any pressing matters in the group that need focused discussion. Try to stay away from things that can be reviewed at an upcoming business meeting and steer toward those issues that require more creativity and processing time.

4. Mission Statement
Create and/or revisit a group mission statement (advisor is encouraged to see sample mission statement following this agenda to give you ideas on one way to guide the discussion).

   A. Get things started by dividing them into small groups of three or four and have them discuss and record their answers to these two questions.
      – Why do we do what we do in our group?
      – Why is that important?

B. Gather the groups together and have them report back. Note similarities and differences.

C. Put people back into groups to brainstorm principles they think the group should live by.

D. Return to the large group. Write down each brainstormed principle on a chalkboard, newsprint, or type on large computer screen. Gauge which principles resonate the best with the group. When similarly worded principles are written by different small groups, attempt to come up with a consensus wording. If the group seems to be missing a key area, ask them a question to see if they think the missing area is important enough to warrant a guiding principle.

E. Note the principles on which everyone agrees. Write and distribute the list to the group at the next meeting for further discussion, consideration, and a consensus decision on adopting the mission statement.

5. Closing Activity

Ask group members to share what they liked the best about the day and the one way they plan to help make the group better in the coming year.

## Mission Statement

Your group may decide to create a mission statement. Alternatively, the members may decide to come up with standards for membership and ask each new member to sign a list of these standards. You or your group might also decide not to do either of these. The examples below provide you with ideas on what such documents can look like.

## Sample Mission Statement for a One in Four Chapter

Our primary mission is to end men's sexual violence against women. To accomplish this goal, we shall follow these principles:

1. To educate men and participate in an outreach that will help break the silence about and end violence against women. We will take an active role in ending rape and encourage others to do the same.

2. To use the most effective, research-proven means to accomplish our primary mission, including but not limited to *The Men's Program*. Accordingly, so long as rigorous social scientific research continues to strongly suggest that sexual-assault peer education is most effective in a single-sex environment, we will limit our membership to an all-male group.

3. To put the needs of survivors first, by respecting their confidentiality and helping to provide support in any manner that will help them in their recovery.

4. To always act in a manner consistent with our teachings and to set an example for all men by treating every woman with respect. We will also reject all forms of discrimination as well as combat attitudes and social norms that lead to sexual violence.
5. To respect and support one another, as well as train a diverse and approachable group, in order to reach as much of the university community as possible.
6. To participate in a larger community of people working for sexual assault education and advocacy while supporting and reinforcing its efforts.

We recognize that the mission outlined above will be difficult, but we are dedicated to hastening the arrival of the day when our group is no longer needed.

# One in Four Member Standards

## *Purpose Statement*

One in Four's primary mission is to end men's sexual violence against women. The Member Standards document was drafted to accomplish this goal. One in Four must hold its members to the highest standards.

## *Standards*

As members of One in Four we have the unique opportunity to make a large difference in the community in which we live. We must have a positive recognition of our influence in shaping men's lives at our institution and beyond. With that in mind, we believe it is important to exemplify the following values:

- A member of One in Four will *always* act in a manner consistent with our teachings and set an example for all men by treating women with respect.
- A member of One in Four will reject all forms of discrimination as well as combat attitudes and social norms that lead to sexual violence.
- A member of One in Four will continually strive to educate men and participate in an outreach that will help break the silence about and end violence against women. He will take an active role in ending rape and encourage others to do the same.
- A member of One in Four will respect and support his fellow members, as well as train a diverse and approachable group, in order to reach as much of the college population as possible.
- A member of One in Four will use the most effective, research-proven means to accomplish the group's primary mission, including but not limited to *The Men's Program*.
- A member of One in Four will put the needs of survivors first, by respecting their confidentiality and helping to provide support in any manner that will help them in their recovery.
- A member of One in Four will actively participate in a larger community of people working for sexual assault education and advocacy while supporting and reinforcing its efforts. This endeavor demands a dedication to this effort both during his time in college and in his future activities.

By placing my name on this document I dedicate myself to the values set forth and pledge to do everything in my power to fulfill my duties as a worthy member of One in Four.

_____          _____

Signature                                                     Date

## One in Four Constitution

Ratified on (date)

### *Article I—Name*

The name of this organization shall be One in Four.

### *Article II—Purpose*

One in Four is an all-male, sexual-assault, peer education group that seeks to educate men about rape and inform them how to help women recover from a sexual assault experience.

### *Article III—Membership*

### *Section 1—Members*

One in Four maintains an open membership to all qualified men enrolled at (name of institution), regardless of age, citizenship, color, disability, race, religion, national origin, political affiliation, sexual orientation, or status as a disabled veteran or veteran of the Vietnam era. New members are selected and approved by the current members and advisor to One in Four.

(If appropriate and approved by www.oneinfourusa.org): This organization is a subsidiary of the national One in Four organization and as such agrees to abide by all such policies, guidelines, and requirements. These requirements include but are not limited to presenting the Men's Program in its current version and having at least 15 hours of training for all members.

### *Section 2—Selection*

Selection of new members shall occur by these procedures:

Recruitment letters shall be sent to administrators, faculty members, and student leaders of organizations to solicit nominations for candidates. These letters shall include a description of the mission of One in Four.

Once nominated, the Selections Coordinator will add each nominee's name to the list of candidates and shall contact each candidate to schedule an interview.

A first interview shall be with multiple group members, and shall consist of objective, conceptual, and contextual questions.

A second interview shall be with the Selections Coordinator and an advisor. The candidate shall present a portion of the script and will be asked a few final questions.

Each interviewer in each interview will score the candidate on a predetermined set of categories. An average score will be determined from the first interview and from the second interview. These two scores will again be averaged for the final candidate score. These scores will be used as a guide—not a mandate—for acceptance or rejection for group membership. Scores will be given in a meeting to all members of One in Four as decisions are made about final selection into the group.

The group shall review the list, discuss each candidate, and come to consensus on which candidates shall be offered membership.

Notification of all candidates shall occur immediately after this meeting, as coordinated by the Selections Coordinator.

## Section 3—Training

After a candidate is selected to become a member of One in Four, he must participate fully in the group's training process. This process includes 1 day in November and 2 days in January. Training shall be led jointly by the Advisor and the Training Coordinator, with significant assistance from current group members.

## Section 4—Expulsion

A member may be expelled from One in Four for:

- Missing 25% of the meetings without prior notice to the President.
- Missing more than 50% of the meetings, regardless of the reasons.
- Conduct unbefitting a member of One in Four, including, but not limited to, committing sexual assault, deliberate deception of the group, or repeated deficiencies in presentations.

Expulsion shall occur by these procedures:

A member of One in Four must present a complaint to the President in writing, e-mail, or by any written or electronic means other than just verbal.

The President must notify in writing or by email the member in question, who must be given at least 24 hours notice to be present at the next meeting to speak on his own behalf. The member shall be given the opportunity to address the complaint, and will then leave the room for the group to deliberate.

The group should attempt to come to a consensus on a decision. If a consensus is not possible, a vote shall be taken with a simple majority required for expulsion.

## Section 5—Active Membership

An active member of One in Four shall consist of a member who is a full-time student. This shall not include someone who is on study abroad or who otherwise has taken a semester off from school. If a member has missed more than

50% of the meetings during the current semester *and* the previous semester in which they were otherwise eligible to vote, they shall be considered an inactive member for the purpose of voting and thus shall not count for the purpose of quorum and shall not be permitted to vote. If said individual wishes to petition the group to restore his voting rights, he may do so. Voting rights may be restored by a simple majority of group members eligible to vote.

## Article IV—Officers

### Section 1—Officers

The officers of One in Four shall consist of a President, Vice President, Training Coordinator, Selections Coordinator, Publicity Coordinator, Alumni Relations Coordinator, Treasurer, and Scribe. All officers will assume their duties at the next-to-last regularly scheduled meeting in the spring.

### Section 2—Removal From Office

An officer may be removed from office for violating the organization's purpose or constitution. Removal shall occur by these procedures:

A member of One in Four must present a complaint in writing, by e-mail, or by any electronic means other than just verbal to the President. If the President is the officer in question, the complaint must be presented to the Advisor.

The President (or Advisor) must notify in writing or by email the officer in question, who must be given the opportunity to be present at the next meeting with at least 24 hours notice to speak on his own behalf.

If an officer is removed from office, a discussion should then immediately take place regarding whether the person should remain a member of the group. The group should attempt to come to a consensus on a decision. If a consensus is not possible, a vote shall be taken with a simple majority required for removal.

If an officer is removed, a special election shall be held to replace that individual at the earliest feasible date.

## Article V—Duties of Officers

### Section 1—President

The President shall:

Organize and preside over all group meetings.
Meet regularly with the Advisor, preferably once per week.

Monitor and guide the organizational activities of all officers, committees, and members.

Be the spokesman for One in Four, meeting regularly with representatives from other student organizations, staff, faculty members, and others involved in rape prevention.

Assist with the training of new members.

## Section 2—Vice President

The Vice President shall:

Schedule all events and programs in which One in Four shall present.

Be the contact for groups and individuals seeking a One in Four presentation.

Keep the group informed about future presentations.

Ensure that as many peer educators as possible are assigned to each presentation. A minimum of two peer educators is required, four is preferred for a typical presentation, as many as possible for open presentations and presentations to large groups.

Preside over group meetings from which the President is absent.

With the President, meet regularly with representatives from other student organizations, staff, faculty members, and others involved in rape prevention.

## Section 3—Training Coordinator

The Training Coordinator shall:

Assist the Advisor in the process of providing training for new members.

Help integrate new members into the group.

Report on new developments and research that might affect the group's mission or further educate its members.

Provide regular in-service training for all members.

## Section 4—Selections Coordinator

The Selections Coordinator shall:

Organize and lead the recruitment and selection of new members in accordance with Article III, Section 2.

Maintain a list of candidates for membership.

Schedule interviews for all candidates and assign group members to conduct the first round of these interviews.

With the Advisor, conduct the second round of candidate interviews.

Lead the selection meeting.

Coordinate the notification of all candidates once member selection is finalized.

## Section 5—Publicity Coordinator

The Publicity Coordinator shall:

Assist organizations that host a One in Four presentation to publicize it to their members.
Publicize the presence and activity of One in Four throughout the university.

## Section 6—Alumni Relations Coordinator

The Alumni Relations Coordinator shall:

Publicize and host a homecoming weekend reception for alumni of the One in Four chapter.
Contact alumni of the chapter at least twice per semester through newsletters, e-mails, or other means to update them about the events of the chapter.
Maintain the accuracy of the alumni e-mail list.
Collect e-mails from graduating seniors prior to their departure from campus to add to the e-mail list.
Coordinate fundraising efforts of the chapter.

## Section 7—Treasurer

The Treasurer shall:

Work with the Advisor to keep the group's financial records.
Authorize purchases and reimbursements.
Oversee financial transactions.

## Section 8—Scribe

The Scribe shall:

Take attendance at all One in Four meetings.
Accurately record the minutes of each meeting.
E-mail the minutes of each meeting to group members within 48 hours of the end of each meeting.

## Article VI – Advisor

The Advisor to One in Four shall:

Be a graduate student or full-time faculty or staff member at the institution.
Provide support and guidance to the organization.

Challenge group members to carry out the mission of One in Four with dedication.

Attend all group meetings unless extenuating circumstances arise.

Lead the training of new members.

With the Selections Coordinator, conduct the second round of candidate interviews.

## Article VII—Meetings

### Section 1—Meetings

Group meetings shall be conducted weekly, at a time and place established by the members and advisor.

The order of business shall be as follows:

Officer reports
Unfinished business
New business
Announcements
Closing circle

### Section 2—Quorum

More than half of the group's active members must be present at a meeting to constitute a quorum. A quorum must be present to make any group decisions, which are made by first attempting consensus and voting if necessary. Quorum is not required at a meeting to assign peer educators to future presentations.

## Article VIII—Elections

The election of new officers shall take place at the first meeting in March by these procedures:

Elections shall be conducted by the retiring President, unless he is seeking another term. In this case, the Advisor shall conduct the presidential election, and the current president will conduct the remaining elections.

As with all group decisions, officer selection shall occur—when possible—by consensus, with a vote taken if necessary. A simple majority of those present and voting is required for election of an officer.

Elections take place office by office in the following order: President, Vice President, Training Coordinator, Selections Coordinator, Publicity Coordinator, Alumni Relations Coordinator, Treasurer, and Scribe.

For each office, candidates must be nominated by a member of the group (this includes self nominations). All nominations must be seconded.

After nominations conclude, each candidate shall speak on his own behalf without other candidates for his office present. The candidates shall not be in the room while the rest of the group deliberates. This still applies when there is only one candidate for an office in the event that the group wishes not to select the one candidate and reopen nominations.

If four or more candidates are running for an office, the group shall narrow the field to two candidates and invite the candidates not in the top two back into the room to be part of the officer selection discussion for that position.

Once a decision has been made by the group, the candidates shall be called back into the room, and the President shall announce the group's decision.

## Article IX—Amendments

This constitution is binding on the members of One in Four. Amendments may be made to meet the changing needs of the group by the following procedures:

A written proposal must be presented to the group.

The group shall decide at the next meeting whether or not to adopt the proposed amendment by a simple majority. If two thirds of the active members agree that the amendment must be voted upon the same day, the rule to delay voting on the amendment until the next meeting can be overridden. If the amendment is adopted, it is effective immediately.

## Article X—Ratification

This constitution was ratified on (date) by consensus of the members of One in Four.

# Ideas for "Closing Circles"

One of the major roles you can play for your group is to keep up the motivation of its members. One of the primary ways to do this is to lead the group in a "closing circle" (think of a group hug combined with a motivational speech) at the end of each meeting. Below are some ideas of things for you to say as you lead "closing circles" at different times of the year.

## *After a Group Finishes Training*

Looking way into the future, my hope is that for each of you, about 30 years from now, your phone will ring. It will be your daughter. She'll be calling from where you went to college. She will have just started going there too. You and your spouse will get on the phone. You'll say, "So, how did your Orientation week go?" She will say, "It was just great! I met lots of incredible people and can't wait to start my classes. People really respect each other here and I feel very safe." You'll respond, "That's great!" Just as you start to tell her stories of your college days, she'll interrupt you and say "Our Orientation Assistant took us all over campus today to see the important parts of campus. We walked into the Student Union and there was an interesting new display." "Really, what was that?" "Well, on this pedestal there was a glass box. Inside the glass box was the sexual assault policy. See, we don't even need it anymore. There was a plaque there dedicating the display to the students who were here in the beginning of the 21st century who fought to make this policy obsolete." You'll then breathe a deep sigh of relief in a way that only your fellow classmates would understand. Your daughter then says, "And you know, below that whole display is another plaque; it reads: First College in the World to End Rape." Okay. "Hey, my hall mates are walking by and I'm going to go join them for dinner." "Have fun sweetheart," you'll say. And you will know that she is safe. Are you willing to work toward making that phone call possible?

If so, then we have work to do. We must all get involved in this fight in the way we find most meaningful. No matter how we get involved, together, we must work to educate this nation about the reality of rape. Let us help those who have suffered this crime to heal, and permanently remove from our schools and campuses those who would so wantonly violate our communities.

We must work to educate all so that they know what rape is, so that they know what they can do to avoid committing rape, so that we all understand rape, and so that we all band together to eradicate it from our communities.

I believe, in the very core of my being, that we really can change the world. Certainly, as we all seek to truly change the world, there will be those who doubt our ability to succeed. If you are committed to ending rape by any ethical means necessary, you will undoubtedly encounter those who doubt your resolve, who doubt your ability, and who doubt the chances that you can be effective. As you encounter these people I encourage you to remember these words: "Don't ever let anyone tell you that you can't change the world, for such is the rally cry of the cynics and the unambitious." (Repeat). Believe it or not, I don't believe that I can change the world. I believe that *we* can change the world. Our world is ever more interconnected and interdependent. In the context in which we work, we must change the world one man at a time, one student group at a time, one high school at a time, one university at a time, one military unit at a time, one community at a time, one country at a time.

Thank you for all you are doing to learn about this issue and all you will do to make our efforts, in time, obsolete. Go forth and make a difference!

## After a Day When Someone Unfairly Questions the Group's Motives

How many of you got into this work because you thought it would be easy? I thought so. You aren't the ones looking for easy work. You are leaders. It is easy to stand on the sidelines and complain. It is much harder to lead. Leaders are moved by principle. In the work that we do, I can think of no higher principle than to commit ourselves to ending rape by the most effective methods we can find as shown by well conducted, scientific research. Indeed, this is the principle upon which the Men's Program was written and One in Four was founded. To select these means we must rely on research over opinion, reason over emotion. Opinion and emotion play a key role in helping to end rape, but can at the same time distract and derail us from achieving our goal.

An all-male peer education group presenting the Men's Program to primarily male audiences may not please everyone, and may not seem to be the most effective thing in everyone's opinion, but it is the best first step we now know. Until another method is shown to be better, it would be unethical and counter to our goal to replace it for any reason other than finding something shown to work better. So remember, don't ever let anyone tell you, you can't change the world.

## For an End-of-the-Year Meeting

For those of you graduating, when you walk across campus on graduation day, I want you to think of this: You will pass many people as you walk. One of them will be a fellow student, a woman. She will be laughing heartily with full joy. Think about the fact that your work here has affected her in ways she may never know. Someone you talked to didn't rape her. Let that feeling move you—not to take yourself too seriously—but to recognize that what you have done and what you continue to do here matters. Next you'll pass another woman. Her disposition will be less animated, but you will sense strength in her presence. You will sense a confidence that has come from growing through a difficult time. This woman is a survivor. This woman talked with a man you educated about how to help her. Because of that, she got more of the help she needed. She was believed. She got counseling. She was listened to. She wasn't doubted. Had you not done that one program that day, her life would be much worse. Think about that too.

At the end of your days here at X University, regardless of what else you did here, where you go, and on what level you continue working for this cause, you can leave with a special feeling within you that you changed this place. That you didn't let people tell you that you can't change the world, that you didn't listen to the rally cry of the cynics and unambitious and turn your head from a complex problem. Rather, you asked what you could do to solve it, you sought opportunities to heal, you sought opportunities to bring people closer together. You modeled for others what ideal men should be—those who love and respect one another, who love and respect women, and who take it upon themselves to live out the motto that binds us all; and that is, to make a difference.

## Sexual Assault Statistics

### How Often Does Rape Happen to Women?

One in four college women has survived either rape or attempted rape in her lifetime. The U.S. Department of Justice published a study in 2006 of more than 4,000 college women. In that survey, 3% of those women had survived rape or attempted rape in a 7-month academic year alone. An additional 21% had survived rape or attempted rape at some point in their lives prior to that academic year. When you take those two figures and add them up—the 3 and the 21—you get 24%, or roughly one in four (Tjaden & Thoennes, 2006).

Every year 5% of college women (300,000) survive rape (Kilpatrick, Resnick, Ruggiero, Conoscenti, & McCauley, 2007; Mohler-Kuo, Dowdall, Koss, & Wechsler, 2004).

Every year in the United States, more than 1 million women survive rape (Kilpatrick et al., 2007).

### Male Survivors

3% of college men report surviving rape or attempted rape as a child or adult (Tjaden & Thoennes, 2006).

### Who Are the Perpetrators?

Between 6 and 9% of men in anonymous surveys admit committing rape (Abbey & McAuslan, 2004; Lisak & Miller, 2002).
One of every 500 college students is infected with HIV, the virus that causes AIDS (Gayle, Keeling, Garcia-Tunon, Kilbourne, Narkunas, Ingram et al., 1990).
Fraternity men and student athletes are more likely to commit rape than other men on college campuses (Murnen & Kohlman, 2007).

Of men who rape, about two thirds report doing so more than once—averaging about six rapes each (Lisak & Miller, 2002).

The more alcohol a man consumes, the more aggressive he is in a sexual situation. More serious cases of sexual assault happen when perpetrators have had four to eight drinks when compared to fewer than four, or more than eight drinks. In addition, the more alcohol a victim has consumed, the more severe the assault against her tends to be (Abbey, Clinton-Sherrod, McAuslan, Zawacki, & Buck, 2003).

## Who Are the Survivors?

False reports of rape are rare, according to a study funded by the U.S. Department of Justice occurring only 2 to 4% of the time (Lonsway, Archambault, & Berkowitz, 2007).

## What Happens After the Rape?

One study found that 16% of rapes in the general population and 12% of rapes in the college population are reported to the police (Kilpatrick et al., 2007). Another found that 5% of rape cases were reported to the police (Fisher, Cullen, & Turner, 2006).

## Prevalence of Rape in the U.S. Military

28% (over one in four) of U.S. women veterans were raped during their military service (Sadler, Booth, & Doebbeling, 2005; Suris & Lind, 2008).

96% of women who experience rape in the U.S. military are raped by a man serving in the U.S. military (Sadler et al., 2005).

38% of active duty women in the Air Force have experienced sexual harassment from their supervisors, a rate that is more than twice as high than that for women in the civilian workforce (Bostock & Daley, 2007).

39% of women who enlist in the Navy have experienced rape or attempted rape prior to their service. This is well over twice as high as the national victimization rate (Stander, Merrill, Thomsen, Crouch, & Milner, 2008).

13% of men enlisting in the Navy report perpetrating rape or attempted rape prior to their service; a rate twice as high as the 6 to 9% national average (Abbey & McAuslan, 2004; Lisak & Miller; 2002; Stander et al., 2008).

Women in the military are four times more likely to be raped if their superior officers tolerate sexual harassment in the workplace or barracks (Sadler, Booth, Cook, & Doebbeling, 2003).

# Recommended Web Sites and Books

## *Web Sites*

Get help: www.rainn.org

Register your group as a One in Four chapter: www.oneinfourusa.org

John Foubert's Web page with all studies on the Men's and Women's programs: http://okstate.academia.edu/JohnFoubert

Get t-shirts, polo shirts, and other regalia with the One in Four logo: www.atlanticembroider.com

Sex trafficking and modern slavery: www.sexandmoneyfilm.com

General information: www.nsvrc.org

Research summaries by independent organization: www.vawnet.org

For victims: www.ncvc.or/ncvc/Main.aspx

## *Recommended Books*

Domitrz, M. (2005). *Voices of courage: Inspiration from survivors of sexual assault.* Greenfield, WI: Awareness Publications.

Eberstadt, M. & Layden, M.A. (2010). *The social costs of pornography: A statement of findings and recommendations.* New York: The Witherspoon Institute.

Fisher, B.S., Daigle, L.E., & Cullen, F.T. (2010). *Unsafe in the ivory tower: The sexual victimization of college women.* Los Angeles: Sage Publ.

Guinn, D.E. (2007). *Pornography: Driving the demand in international sex trafficking.* U.S.A.: International Human Rights Law Institute and Captive Daughters Media.

Jensen, R. (2007). *Getting off: Pornography and the end of masculinity.* Cambridge, MA: South End Press.

Katz, J. (2006). *The macho paradox: Why some men hurt women and how all men can help.* New York: Sourcebooks.

Malarek, V. (2009). *The Johns: Sex for sale and the men who buy it.* New York: Arcade Publishing.

Sebold, A. (2002). *Lucky.* London: Picador.

# Chapter 8

## Summary of Research on the Men's Program and the Women's Program

One of the distinguishing factors of both the Men's Program and the Women's Program is the research on their effectiveness. Given that the Men's Program has been in use for a much longer time, it has much more research to substantiate its impact. Still, both programs have data to substantiate their impact. This chapter provides you with brief summaries of studies done on both programs. A longer list of citations is included at the end of this chapter that includes these and other studies done on the Men's Program and the Women's Program. In addition, copies of these articles, along with additional articles published subsequent to this book, are and will be posted on http://okstate.academia.edu/ JohnFoubert under the category "papers."

### The Women's Program

**Foubert, J. D., Langhinrichsen-Rohling, J., Brasfield, H., & Hill, B. (in press). Effects of a rape awareness program on college women: Increasing bystander efficacy and willingness to intervene.** *Journal of Community Psychology.*

This study measured whether the Women's Program could produce results whereby women would report greater efficacy and willingness to prevent rape from happening to other women when they themselves were in the bystander position, and whether women's rape myth acceptance would decline after seeing the program. Prior studies have viewed women's roles as limited to reducing their individual risk for rape, consequently leaving much of the prevention work to men (Katz, 2006). This study sought to document the efficacy of a program envisioning a broader role for women in ending sexual assault: from reducing personal risk for rape to teaching women bystander intervention techniques, which would conceivably increase the safety of all women in a culture.

A comprehensive review of the research literature (Banyard, Plante, & Moynihan, 2004) revealed that several factors have been shown to increase the likelihood that people will intervene as bystanders. These include being aware of a situation in which someone is being victimized, making a prior commitment to help, having a sense of partial responsibility for helping, believing that the victim has not caused the situation to occur, having a sense of self efficacy related to possessing the skills necessary to do something, and seeing others model prosocial behavior. Potential bystanders are also likely to weigh the costs and benefits of intervention relative to how they personally believe it will affect their status in a reference group (Banyard et al., 2004).

The more that a woman can recognize threatening cues in a situation that could turn into a sexual assault situation, the more likely she can resist or escape (Turchik, Probst, Chau, Nigoff, & Gidycz, 2007). Thus, preparing women to respond assertively to threatening situations has the potential for helping women to resist assaults (Turchik et al., 2007). Simultaneously, teaching women bystander intervention strategies empowers women to help all others to begin to be free from the societal burden of rape (Banyard, Moynihan, & Plante, 2007).

## Method

### Participants

A total of 279 women participated in the study, with 189 participating in the treatment group and 90 participating in the control group. The majority of participants identified themselves as first-year students ($n = 266$), followed by sophomores ($n = 6$), juniors ($n = 2$), seniors ($n = 1$), and other ($n = 1$). The mean age of participants was 18.87 years (SD = 3.17, range = 17 to 46).

### Materials

### Illinois Rape Myth Acceptance Scale – Short Form (IRMA – SF)

Participant's attitudes toward sexual assault were measured using the short form of the Illinois Rape Myth Acceptance Scale (Payne, Lonsway, & Fitzgerald, 1999). This scale includes 20 items scored on a scale of 1 (not at all agree) to 7 (very much agree). Scores at the higher end of this scale indicate stronger belief in rape myths.

### Bystander Efficacy Scale

Willingness to intervene as a bystander was measured by the bystander efficacy scale developed by Banyard, Plante, and Moynihan (2005). This measure asks participants to indicate whether they believe that they could do each of 18 bystander behaviors and if so to indicate their level of confidence in performing each behavior. This scale yielded an alpha reliability of .89 in the current sample of women at pretest. The coefficient alpha for this scale at posttest was .92.

## Bystander Willingness to Help Scale

The Willingness to Help Scale was developed by Banyard et al. (2005) and measures participants' degree of likelihood of engaging in 12 bystander behaviors on a 7-point scale. Items came from research literature and from discussions with advocates and professionals working in the field of sexual violence. The alpha reliability for these 12-items was .82 in the present sample at pretest and .88 at posttest.

## *Procedure*

Institutional Review Board (IRB) approval was obtained for the procedure used to collect this data and all participants gave informed consent prior to their participation. Participation was voluntary and all data was collected anonymously. Participants in this study were enrolled in one of many freshman orientation seminars ($n = 64$, taught by a total of 49 professors) at a moderately sized university in the southeastern United States.

Program participants completed surveys before and after seeing the Women's Program. Control participants completed surveys before and after an unrelated stress management program.

## *Results*

### *Bystander Intervention*

As predicted, female participants who experienced the Women's Program reported significantly greater increases in their bystander efficacy over time than did female participants who experienced the control condition.

An analysis of the bystander efficacy scale revealed that the pretest–posttest comparisons were significant within the treatment group, $F(1, 157) = 159.93$, $p < .001$, partial $\eta^2 = .50$ and within the control group, $F(1, 83) = 7.45$, $p = .01$, partial $\eta^2 = .08$, as was the treatment–control comparison under the posttest condition, $F(1, 240) = 22.28$, $p < .001$, partial $\eta^2 = .08$. The only simple main effect that was not significant for the BES was treatment–control contrast under the pretest condition, $F(1, 240) = .07$, $p = .80$.

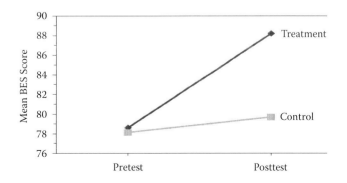

As was found with the BES, female participants who experienced the Women's Program reported significantly greater increases over time in their willingness to help a potential victim when in the bystander role than did female participants who experienced the control condition.

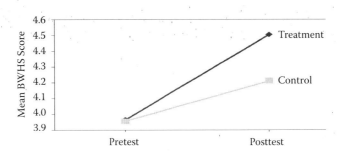

The pretest–posttest contrast within the treatment group, $F(1, 157) = 210.28$, $p < .001$, partial $\eta^2 = .57$ as well as within the control group, $F(1, 83) = 36.55$, $p < .001$, partial $\eta^2 = .31$ were significant. The treatment–control group comparison within the posttest occasion of measurement was significant, $F(1, 240) = 16.07$, $p < .001$, partial $\eta^2 = .06$, but it was not at pretest, $F(1, 240) = .02$, $p = .89$.

## Rape Myth Acceptance

As predicted, these tests revealed a significant decrease in the mean score of the IRMA-SF from the pretest to posttest within the treatment group [$F(1, 213) = 42.906$, $p < .001$, partial $\eta^2 = .168$]. Furthermore, and consistent with the lack of rape-related content in the control condition, the pretest–posttest comparison on the rape myth acceptance scale within the control group was not significant [$F(1, 213) = .101$, $p = .75$].

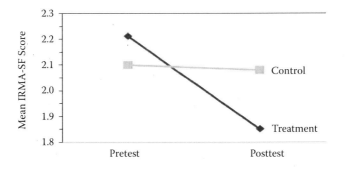

Unlike women experiencing the Women's Program, female participants in the control condition did not experience a significant reduction in their rape myth acceptance. The treatment versus control contrast for the pretest scores was not significant [$F(1, 213) = .809$, $p = .369$]. Unfortunately, the contrast between the groups failed to reach significance at the posttest occasion [$F(1, 213) = 2.618$, $p = .107$]. This pattern shows that the focal point for the interaction is the pretest-to-posttest drop in the mean IRMA-SF score for the treatment group.

## *Discussion*

As expected, results indicated that the program significantly decreased female attendee's endorsement of rape myths. Although the experimental group had lower rape myth acceptance than the control group at the post-assessment period, this difference was not significant. This suggests that even successful programs such as the Women's Program need to continue to enhance their efficacy. It is also possible that measures of rape myth acceptance could be enhanced to be more sensitive to change.

Results regarding changes in bystander behavior were precisely as expected. As we predicted, participation in the Women's Program significantly increased both women's confidence in their ability to intervene as a bystander, and their perceived willingness to help a potential abuse victim.

## Research on The Men's Program

Well over a dozen studies have been published evaluating the effects of the Men's Program. Citations for all of those currently available are included at the end of this chapter.

This section of Chapter 8 includes highlights of some of the most important studies published thus far.

**Foubert, J. D., & Cowell, E. A. (2004). Perceptions of a rape prevention program by fraternity men and male student athletes: Powerful effects and implications for changing behavior. *NASPA Journal, 42,* 1–20.**

An earlier version of the Men's Program (before bystander intervention material was included) was seen by members of several fraternities and athletic teams. These men then participated in focus groups assessing their reactions.

Four focus groups were conducted: two of fraternity men and two of student athletes. Four major themes emerged from the analysis of participant comments.

1. Participants overwhelmingly reported they learned more about how rape feels through seeing the video in the Men's Program that describes a male-on-male rape situation.
2. Participants reported they felt much more able to help a survivor. In particular, participants reported greater sympathy, greater understanding of how to be supportive, greater awareness of the need to help the victim regain control, and an increased understanding of what not to do when a survivor approached them for help.
3. The third theme of comments included those where participants showed they would have a greater awareness of their behavior in intimate situations, they were more likely to believe survivors, and they were less likely to tell rape jokes.

4. The final theme included feedback for program revisions. The most critical element of this feedback was to deal more directly with alcohol and consent. This feedback was used to update a subsequent version of the Men's Program.

**Foubert, J. D., & Perry, B. C. (2007). Creating lasting attitude and behavior change in fraternity members and male student athletes: The qualitative impact of an empathy-based rape prevention program. *Violence Against Women, 13,* 70–86.**

In a follow-up study to Foubert and Cowell (2004), this article contains the results of a survey 5 months after fraternity men and student athletes saw the Men's Program. Of the participants in this study:

- 100% of participants in earlier focus groups completed a 5-month follow-up survey.
- 92% reported lasting attitude change.
- 75% reported behavior change.
- All reported either attitude or behavior change.

Results for this study are reported in themes in four areas. Themes are reported for attitude change over 5 months and behavior change over 5 months. In addition, for both attitude and behavior change, results are reported for what about the program led to the change.

## Reported Attitude Change 5 Months After Seeing the Men's Program

Theme 1: The program increased my understanding of what rape feels like. Better understanding of what rape survivors go through, increased empathy toward survivors, more sensitivity toward rape in general.
Theme 2: I now have a greater understanding of how to support survivors.
Theme 3: Understanding the gravity of the term *rape*. Newfound appreciation for the misuse of the word *rape* in everyday conversation.
Theme 4: The program strengthened my existing beliefs.

## What Changed Them?

Theme 1: The video of a male-on-male rape.
Theme 2: The statistics provided throughout the program.
Theme 3: The section on confronting rape jokes and changing sexist behaviors.

## Changed Behavior 5 Months Later

Theme 1: No more rape jokes.
Theme 2: My behavior has not yet changed, but I would act differently in the future. Better prepared to help survivors or they would react differently to rape jokes.

Theme 3: I behaved differently when I helped a sexual assault survivor. Helped survivors since seeing the program.
Theme 4: I am more protective of my female friends.

## What Changed Them?

Theme 1: The video changed my behavior.
Theme 2: The section on confronting rape jokes and challenging sexist behaviors.
Theme 3: The program in general.

The following are comments written by study participants 5 months after seeing the Men's Program:

> "I now have a much greater understanding for what it must feel like to be in a sexual assault or rape situation. Just from watching the video I was frozen like they said young women are in those situations. I was utterly speechless and shocked. I now understand the importance of being a listener and not trying to make the victim do anything she doesn't feel comfortable doing, like immediately going to the hospital or talking about the situation. More than anything, I have tried to watch my mouth and not make comments after tests or a game like, 'they raped us.' I really think the approach One in Four takes of teaching how to help rather than how not to be an offender made me look at this a lot differently. I now feel a responsibility to help rather than just the normal response of 'I would never do that, so I don't really need to listen.'"
>
> "I've certainly become more aware of language that reinforces improper male attitudes toward sexual abuse (i.e., "I was raped by that test"). I was never big into using such terminology but now it strikes me more as immaturity and ignorance and is completely unappealing for colloquial language. Since then I've seen a number of videos on sexual assault, especially of kids, and I think you don't necessarily think about the harm to the quality of life of the victims without such presentations. The most important aspect of such a presentation is to alarm the viewers with a striking example that they can relate to, which One-in-Four does. The best way to make people change is to put them in the others' shoes. Knowing the psychology behind recovering from rape is quintessential to helping a rape victim, I feel. Also, trying to get people to change their daily behavior (like the language example) will undermine the rape subculture of groups and will help achieve the desired results. The emphasis of the program on startling the audience with real-life examples and ways to change both the subculture and daily behaviors is the key to education. Once you understand the harm done to the victim and the pain she will feel the rest of her life, you can't help but feel her pain and want to change such an awful aspect of culture."

"I think the biggest thing that changed for me is the magnitude of the effect that assault can bring to the women. Consequently, I am far more—I guess sympathetic, but more empathetic too—toward survivors. My behavior was a lot more confident in one incident that I have dealt with since the program. I feel a lot more capable as to what to say in terms of providing comfort and working toward a solution. And I suspect that comes across in my mannerisms which only helps comfort more."

"My attitude toward how I would react to someone close to me being raped is one of the big changes. Before the program I believe that if any one of my close friends were raped I would go out and try to fight the one responsible. But after the program I know that it is better to comfort my friend, the victim, and not make the situation worse for her. Actually one of my friends told me a few months after the program that a long time ago she had been sexually assaulted by some schoolmates and luckily she was able to get out in time before things got worse. Before the program I feel I would have just asked her questions and not thought too much about it. But since I did go to the program, I felt very sorry for my friend and tried to make her feel comfortable about it and tried to imagine how horrible it must have been for her."

"There was a significant change in the way I understood sexual assault. I didn't realize how common it really is. I used to believe false accusations were more common than they really are. My grasp of the subject as a whole is much more solid."

**Foubert, J. D., & Newberry, J. T. (2006). Effects of two versions of an empathy-based rape prevention program on fraternity men's rape survivor empathy, rape myth acceptance, likelihood of raping, and likelihood of committing sexual assault. *Journal of College Student Development, 47,* 133–148.**

This study tested two experimental versions of the Men's Program, including its present version, the one including a bystander intervention component.

All fraternities at a midsized public institution volunteered to participate in the study; 67% of the total population of members completed surveys before and after and were part of either the program condition or the control group (261 of 388 men). Participants completed measures of their attitudes toward rape (the Illinois Rape Myth Acceptance Scale), their likelihood of committing rape and sexual assault (Malamuth Sexual Aggression Scale), and their degree of empathy toward female rape survivors (Rape Empathy Scale).

The present version of the Men's Program was found to lead to

- Declines in rape myth acceptance among program participants ($p < .001$) that were significantly different from a control group ($p < .01$).
- Increased empathy toward female rape survivors ($p < .001$) that was significantly greater than a control group ($p < .05$).

- A decline in men's likelihood of raping ($p < .01$) (very low rape likelihood in the control group precluded significant difference between the control and experimental group).
- A decline in men's likelihood of committing sexual assault ($p < .001$), that was significantly lower than a control group ($p < .05$).

Of the men in this study, 13% reported some likelihood of raping. Of these men, 73% declined in their likelihood of raping after seeing the Men's Program; 62% fell to no likelihood of raping.

Of the men in this study, 30% reported some likelihood of committing sexual assault. Of these men, 73% declined in their likelihood of committing sexual assault after seeing the Men's Program; 63% fell to no likelihood of committing sexual assault.

**Foubert, J. D., & Cremedy, B. J. (2007). Reactions of men of color to a commonly used rape prevention program: Attitude and predicted behavior changes. *Sex Roles: A Journal of Research, 57,* 137–144.**

Men of color saw the Men's Program and responded to a series of open-ended stimulus questions gauging whether and how they expected the program would change their behavior and how it would change their attitudes. Approximately three of four men of color stated that it would change their behavior; half said it changed their attitudes.

Five main themes came out of the analysis of results. These included that the program reinforced their current beliefs and/or no change, increased awareness of rape and its effects on survivors, increased understanding of consent, plans to intervene if a rape might occur, and plans to change behavior in intimate situations. It was particularly interesting that more said they would change their behavior than said their attitudes would change. Their behaviors they said would change focused on intervening to help prevent rape or helping a survivor differently. On the whole, there was remarkable similarity among racial groups' responses, and tremendous similarity between the responses of these men of color to the program and those of the mostly white participants in other evaluation studies of the Men's Program (Foubert & Cowell, 2004; Foubert, Tatum, & Donahue, 2006).

**Foubert, J. D., Newberry, J. T., & Tatum, J. L. (2007). Behavior differences seven months later: Effects of a rape prevention program on first-year men who join fraternities. *NASPA Journal, 44,* 728–749.**

This is the most important study conducted thus far about the Men's Program. It provides strong evidence for behavior change resulting from the program.

All first-year men at a midsized public university participated in an evaluation study of the Men's Program. Fully 90% of participants completed surveys on all testing occasions: before seeing the program, afterward, and at the 7-month, year-end follow-up. The same response rate was achieved for the control group. Three times as many men who joined fraternities committed sexual assault than men who did not join fraternities.

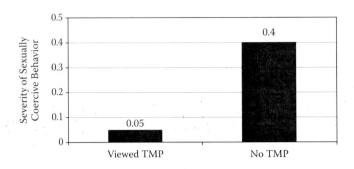

**Fraternity men's sexually coercive behavior.**

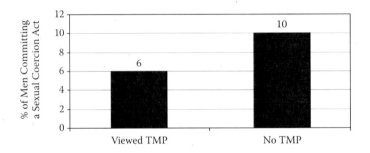

**Percentage of fraternity men's sexually coercive behavior.**

Men who joined fraternities during their first year of college and who saw the Men's Program at the beginning of that year reported committing fewer and less severe cases of sexually coercive behavior when the year was over, than did fraternity men who did not see the Men's Program. In fact, the only incidents of sexually coercive behavior reported by fraternity men who saw the Men's Program were the least severe possible on the scale, unwanted sexual contact ($p < .05$).

These results showed that 10% of untreated fraternity men committed sexual assault, whereas 6% of treated men committed sexual assault. Moreover, the severity of the acts of sexual assault committed by untreated men was eight times more severe than those who saw the Men's Program.

**Foubert, J. D., Godin, E., & Tatum, J. (in press). In their own words: Sophomore college men describe attitude and behavior changes resulting from a rape prevention program two years after their participation. *Journal of Interpersonal Violence*. Note: will appear in December 2010 issue.**

Two academic years after seeing the Men's Program, sophomore college men completed surveys at the end of the year including four open-ended questions asking for them to write about whether the program had changed their attitudes or behavior during the last 2 years.

Of 184 college men, 79% reported either attitude or behavior change due to the program's effects, or that the program reinforced their original beliefs. Furthermore, a multistage inductive analysis revealed that, after seeing the Men's Program, men intervened to prevent rapes from happening. Participants also modified their behavior to avoid committing sexual assault when they or a potential partner were under the influence of alcohol. Comments from participants, written two academic years after program participation, included the following:

- There was one time when a friend was going to engage in sexual activity with a girl who was really drunk. Me and a couple of other guys intervened because the girl seemed out of it (also, she was another friend's sister). They ended up not having sex.
- Mostly as a result of the One in Four program I am very cautious about initiating any kind of sexual activity while under the influence of alcohol.
- My attitude is pretty much to avoid alcohol mixing with sex and One in Four definitely helped me commit to that idea.
- I have helped a girl friend get out of a potentially scary situation.
- Yes. Drunk girl asked me to take her home, then tried to hook up with me and I said no.
- Yes, I have refused sex with a girl who was asking for it but was more drunk that I was.
- I have been more aware not only of my own sobriety, but of the sobriety of the girl and acted accordingly by suggesting that we're both too drunk.
- Yes—A woman had consumed alcohol, and although she wasn't passing out drunk and seemed coherent, we refrained from sexual activity. Regardless of my personal views of rape and alcohol, I'm aware that situations can easily be misconstrued and get out of control, and I don't want to risk having that happen to a woman, or me.
- Yes, I turned down sex because the girl was very intoxicated. She thanked me afterward and things progressed how I wanted them to.

**Langhinrichsen-Rohling, J., Foubert, J. D., Brasfield, H., Hill, B., & Shelley-Tremblay, S. (in press). Effects of the men's rape prevention program: Does it impact college men's bystander behavior and willingness to intervene? *Violence Against Women.***

College men (mostly first-year students) at a large southern public university were randomly selected to be in control a group ($n = 94$) or they experienced the rape prevention program condition ($n = 119$). Results indicated college men who experienced the Men's Program significantly increased their willingness to help as a bystander, and their bystander behavior efficacy in comparison to college men randomly selected to experience a control condition.

## Bystander Willingness to Help

As shown in the next figure, men who saw the Men's Program significantly increased their willingness to intervene as a bystander after the program ($p < .001$) with a moderate effect size (partial $\eta^2 = .54$). The control group, who saw a stress management program, experienced an unexpected increase in willingness to intervene as a bystander ($p < .001$) with a low effect size (partial $\eta^2 = .23$). Still, the program group and control group were statistically equivalent prior to the study and those who saw the Men's Program were significantly more likely to be willing to intervene as bystanders ($p < .001$ with a low effect size, partial $\eta^2 = .17$) than men in the control group.

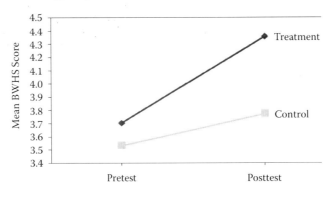

**Mean-bystander-willingness-to-help score by program pretest/posttest.**

### Bystander Efficacy

With regard to the bystander efficacy, program participants increased in their perceived ability to intervene as shown below.

Results for bystander efficacy were clearer than those for bystander willingness to intervene. Men who saw the Men's Program significantly increased in their bystander efficacy ($p < .001$, partial $\eta^2 = .12$), this significantly differed from the control group ($p < .001$, partial $\eta^2 = .42$), and there was no significant change within the control group from pre- to posttest.

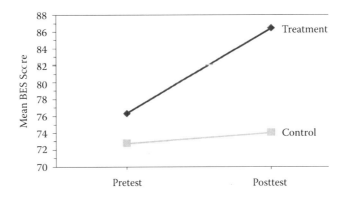

**Mean bystander efficacy by program pretest/posttest.**

Thus, when it comes to bystander intervention, there is tangible evidence that seeing the Men's Program increases men's willingness to intervene as a bystander in sexual assault situations. There is stronger evidence that seeing the Men's Program increases men's efficacy when intervening as a bystander. It is important to do additional research to confirm these findings to establish their validity and to confidently generalize them.

## Citations of Available Studies

### Study on the Women's Program

Foubert, J. D., Langhinrichsen-Rohling, J., Brasfield, H., & Hill, B. (in press). Effects of a rape awareness program on college women: Increasing bystander efficacy and willingness to intervene. *Journal of Community Psychology.*

### Studies on the Men's Program

Foubert, J. D. (2000). The longitudinal effects of a rape-prevention program on fraternity men's attitudes, behavioral intent, and behavior. *The Journal of American College Health, 48,* 158–163.

Foubert, J. D., & Cowell, E. A. (2004). Perceptions of a rape prevention program by fraternity men and male student athletes: Powerful effects and implications for changing behavior. *NASPA Journal, 42,* 1–20.

Foubert, J. D., & Cremedy, B. J. (2007). Reactions of men of color to a commonly used rape prevention program: Attitude and predicted behavior changes. *Sex Roles: A Journal of Research, 57,* 137–144.

Foubert, J. D., Garner, D. G., & Thaxter, P. J. (2006). An exploration of fraternity culture: Implications for programs to address alcohol-related sexual assault. *College Student Journal, 40,* 361–373.

Foubert, J. D., Godin, E., & Tatum, J. (in press). In their own words: Sophomore college men describe attitude and behavior changes resulting from a rape prevention program two years after their participation. *Journal of Interpersonal Violence.*

Foubert, J. D., & LaVoy, S. L. (2000). A qualitative assessment of The Men's Program: The impact of a rape prevention program on fraternity men. *NASPA Journal, 38,* 18–30.

Foubert, J. D., & Marriott, K. A. (1996). Overcoming men's defensiveness toward sexual assault programs: Learning to help survivors. *Journal of College Student Development, 37,* 470–472.

Foubert, J. D., & Marriott, K. A. (1997). Effects of a sexual assault peer education program on men's belief in rape myths. *Sex Roles: A Journal of Research, 36,* 257–266.

Foubert, J. D., & McEwen, M. K. (1998). An all-male rape-prevention peer education program: Decreasing fraternity men's behavioral intent to rape. *Journal of College Student Development, 39,* 548–556.

Foubert, J. D., & Newberry, J. T. (2006). Effects of two versions of an empathy-based rape prevention program on fraternity men's rape survivor empathy, rape myth acceptance, likelihood of raping, and likelihood of committing sexual assault. *Journal of College Student Development, 47,* 133–148.

Foubert, J. D., Newberry, J. T., & Tatum, J. L. (2007). Behavior differences seven months later: Effects of a rape prevention program on first-year men who join fraternities. *NASPA Journal, 44,* 728–749.

Foubert, J. D., & Perry, B. C. (2007). Creating lasting attitude and behavior change in fraternity members and male student athletes: The qualitative impact of an empathy-based rape prevention program. *Violence Against Women, 13,* 70–86.

Foubert, J. D., Tatum, J., & Godin, E. (in press). First-year men's perceptions of a rape prevention program seven months after their participation: Attitude and behavior changes. *Journal of College Student Development.*

Foubert, J. D., Tatum, J. L., & Donahue, G. A. (2006). Reactions of first-year men to a rape prevention program: Attitude and predicted behavior changes. *NASPA Journal, 43,* 578–598.

Langhinrichsen-Rohling, J., Foubert, J. D., Brasfield, H., Hill, B., & Shelley-Tremblay, S. (in press). Effects of the men's rape prevention program: Does it impact college men's bystander behavior and willingness to intervene? *Violence Against Women.* Note: due out in early 2011.

# References

Abbey, A., Clinton-Sherrod, A. M., McAuslan, P., Zawacki, T., & Buck, P. O. (2003). The relationship between the quantity of alcohol consumed and the severity of sexual assaults committed by college men. *Journal of Interpersonal Violence, 18*, 813–833.

Abbey, A., & McAuslan, P. (2004). A longitudinal examination of male college students' perpetration of sexual assault. *Journal of Consulting and Clinical Psychology, 72*, 747–756.

Abbey, A., McAuslan, P., Zawacki, T., Clinton, A. M., & Buck, P. O. (2001). Attitudinal, experimental, and situational predictors of sexual assault perpetration. *Journal of Interpersonal Violence, 16*, 784–807.

Banyard, V. L., Moynihan, M. M., & Plante, E. G. (2007). Sexual violence prevention through bystander education: An experimental evaluation. *Journal of Community Psychology, 35*(4), 463–481.

Banyard, V. L., Plante, E. G., & Moynihan, M. M. (2004). Bystander education: Bringing a broader community perspective to sexual violence prevention. *Journal of Community Psychology, 32*(1), 61–79.

Banyard, V. L., Plante, E. G., & Moynihan, M. M. (2005). Rape prevention through bystander education: Final report to NIJ for grant 2002-WG-BX-0009. Retrieved June 1, 2007, from www.ncjrs.org0pdffiles10nij0grants0208701.pdf.

Bergner, R. M., & Bridges, A. J. (2002). The significance of heavy pornography involvement for romantic partners: Research and clinical implications. *Journal of Sex and Marital Therapy, 28*, 193–206.

Bernat, J. A., Calhoun, K. S., & Stolp, S. (1998). Sexually aggressive men's responses to a date rape analogue: Alcohol as a disinhibiting cue. *Journal of Sex Research, 35*(4), 341–348.

Boeringer, S. B. (1994). Pornography and sexual aggression: Associations of violent and nonviolent depictions with rape and rape proclivity. *Deviant Behavior, 15*, 289–304.

Bostock, D. J., & Daley, J. G. (2007). Lifetime and current sexual assault and harassment victimization rates of active-duty United States air force women. *Violence Against Women. 13*(9), 927–944.

Brecklin, L. R., & Forde, D. R. (2001). A meta-analysis of rape education programs. *Violence and Victims, 16*, 303–321.

Carr, J. L., & VanDeusen, K. M. (2004). Risk factors for male sexual aggression on college campuses. *Journal of Family Violence, 19*(5), 279–289.

Carroll, J. S., Padilla-Walker,, L. M., Nelson, L. J., Olson, C. D., Barry, C. M., & Madsen, S. D. (2008). Generation XXX: Pornography acceptance and use among emerging adults. *Journal of Adolescent Research, 23*, 6–30.

Douglas, C. A., & Holsopple, K. (1998). Beyond the sex wars? *Off Our Backs, 28.* National Women's Studies Association.

Douglas, K. A., Collins, J. L., Warren, C., Kann, L., Gold, R., Clayton, S., Ross, J. G., & Kolbe, L. J. (1997). Results from the 1995 national college health risk behavior survey. *Journal of American College Health, 46*(2), 55–66.

Ekberg, G. S. (2002, November). The international debate about prostitution and trafficking in women: Refuting the arguments. Seminar on the effects of legislation of prostitution activities—A critical analysis. Stockholm, Sweden.

Farley, M., Cotton, A., Lynne, J. Zumbeck, S., & Spiwak, F. (2003). *Prostitution in nine countries: Update on violence and posttraumatic stress disorder.* New York: Haworth Press.

Fisher, B. S., Cullen, F. T., & Turner, M. G. (2006). *The sexual victimization of college women.* Washington, DC: National Institute of Justice, U.S. Department of Justice.

Foubert, J. D. (2000). The longitudinal effects of a rape-prevention program on fraternity men's attitudes, behavioral intent, and behavior. *Journal of American College Health, 48,* 158–163.

Foubert, J. D., & Cowell, E. A. (2004). Perceptions of a rape prevention program by fraternity men and male student athletes: Powerful effects and implications for changing behavior. *NASPA Journal, 42,* 1–20.

Foubert, J. D., & Cremedy, B. J. (2007). Reactions of men of color to a commonly used rape prevention program: Attitude and predicted behavior changes. *Sex Roles: A Journal of Research, 57,* 137–144.

Foubert, J. D., Garner, D. G., & Thaxter, P. J. (2006). An exploration of fraternity culture: Implications for programs to address alcohol-related sexual assault. *College Student Journal, 40,* 361–373.

Foubert, J. D., Godin, E., & Tatum, J. (in press). In their own words: Sophomore college men describe attitude and behavior changes resulting from a rape prevention program two years after their participation. *Journal of Interpersonal Violence.*

Foubert, J. D., Langhinrichsen-Rohling, J., Brasfield, H., & Hill, B. (in press). Effects of a rape awareness program on college women: Increasing bystander efficacy and willingness to intervene. *Journal of Community Psychology.*

Foubert, J. D., & LaVoy, S. L. (2000). A qualitative assessment of The Men's Program: The impact of a rape prevention program on fraternity men. *NASPA Journal, 38,* 18–30.

Foubert, J. D., & Marriott, K. A. (1996). Overcoming men's defensiveness toward sexual assault programs: Learning to help survivors. *Journal of College Student Development, 37,* 470–472.

Foubert, J. D., & Marriott, K. A. (1997). Effects of a sexual assault peer education program on men's belief in rape myths. *Sex Roles: A Journal of Research, 36,* 257–266.

Foubert, J. D., & McEwen, M. K. (1998). An all-male rape-prevention peer education program: Decreasing fraternity men's behavioral intent to rape. *Journal of College Student Development, 39,* 548–556.

Foubert, J. D., & Newberry, J. T. (2006). Effects of two versions of an empathy-based rape prevention program on fraternity men's rape survivor empathy, rape myth acceptance, likelihood of raping, and likelihood of committing sexual assault. *Journal of College Student Development, 47,* 133–148.

Foubert, J. D., Newberry, J. T., & Tatum, J. L. (2007). Behavior differences seven months later: Effects of a rape prevention program on first-year men who join fraternities. *NASPA Journal, 44,* 728–749.

Foubert, J. D., & Perry, B. C. (2007). Creating lasting attitude and behavior change in fraternity members and male student athletes: The qualitative impact of an empathy-based rape prevention program. *Violence Against Women, 13,* 70–86.

Foubert, J. D., Tatum, J. L., & Donahue, G. A. (2006). Reactions of first-year men to a rape prevention program: Attitude and predicted behavior changes. *NASPA Journal, 43,* 578–598.

Foubert, J. D., Tatum, J., & Godin, E. (in press). First-year men's perceptions of a rape prevention program seven months after their participation: Attitude and behavior changes. *Journal of College Student Development.*

Gayle, H.D., Keeling, R.P., Garcia-Tunon, M., Kilbourne, B.W., Narkunas, J.P., Ingram, F.R. et al. (1990). Prevalence of the human immunodeficiency virus among university students. *New England Journal of Medicine,* 323, 1538–1541.

Grube, J. W., Mayton, D. M., & Ball-Rokeach, S. J. (1994). Inducing change in values, attitudes, and behaviors: Belief system theory and the method of value self-confrontation. *Journal of Social Issues, 50,* 153–173.

Hald, G. M., Malamuth, N. M., & Yuen, C. (2009). Pornography and attitudes supporting violence against women: Revisiting the relationship in nonexperimental studies. *Aggressive Behavior,* 14–20.

Holsopple, K. (1999a). Pimps, tricks, and feminists. *Women's Studies Quarterly, 27,* 47–52.

Holsopple, K. (1999b). The Freedom and Justice Center for Prostitution Resources: A Program of the Volunteers of America of Minnesota, October 16, 2007. http://www.ccv.org/downloads/pdf/Strip_club_study.pdf.

Jensen, R. (2007). *Getting off: Pornography and the end of masculinity.* Cambridge: South End Press.

Katz, J. (2006). *The macho paradox: Why some men hurt women and how all men can help.* New York: Sourcebooks, Inc.

Kilpatrick, D. G., Resnick, H. S., Ruggiero, K. J., Conoscenti, L. M., & McCauley, J. (2007). *Drug facilitated, incapacitated and forcible rape: A national study.* Charleston, SC: National Crime Victims Research & Treatment Center,

Koss, M. P., Gidycz, C. A., & Wisniewski, N. (1987). The scope of rape: Incidence and prevalence of sexual aggression and victimization in a national sample of higher education students. *Journal of Consulting and Clinical Psychology, 55,* 162–170.

Langhinrichsen-Rohling, J., Foubert, J. D., Brasfield, H., Hill, B., & Shelley-Tremblay, S. (in press). Effects of the men's rape prevention program: Does it impact college men's bystander behavior and willingness to intervene? *Violence Against Women.*

Lisak, D., & Miller, P. (2002). Repeat rape and multiple offending among undetected rapists. *Violence and Victims, 17*(1), 73–84.

Lonsway, K. (2009, January). *Rape prevention and risk reduction: Review of the research for practitioners.* Harrisburg, PA: VAWnet, a project of the National Resource Center on Domestic Violence/Pennsylvania Coalition Against Domestic Violence. Retrieved February 13, 2009, from http://www.vawnet.org.

Lonsway, K.A., Archambault, J. & Berkowitz, A. (2007). False reports: Moving beyond the issue to successfully investigate and prosecute non-stranger sexual assault. *The Voice, 3*(1), 2–11.

Malamuth, N., Addison, T., & Koss, M. (2000). Pornography and sexual aggression: Are there reliable effects and can we understand them? *Annual Review of Sex Research, 11,* 26–94.

Malarek, V. (2009). *The johns: Sex for sale and the men who buy it.* New York: Arcade Publishing.

Manning, J. C. (2006). Impact of Internet pornography on marriage and the family: A review of the research. *Sexual Addiction & Compulsivity, 13*(2), 131–165.

McIntosh, P. (1998). White privilege and male privilege: A personal account of coming to see correspondences through work in women's studies. In M. Kimmel & A. Ferber (Eds.) *Privilege: A reader* (pp. 147–160). Cambridge, MA: Westview Press.

Messman-Moore, T. L., & Brown, A. L. (2006). Risk perception, rape, and sexual revictimization: A prospective study of college women. *Psychology of Women Quarterly, 30,* 159–172.

Miller, A. K., Markman, K. D., & Handley, I. M. (2007). Self-blame among sexual assault victims prospectively predicts revictimization: A perceived sociolegal context model of risk. *Basic and Applied Social Psychology, 29,* 129–136.

Mizus, M., Moody, M., Privado, C., & Douglas, C. A. (2003). Germany, U.S. receive most sex-trafficked women. *Off Our Backs, 33*(7/8), 4.

Mohler-Kuo, M., Dowdall, G. W., Koss, M. P., & Wechsler, H. (2004). Correlates of rape while intoxicated in a national sample of college women. *Journal of Studies on Alcohol, 9,* 37–43.

Murnen, S. K., & Kohlman, M. H. (2007). Athletic participation, fraternity membership, and sexual aggression among college men: A meta-analytic review. *Sex Roles, 57,* 145–157.

Norris, J., George, W. H., Davis, K. C., Martel, J., & Leonesio, R. J. (1999). Alcohol and hypermasculinity as determinants of men's empathic responses to violent pornography. *Journal of Interpersonal Violence, 14*(7), 683–700.

O'Connor, M., & Healy, G. (2006). The links between prostitution and sex trafficking: A briefing handbook. Prepared for the Joint Project Coordinated by the Coalition Against Trafficking in Women (CATW) and the European Women's Lobby (EWL) on Promoting Preventative Measures to Combat Trafficking in Human Beings for Sexual Exploitation: A Swedish and U.S. Governmental and Non-Governmental Organization Partnership.

Oddone-Paolucci, E., Genius, M., and Violato, C. (2000). A meta-analysis of the published research on the effects of pornography. In M. Genius, E. Oddone-Paolucci, & C. Violato (Eds.), *The changing family and child development* (pp. 48–59). Aldershot, UK: Ashgate.

Office on Violence Against Women. (2000). *Victims of Trafficking and Violence Prevention Act of 2000.* Washington, DC: U.S. Department of Justice.

Payne, D. L., Lonsway, K. A., & Fitzgerald, L. F. (1999). Rape myth acceptance: Exploration of its structure and its measurement using the Illinois Rape Myth Acceptance Scale. *Journal of Research in Personality, 33,* 27–68.

Petty, R. E., & Cacioppo, J. T. (1986). *Communication and persuasion: Central and peripheral routes to attitude change.* New York: Springer-Verlag.

Raymond, J., d'Cunha, J., Ruhaini Dzuhayatin, S., Hynes, H. P., Ramirez Rodriguez, Z., & Santos, A. (2002). *A comparative study of women trafficked in the migration process: Patterns, profiles and health consequences of sexual exploitation in five countries (Indonesia, the Philippines, Thailand, Venezuela and the United States).* N. Amherst, MA: Coalition Against Trafficking in Women (CATW).

Rozee, P. D., & Koss, M. P. (2001). Rape: A century of resistance. *Psychology of Women Quarterly, 25,* 291–311.

Sabina, C., Wolnak, J., & Finkelhor, D. (2008). The nature and dynamics of Internet pornography exposure for youth. *Cyberpsychology and Behavior, 11,* 691–693.

Sadler, A. G., Booth, B. M., Cook, B. L., & Doebbeling, B. N. (2003). Factors associated with women's risk of rape in the military environment. *American Journal of Industrial Medicine, 43,* 262–273.

Sadler, A. G., Booth, B. M., & Doebbeling, B. N. (2005). Gang and multiple rapes during military service: Health consequences and health care. *Journal of American Medical Women's Association, 60*(1), 33–41.

Scheel, E. D., Johnson, E. J., Schneider, M., & Smith, B. (2001). Making rape education meaningful for men: The case for eliminating the emphasis on men as perpetrators, protectors, or victims. *Sociological Practice: A Journal of Clinical and Applied Sociology, 3*(4), 257–278.

Schewe, P. A. (2007). Interventions to prevent sexual violence. In L. Doll, S. Bonzo, J. Mercy, & D. Sleet (Eds.), *Handbook on injury and violence prevention interventions* (pp. 223–240). New York: Kluwer Academic/Plenum Publishers.

Schneider, J. P. (2000). A qualitative study of cybersex participants: Gender differences, recovery issues, and implications for therapists. *Sexual Addiction & Compulsivity, 7,* 249–278.

Söchting, I., Fairbrother, N., & Koch, W. J. (2004). Sexual assault of women: Prevention efforts and risk factors. *Violence Against Women, 10,* 73–93.

Stack, S., Wasserman, I., & Kern, R. (2004). Adult social bonds and use of Internet pornography. *Social Science Quarterly, 51,* 75–88.

Stander, V. A., Merrill, L. L., Thomsen, C. J., Crouch, J. L., & Milner, J. S. (2008). Premilitary adult sexual assault victimization and perpetration in a Navy recruit sample. *Journal of Interpersonal Violence, 23,* 1636–1653.

Stein, J. L. (2007). Peer educators and close friends as predictors of male college students' willingness to prevent rape. *Journal of College Student Development, 48,* 75–89.

Suris, A., & Lind, L. (2008). Military sexual trauma: A review of prevalence and associated health consequences in veterans. *Trauma, Violence, and Abuse, 9*(4), 250–269.

Tjaden, P., & Thoennes, N. (2006). Prevalence, incidence, and consequences of violence against women: Findings from the national violence against women survey. Research in Brief, Washington, DC: National Institute of Justice, U.S. Department of Justice.

Turchik, J. A., Probst, D. R., Chau, M., Nigoff, A., & Gidycz, C. A. (2007). Factors predicting the type of tactics used to resist sexual assault. *Journal of Consulting and Clinical Psychology, 75,* 605–614.

U.S. Department of Justice, Office of Justice Programs, Bureau of Justice Statistics. (2010). Criminal Victimization in the United States, 2007 Statistical Tables (NCJ Publication No. 22-7669). Retrieved from http://bjs.ojp.usdoj.gov/content/pub/pdf/cvus0702.pdf

Weiss, D. S., Marmar, C. R., Schlenger, W. E., Fairbank, J. A., Jordan, B. K., Hough, R. L., & Kulka, R. A. (1992). The prevalence of lifetime and partial post-traumatic stress disorder in Vietnam theater veterans. *Journal of Traumatic Stress, 5,* 365–376.

Zawacki, T., Abbey, A., Buck, P. O., McAuslan, P., & Clinton-Sherrod, A. M. (2003). Perpetrators of alcohol-involved sexual assaults: How do they differ from other sexual assault perpetrators and nonperpetrators? *Aggressive Behavior, 29,* 366–380.

Zillmann, D. (2000). Influence of unrestrained access to erotica on adolescents and young adults dispositions toward sexuality. *Journal of Adolescent Health, 27*(2), 41–44.

# JOHN D. FOUBERT'S PEER EDUCATION PROGRAM

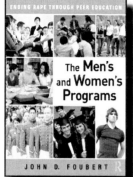

## THE MEN'S AND WOMEN'S PROGRAMS
Ending Rape Through Peer Education

This is a guide for college officials,community leaders, and military personnel looking to create a sexual assault prevention and education program to provide men and women with the knowledge, skills, and support systems needed to become active participants in the prevention of rape. It contains detailed scripts which outline how to set up and implement a program and provides instructions on running a training course and recruiting peer educators. Handouts and worksheets are included to assist in the training process, as well as for peer educators to use when working with participants. This revised version of the program features the inclusion of a program targeted at female participants, as well as completely updated scripts, handouts, and resources.

September 2010 ● 978-0-415-88105-0 ● 160pp ● $39.95

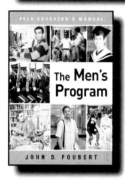

## THE MEN'S PROGRAM
Peer Educator's Manual
978-0-415-88106-7
September 2010 ● 105pp.
$100.00 for 10 manuals

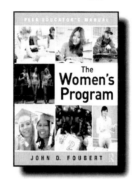

## THE WOMEN'S PROGRAM
Peer Educator's Manual
978-0-415-88107-4
September 2010 ● 105pp.
$100.00 for 10 manuals

Intended to be used in either an all-female or all-male peer education group, these manuals contain the training materials necessary for the peer educator. While they complement the guide for administrators, they are designed to be a self-contained manual and include all of the program scripts and handouts, as well as advice for running the program. The program scripts lay out each session in detail for the leader. Participants will learn how to recognize and identify dangerous men, how to help a friend who is a survivor of rape, and about ways to be an active bystander.

## POLICE RAPE TRAINING VIDEO
*by One In Four, Inc*

An integral part of presenting The Men's Program, this powerful DVD is a presentation of a police officer talking to new officers about how to handle rape cases. In doing so, Sgt. Ramon shares the story of a male police officer who went about his everyday business and was raped by two men. Afterward, other officers didn't believe it happened as he said it did, couldn't understand why he didn't fight back, and blamed him for what happened. This DVD is especially useful for helping men understand what it might feel like to be raped, and ideally suited for presentation in conjunction with The Men's Program to universities, the military, high schools, prisons, and community outreach organizations.

September 2010 ● 978-0-415-88419-8 ● 20 mins ● $50.00

## HOW TO HELP A SEXUAL ASSAULT SURVIVOR
*by One In Four, Inc.*

This video is a performance of The Men's Program by experienced peer educators and it includes the complete Police Rape Training video presentation. Men who watch the video will discover what rape is, what it might feel like, what women tend to experience before, during, and after being raped, how to help a woman recover from a rape experience, what they can do to modify their own behavior in their intimate encounters, and will be encouraged to confront their peers when necessary. Thought-provoking and provocative, this video is great for use with fraternities, sports teams, men's residence halls, military units, community organizations, high school boys, or any group of men who want to learn how to help women recover from rape. Women looking to present to men who can't find a male presenter could find it useful to show and then take questions or discuss other material. It is a very helpful tool to use in training sexual-assault peer educators, or to help a peer education program get off the ground.

September 2010 ● 978-0-415-88429-7 ● 45 mins ● $150.00

## www.routledgementalhealth.com